EDISON RECORD
THE NEW MOLDED RECORD
FROM
John Arnold
EVERYTHING IN MUSIC.
PIANOS · ORGANS
WAGONER
ROCHESTER
TALKING MACHINES
Thomas A. E
Talking Machines
GREGORY'S MUSIC HOUSE
ECHO ALL OVER THE WORLD.
CHAS. W. YOUNG
Talking Machines
EDISON
Machines
BUFFALO, N.Y.

ANTIQUE PHONOGRAPH ADVERTISING

An Illustrated History

TIMOTHY C. FABRIZIO & GEORGE F. PAUL

ANTIQUE PHONOGRAPH ADVERTISING

An Illustrated History

With photographs by the authors

Schiffer® Publishing Ltd

4880 Lower Valley Road, Atglen, PA 19310 USA

Dedication

To those whose impact was felt in phonograph and record marketing, Edward Easton, Frank Seaman, Leon Douglass, and countless unsung others, this book is dedicated.

Frontispiece: Wednesday, August 15, 1894, was the day of Mount Morris, New York's centennial celebration. As the parade began at 1:00 that afternoon, the streets were lined with people from all over Livingston County, some sheltering from the sun beneath umbrellas or on shady porches. Children, dressed in their Sunday best, were looking forward to the bicycle and foot races. Babies were held high to see the floats and beautifully groomed horses. There was a feeling of festival in the air. There would be orations at the Opera House, a ball game, wheelbarrow races, music by the Seymore Opera Band, and finally, once darkness fell, the finest display of fireworks ever seen in the county. It was a great day for a parade. Around 1:30, Mr. Howland drove by with his attractive four-in-hand tally-ho coach loaded with young ladies from the village. At that instant, Mr. Wright snapped the shutter of his camera, freezing the moment. Included in this tableau is a board fence to the right. It is covered with numerous bills, broadsides, and a ten-foot banner with its hand-lettered advertisement for an exhibition of "Edison's Phonograph."

Library of Congress Cataloging-in-Publication Data

Fabrizio, Timothy C.
Antique phonograph advertising : an illustrated history / Timothy C. Fabrizio & George F. Paul.
p. cm.
ISBN 0-7643-1517-X
1. Advertising--Phonographs--History. 2. Phonograph--History.
3. Advertising--History. I. Paul, George F. II. Title.
HF6161.P33 F33 2002
659.1'962138933--dc21
2001005740

Designed by Bonnie M. Hensley
Cover design by Bruce M. Waters
Type set in Galleria/Korinna BT

ISBN: 0-7643-1517-X
Printed in China
1 2 3 4

Published by Schiffer Publishing Ltd.
4880 Lower Valley Road
Atglen, PA 19310
Phone: (610) 593-1777; Fax: (610) 593-2002
E-mail: Schifferbk@aol.com
Please visit our web site catalog at **www.schifferbooks.com**
We are always looking for people to write books on new and related subjects. If you have an idea for a book please contact us at the above address.

This book may be purchased from the publisher.
Include $3.95 for shipping.
Please try your bookstore first.
You may write for a free catalog.

In Europe, Schiffer books are distributed by
Bushwood Books
6 Marksbury Ave.
Kew Gardens
Surrey TW9 4JF England
Phone: 44 (0) 20 8392-8585; Fax: 44 (0) 20 8392-9876
E-mail: Bushwd@aol.com
Free postage in the U.K., Europe; air mail at cost.

CONTENTS

ACKNOWLEDGMENTS

The authors would like to acknowledge those whose items appear anonymously and under the following attributions: Tom and Joanna Broome, Martin F. Bryan, Bob Carver, R. Chase, Dom Coladonato, the Scott and Denise Corbett collection, the Domenic DiBernardo collection, the John and Nancy Duffy family, Jen and Ken Flaherty, the Gfell family collection, H. Duane Goldman, David P. Graber, Fred Guenther, the collection of Michael S. Hatfield, the collection of Howard Hazelcorn, Nina and Dave Heitz, Neal Hinchman, the Charles Hummel collections, Brady Jeffcoat, Pat and Jamie Jones, Michael F. Khanchalian, Jim Kintzel, the Jerry Koch collection, Philippe Le Ray, the Scott Malawski collection, Richard and Christine Mazur, Charles McCarn, the Tom and Sandi McCarthy collection, William G. Meyer, Alan H. Mueller, Walter and Carol Myers, Gilbert (Bert) Pasley, the Babcock House Museum and John H. Perschbacher, Bruce and Linda Peterson, Dennis Peterson, Ray Phillips, Rae Ann Rieping, Robin and Joan Rolfs, Leslie Rosenfeld, Steve and Ellie Saccente, Wilfried Sator, Ron Seavers, Sam Sheena, Bob and Karyn Sitter, David Werchen.

We also extend our gratitude to Robert Baumbach, Tim Brooks, the enthusiastic W.C. Chin, David Giovannoni, Mike Hatfield for his efforts "above and beyond the call of duty," and John Levin. Very special thanks to Kurt Nauck, the ever-supportive Barbara, Jess, and Tim Paul, and of course, Peter and Nancy Schiffer and their friendly staff.

Chapter One

THE FIRST WAVE: 1877~1900

The late nineteenth century was a time of momentous inventions. Alexander Graham Bell's telephone (1876) and Edison's electric light (1879) were perhaps the two best-known achievements of the age. Newspaper columns, pamphlets, and books celebrated these and other scientific and technical advancements, foretelling the benefits (both real and imagined) that would accrue to mankind. It was a time of optimism and confidence. Interestingly, it was also a brief cusp wherein the age of invention had not yet developed into big business.

Different from most other practical and often utilitarian inventions of the time was the phonograph. Despite its innocuous appearance and simple, non-electrical principles, Edison's Phonograph captured the popular imagination in a way that the telephone and electric light could not. It was a *romantic* invention. Nothing better illustrates this than the epithet commonly applied to the device for many years: the Talking Machine.

From the perspective of the twenty-first century, the phrase, "talking machine" may seem ingenuous and quaint. In the context of the time, however, this term was eminently descriptive for its users, much like "horseless carriage" for an automobile or "wireless" for radio. Unlike the latter two examples, which described common articles *minus* a heretofore-integral part, the "talking machine" appended an *additional* characteristic to a mechanical object. The adjective was uniquely human. Nothing else talked. To hear speech had always implied the presence of a human being. And yet, like a carriage without a horse, or a telephone without wires, here was a simple machine that *talked* without lips, teeth, tongue, or larynx. From the outset, this seemingly magical ability set the phonograph apart from inventions such as the telephone and electric light. For all their utility, none of the other inventions of the time could raise the voice of the dead, play any instrument, or freeze time aurally. Phonograph advertising would capitalize on these attributes for many, many years.

The earliest advertising for the phonograph was provided free of charge by newspaper and magazine writers. Perhaps best known are the articles that appeared in the *Scientific American* at the time of the phonograph's invention. Enterprising reporters who rode the train out to Menlo Park, New Jersey, and managed to "coax" Edison into expounding on the invention wrote glowing essays in the *New York Daily Graphic* and the *New York Sun*. Never shy about self-promotion, the "Wizard of Menlo Park" could wax enthusiastic, knowing that his prognostications would be read in the next morning's edition by thousands of people. Magazines and newspapers commonly used woodcuts or engravings to illustrate articles describing the phonograph and its great inventor.

First Faltering Steps

The Edison Speaking Phonograph Company (note the variation of "talking" used here; sure proof of the perceived marketability of the "talking machine" terminology) was organized in the

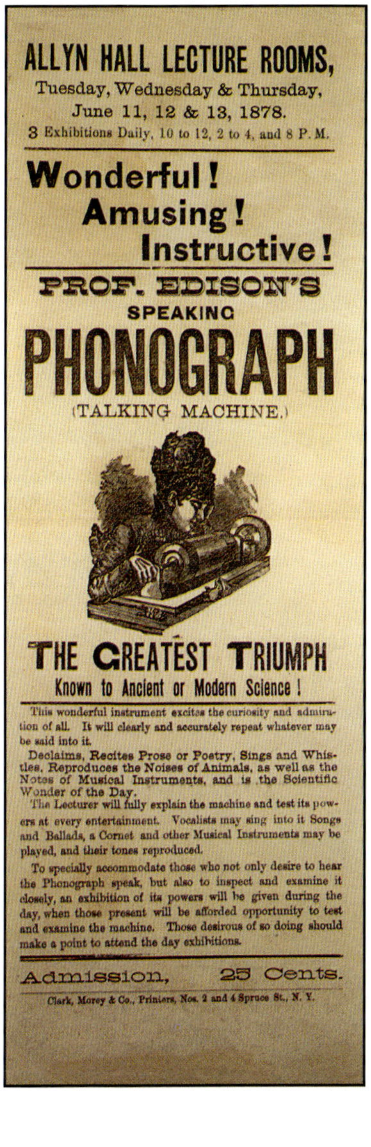

1-1. The Phonograph was only six months old when this series of exhibitions was given. The fact that three shows were scheduled daily at 25 cents admission (a substantial sum for entertainment in 1878) speaks to the allure of "Professor Edison's Speaking Phonograph" in its earliest days. This broadside measures 4 1/4" x 12 1/4". *Courtesy of the collection of Howard Hazelcorn.* (Value code: VR)

spring of 1878, initially for the purpose of exhibiting Edison's phonograph. Formal advertisements by this company are virtually unknown beyond postal card form responses and handbills, both quite rare today. Most advertising of this period was done on a local basis by traveling exhibitors. Much like snake-oil salesmen, they might send a canvasser ahead to the next town to post bills and drum up excitement for the coming phonograph exhibition. Local newspapers might carry small items advertising the show, but more often the enterprising showman would submit a stock "filler" to be printed in the guise of "news." Such shoestring publicity lasted only two or three years, as interest in these exhibitions flickered out.

Not until 1888 would the public see phonographic publicity printed in newspapers and magazines once again. The formation of the North American Phonograph Company, marketing the Edison Phonograph and the Bell-Tainter Graphophone, resulted in catalogues, illustrated circulars, and posters advertising the lease and later sale of Phonographs and Graphophones. These materials still utilized line-cuts of the machines, although rare period examples of brochures exist featuring early half-tone photographs. And yet, there are very few North American advertisements to be found in newspapers or magazines of 1888-1894.

Berliner: Merchandise and Medium

Emile Berliner's disc-playing talking machine, the Gramophone, was gradually introduced to the American public during the mid-1890s. It is ironic that, while the Gramophone had no organized advertising campaign to promote it in 1894 and 1895, the device itself was immediately recognized as an advertising tool by its developers. During this brief period, Berliner was attempting to attract financial backers, and the Gramophone's purported ability to advertise the goods of others was seen as an enticement to potential investors. A flyer of 1894-1895 was titled, "The Gramophone as an Advertising Medium" and made the following points:

> *Parties desiring to advertise their wares will find in the Gramophone a most valuable medium.*
>
> *We will make for you any special plate* [record], *containing, besides an interesting musical piece, etc., a bit of advertising such as you may suggest; manufacture as many hard rubber copies as you may order at regular wholesale rates; and destribute* [sic] *them gratis to people buying Gramophones.*
>
> *Prices for the original plate for advertising purposes will vary according to the special expenses incurred in making it, the talent to be employed, preparations, etc.*
>
> *When less than 1000 copies are ordered the expense for making the matrix or press form (about $10,) will be added.*
>
> *Nobody will refuse to listen to a fine song or concert piece, or an oration – even if interrupted by a modest remark: "Tartar's Baking Powder is the Best," or "Wash the Baby with Orange Soap," etc.*

A year or so later, the Berliner Gramophone Company followed its own advice. It recorded a selection entitled "On the Gramophone" (by George Graham, No.637[W], December 2, 1896). This 7" diameter recording consisted of a recitation: a humorous poem celebrating the merits of Mr. Berliner's extraordinary invention. It perhaps was based on an even earlier (5" diameter) Berliner disc called "My Name Is the Gramophone," which had known very limited circulation in Great Britain.

Dealers certainly must have employed "On the Gramophone" as a sales tool, playing it for the amusement of prospective customers. However, since the disc was also sold to Gramophone owners, it had the potential to inspire interest from a much wider range of casual listeners. A complete transcription of this historical artifact may be read in *The Talking Machine, an Illustrated Compendium, 1877-1929* by Fabrizio and Paul, Schiffer Publishing Ltd., 1997.

1-2. Berliner record: "On the Gramophone," recorded December 2, 1896.

Another interesting result of the record-as-advertising concept was Berliner record No. 641, "Oven Rising Plant's Baking Powder" by George Graham. Although evidently not intended as a legitimate advertising record (Graham was a humorous monologist, and no Plant's Baking Powder Company is known), the disc nevertheless demonstrated its advertising potential, while simultaneously entertaining its audience:

Frank Seaman: Father of Phonograph Advertising

The year 1896 may be considered a watershed in the history of phonograph advertising. On October 1, the United States government instituted Rural Free Delivery, which provided free mail service in rural areas. This opened up a huge market, comprising the majority of Americans at the time. In this same year, 1896, an advertising man named Frank Seaman was hired to promote Emile Berliner's Gramophone. Seaman, who had advertised Kodak cameras for several years, touted the Gramophone with splashy full-page ads, some with tinted halftone photographs of people listening to the machine. Most other talking machine advertisements of the time consisted of tiny, boxed displays set in columns on the page. Illustrations of Edison Phonographs or Columbia Graphophones, when shown at all, utilized small line drawings of the machines. Although seemingly second nature to us over a century later, Seaman's innovative brashness in size, color, and the all-important human element set him apart in his field. He may justifiably be considered the father of phonograph advertising.

1-3. Berliner record: "Oven Rising Plant's Baking Powder," recorded May 26, 1896.

Now, friends; a few words to you about baking powder. I wish to say something about Dr. Plant's Cream of Tartar Baking Powder. This is absolutely the purest and best baking powder on the market today. Now, the public asked for its relief against buying these cheap powders, which contain alum and ammonia. Now, you all know that ammonia is made from the hoofs of dead and decayed animals. And friends, think of that! Think of that! Think of that! A preparation like that being used in a baking powder! Now, this baking powder – Dr. Plant's Baking Powder – is a pure cream of tartar baking powder. Now, you want something to raise the bread properly; you want good bread; bread is the Staff of Life, yes! But consequently, you want good bread. Now, how are you going to get good bread if you haven't got good baking powder? Plant's Cream of Tartar Baking Powder is the powder you want. It's sold everywhere; it costs a little more than the ordinary powders, but friends, it does the work, and that's what you want. What is a few cents on a can of baking powder when you get a baking powder that will achieve the proper results? And that's what Plant's Cream of Tartar Baking Powder will do. Now, I'll tell you friends, there's nothing like a good baking powder – and I'm gonna say again that Plant's Cream of Tartar Baking Powder is a proper baking powder to use – that's all I can say – I can say Plant's Cream of Tartar Baking Powder! Well, friends, I couldn't say anything better for making good bread. It makes good, wholesome biscuits; makes biscuits that you can eat! Does not make any of these plaster-Paris leaden biscuits, no! It makes good, light, wholesome biscuits – biscuits that you can eat! Now, friends, you know perfectly well if you've got good biscuits, and good butter, and a good cup of coffee, you can make a meal. And I'll tell you you'll have good biscuits if you use Plant's Cream of Tartar Baking Powder; you can tend to the coffee yourself.

A RAY OF LIGHT

intensified and thrown upon a section of human skin which has been persistently bathed with VELVET-SKIN SOAP, shows the skin to be free from all impurities, fine, smooth and velvet-like in texture—hence the name, VELVET-SKIN SOAP.

COSTS 25c. A CAKE AND IS WORTH IT

SEND TEN CENTS IN STAMPS FOR SAMPLE OF SOAP AND POWDER.

THE PALISADE MAN'F'G CO. Yonkers, N. Y.

Talking Machines

~IT TALKS~

GRAPHOPHONE

Phonographs Graphophones *Reproduce* Songs, Bands Orchestras and your own voice

Send for circular. Agents wanted.

ONLY $40

Chicago Talking Machine Co., 107 Madison Street CHICAGO

The Capital Self-playing Music Box

Plays any number of tunes. Standard and popular airs.

AMERICAN MANUFACTURE

Interchangeable Cylinders

Size A, 15x12x7 inches, 44 teeth in comb, with 8 tunes, $15 00
Size B, 21x14x9 inches, 58 teeth in comb, with 10 tunes, 28 00
Size C, 26x17x10 inches, 81 teeth in comb, with 12 tunes, 40 00
Style F, 28x17x12 inches, 162 teeth in comb, with 12 tunes, 75 00

Extra tunes, 20 cents, 30 cents and 40 cents
Sent on receipt of price or C. O. D. by
F. G. OTTO & SONS, 44 to 50 Sherman Ave., Jersey City, N. J.
Or can be bought from any Dealer in Musical Merchandise.
Send for Handsomely Illustrated Catalogue.

VOSE ESTABLISHED 1851 PIANOS

MADGE H.—If you will send us a sta
addressed envelope repeating your reque
send you the information you desire.

PROFESSORS BROWN AND PAINE—Pader
widower. See article in the March issu
LADIES' HOME JOURNAL for information
son.

IGNATIUS AURELIUS—Both Madame Z
Paderewski are great artists. We cannot
any discussion of their respective talents
cesses here.

W. G. P.—Most voices gain in range as
quality under proper instruction, and it
likely that at the age of seventeen your vo
manently fixed in its range.

MAY BIRD—We do not believe that s
progress can be made in the study of any
music without competent instruction.

WAGNER—The word "Tannhäuser"
nounced "Ton-hoy-zur" as nearly as ca
in English spelling. The second syllable
between "how" and "ny."

VIOLIN—We consider Grove's "Dic
Music and Musicians" the most complete
kind published. (2) Anton Rubinstein die
hoff, Russia, in November, 1894.

MISS A. J. M. D.—You can, perhaps,
the words which you think suitable for
writing directly to some of the best-k
writers, offering the poem for sale.

DORIS—The JOURNAL will examine a
manuscript submitted to it for purchase
as it publishes so few compositions, and
these are ordered, the opportunities of pu
few.

ANXIOUS AMATEUR—If your instructor a
to continue your piano studies you shoul
do so. He is the best judge of your gai
and one can always add to his store of
to his general knowledge.

GIRLS—Sousa's "Manhattan Beach,"
Bell" and "El Capitan" marches, Sup
caccio" march and Gilmore's "Twe
Regiment March" are all compositions
marching rhythm strongly marked.

MRS. H. K.—As far as we have been a
Lillian Nordica had one sister who h
promising voice. We understand that
Lillian Nordica studied first with John
Boston and afterward with Sangiovanni i

LULU W. CHILDS—"Valse Brilliante,"
kowski; "Polonaise," by Moszkowsk
from "Birthday Music," by Bohm
d'Amore," by Vilback, and "Caprice
Saint-Saens, are a few brilliant pian
medium difficulty suitable for public perf

LOVER OF MUSIC—Other things being
not consider that the sex of a piano instr
in any way his or her ability. We imagi
would, under the circumstances you men
greater satisfaction from private lessons.
recommend instructors in this column.

A. L. A.—Transposing music can be
ways, according to the laws of harmon
The latter method is unmusicianly and
tory. Take a course of lessons in h
you will be able to transpose any comp
you have obtained the necessary practice
edge.

J. L. R.—The teachers whose names
in your letter are both able representati
is called the Italian method of singin
give you no better advice than to sugges
to the gentleman with whom you la

1-4. A page extract from the October 1896 *Ladies' Home Journal* illustrated the typically small scale of talking machine advertising before Frank Seaman revolutionized the medium. (Value code: H)

Frank Seaman's impact on the tiny talking machine industry was immediate. Fueled by his relentless magazine advertising, much of it full-page, sales of Berliner Gramophones accelerated throughout 1897 and 1898. Readers of popular magazines became accustomed to seeing the Gramophone touted in large ads featuring attractive half-tone photographs and splashy headlines such as, "THE TALKING MACHINE THAT TALKS TALK!" The quality of the advertising lent some prestige to the relatively new Gramophone, and its growing success was observed with concern by the Edison and Columbia forces. From 1898 onward, both of these companies gradually began to

1-5. In December 1896, while Edison and Columbia were employing simple, line drawings in their print advertising, Frank Seaman was promoting the Gramophone with real photos of average Americans enjoying Mr. Berliner's invention. This distinctively tinted quarter-page ad appeared in *Ladies' Home Journal*. (Value code: H)

emulate the innovative advertising tactics of Frank Seaman.

By the close of 1900, phonograph and record advertising was developing at the pace of the evolving industry it represented. Substantial ads with detailed images reached out from the pages to entice prospective customers. Large typeface proclaimed the marvelous virtues of various talking machines. In short, *visual* attractions were being seriously employed to market an *acoustic* device. Evolving like the decorative cabinets and horns of the talking machine, advertising was gradually assuming a mantle of sophistication. The earliest stage of phonographic advertising was over.

1-6. A Gramophone advertisement from early 1897. The emphasis of Berliner advertising was less on the machine and more on the domestic joys it inspired. (Value code: H)

1-7. A Graphophone ad from June 1898. In the depiction of ordinary people, the influence of marketer Frank Seaman's style can be recognized. (Value code: H)

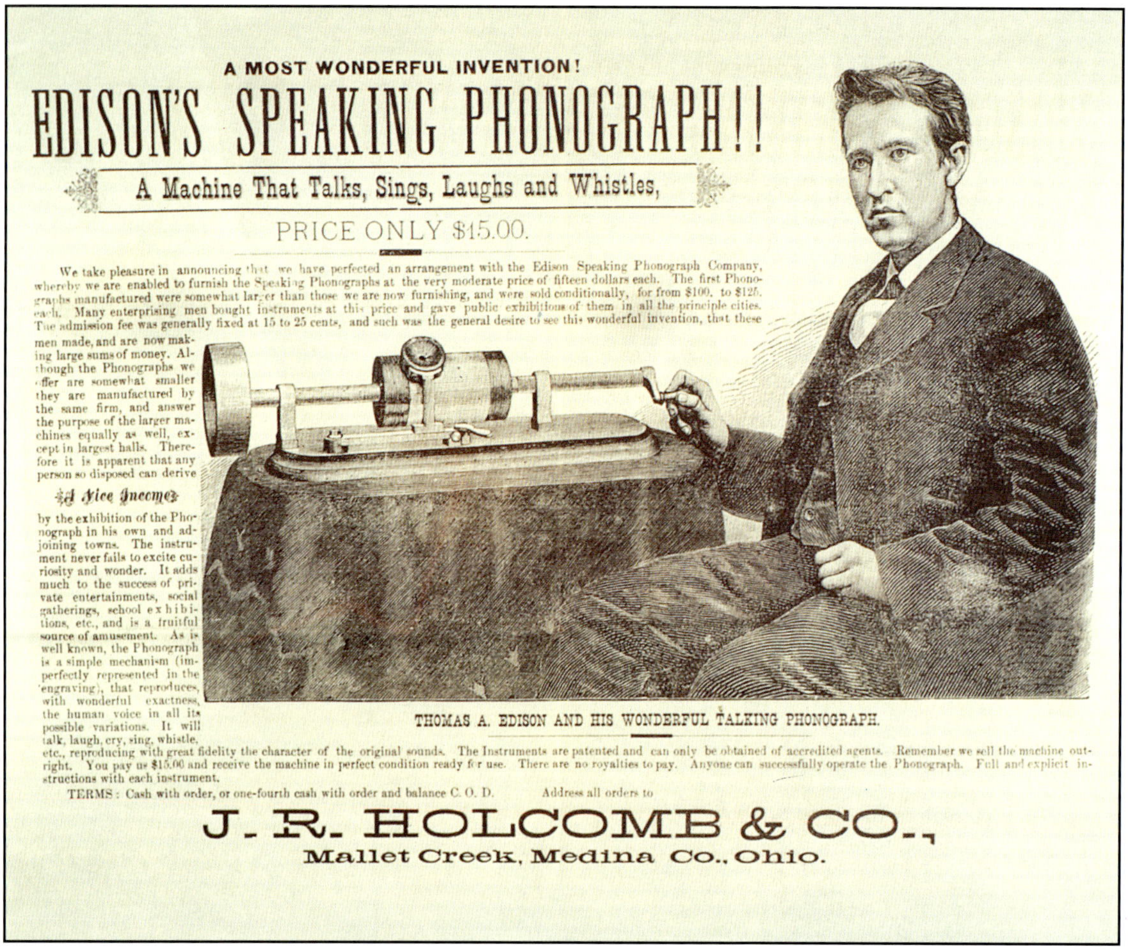

1-8. This flyer, the earliest known advertisement offering phonographs for sale, dates from late 1878 or early 1879. Below the engraving of a rather dazed-looking Thomas Edison with the large "second model" of his invention, the text carefully pointed out that, *"The first Phonographs manufactured were somewhat larger than those we are now furnishing…"* Additionally, the ad stated that, *"Although the Phonographs we offer are somewhat smaller[,] they are manufactured by the same firm…"* This makes it clear that the machines being offered for $15.00 were the small Bergmann models: a fraction of the size of the machine pictured. Interestingly, the text includes the suggestion that the fortunate owner might generate *"…A Nice Income by the exhibition of the Phonograph in his own and adjoining towns."* Measures 8 3/8" x 11". *Courtesy of René Rondeau.* (Value code: VR)

1-9. Free publicity, such as these engravings in the *Illustrated London News* of Edison's Phonograph being exhibited in Paris in 1889, was far more effective than the meager advertising of the North American Phonograph Company. (Value code: VR)

1-10. The founding of the American Graphophone Company in 1887, and the commercial introduction of the Graphophone, had caught Edison napping. He and his associates had developed a series of improved Phonographs, culminating in the venerable Class "M" electric model, which was rapidly put into production. The great Paris industrial exposition of 1889 presented a perfect opportunity for Edison to showcase his latest Phonograph. Crowds of people, such as these smartly attired exhibition-goers, came to listen to cylinder records being played through banks of rubber ear-tubes. This souvenir plate measures 8 1/2" in diameter. (Value code: E)

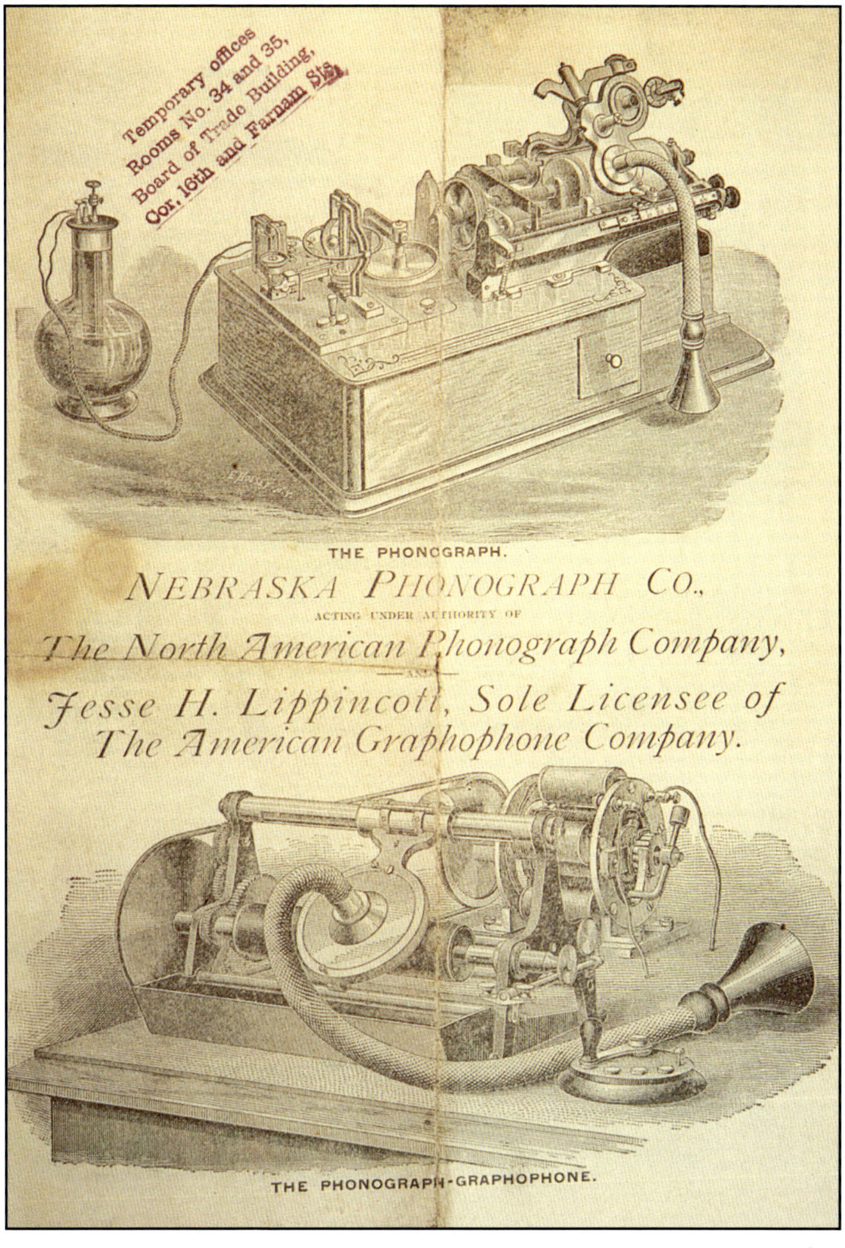

1-11. The North American Phonograph Company must have been born under a bad sign. Much of its misfortune stemmed from its ill-starred attempt to market two competing talking machines produced by mutually antagonistic manufacturers. This 6 1/2" x 9 1/2" flyer from one of North American's branches, the Nebraska Phonograph Company, illustrated the Phonograph and the Graphophone in their earliest commercial incarnations, circa 1889. (Value code: VR)

1-12. This book, published by Allen & Ginter under the guise of public edification, capitalized on Thomas Edison's fame, as well as the popularity of his inventions. The cover of this book illustrates the incandescent lamp, the improved telephone transmitter, and the Phonograph. Such publicity aided public acceptance of Edison's various commercial products, particularly the Phonograph. (Value code: VR)

1-13. Edison's visage could be found on later promotional items such as this "Inventor" cigar box label, and a card which accompanied a pack of Ogden's Guinea Gold Cigarettes. *Courtesy of Sam Sheena*. (Value code: F)

1-14. The likeness of Thomas Edison was recognizable the world over. This French trade card depicted the famous inventor listening to his Phonograph. On the reverse side, merchant A.A. Anderson described his wares, wholly unrelated to this promotional image. *Courtesy of the Tom and Sandi McCarthy collection.* (Value code: F)

1-15. The rear cover of an 1890 North American Phonograph Company brochure, 6 3/4" x 9 1/4", illustrated the entire mechanism of the Graphophone, including treadle-power stand. *Courtesy of Tom and Sandi McCarthy collection.* (Value code: VR)

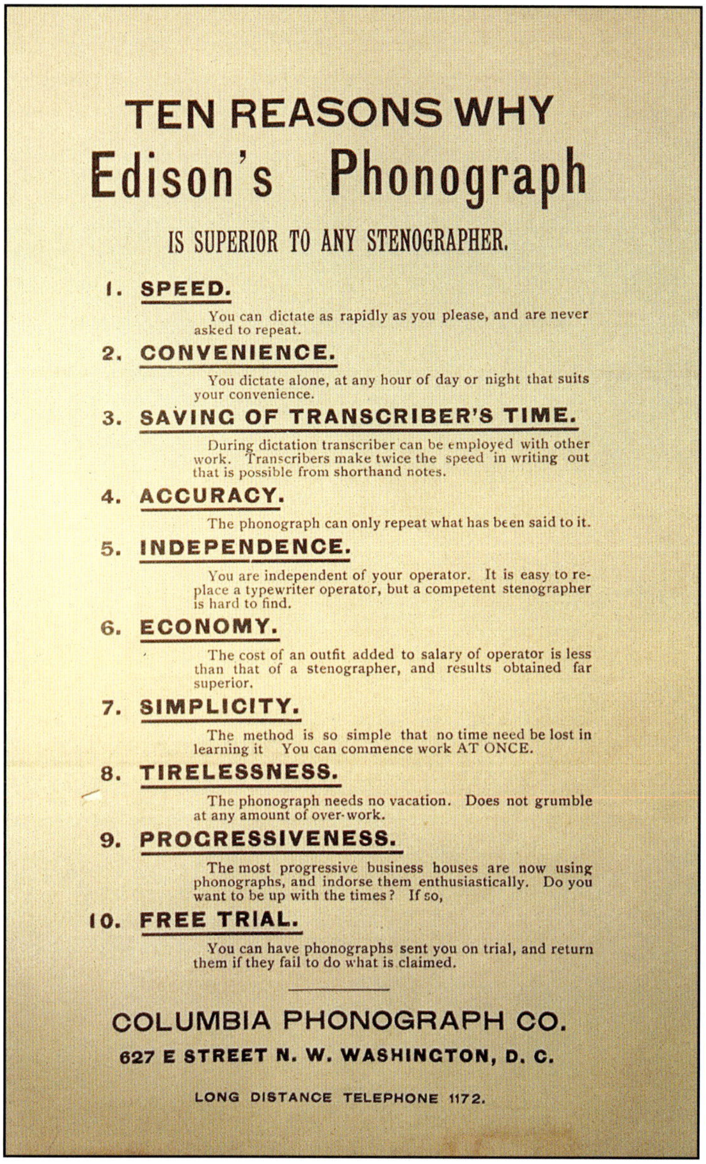

TEN REASONS WHY
Edison's Phonograph
IS SUPERIOR TO ANY STENOGRAPHER.

1. SPEED.
You can dictate as rapidly as you please, and are never asked to repeat.

2. CONVENIENCE.
You dictate alone, at any hour of day or night that suits your convenience.

3. SAVING OF TRANSCRIBER'S TIME.
During dictation transcriber can be employed with other work. Transcribers make twice the speed in writing out that is possible from shorthand notes.

4. ACCURACY.
The phonograph can only repeat what has been said to it.

5. INDEPENDENCE.
You are independent of your operator. It is easy to replace a typewriter operator, but a competent stenographer is hard to find.

6. ECONOMY.
The cost of an outfit added to salary of operator is less than that of a stenographer, and results obtained far superior.

7. SIMPLICITY.
The method is so simple that no time need be lost in learning it You can commence work AT ONCE.

8. TIRELESSNESS.
The phonograph needs no vacation. Does not grumble at any amount of over-work.

9. PROGRESSIVENESS.
The most progressive business houses are now using phonographs, and indorse them enthusiastically. Do you want to be up with the times? If so,

10. FREE TRIAL.
You can have phonographs sent you on trial, and return them if they fail to do what is claimed.

COLUMBIA PHONOGRAPH CO.
627 E STREET N. W. WASHINGTON, D. C.
LONG DISTANCE TELEPHONE 1172.

1-16. In 1892, the North American Phonograph Company was made up of 32 local branches that handled both Phonographs and Graphophones. The Columbia Phonograph Company's sales territory comprised Delaware, Maryland, and the District of Columbia. In the few years following its introduction in 1888, the Graphophone had proved unreliable, unpopular and, ultimately, non-saleable. Although the Columbia Phonograph Company would eventually become inextricably associated with the development and improvement of the Graphophone, in September 1892 when this 5 1/2" x 9 1/4" flyer was issued, Edison's Phonograph was the only viable talking machine that Columbia had to offer. *Courtesy of Ray Phillips.* (Value code: VR)

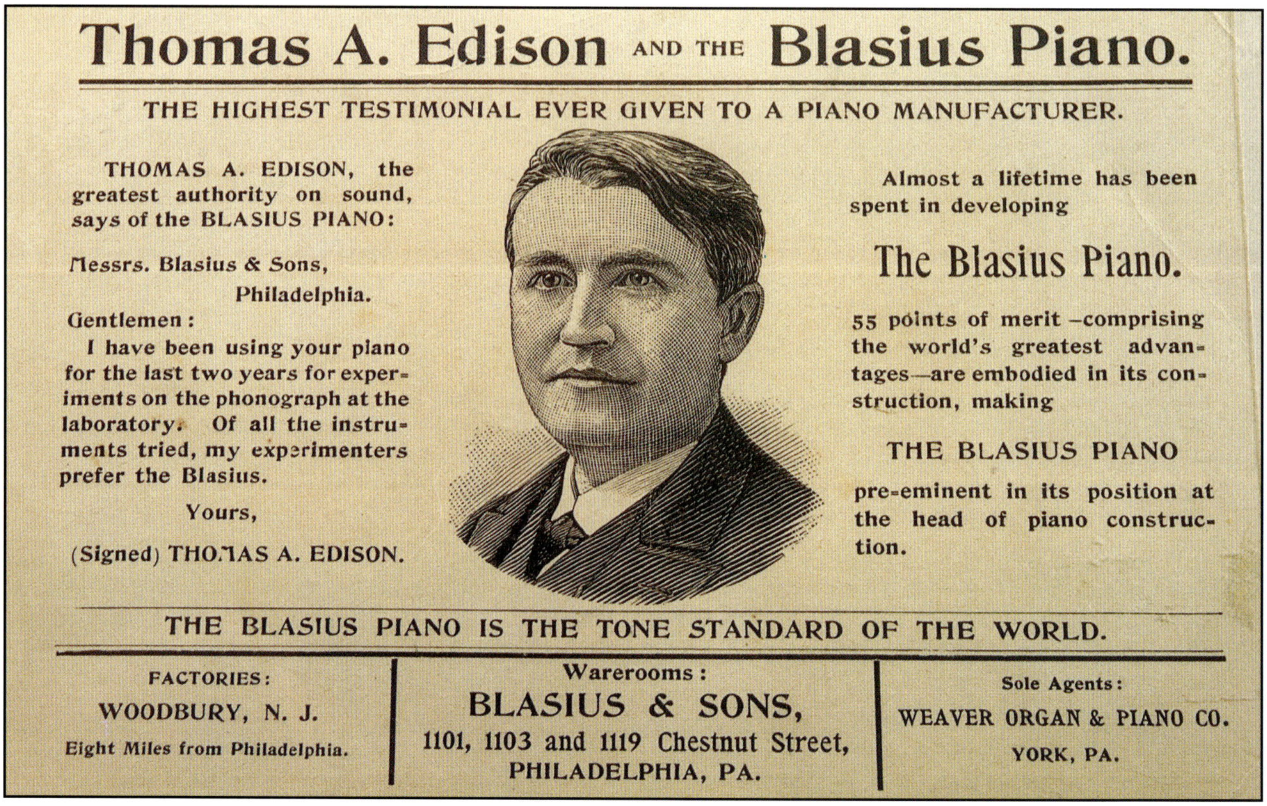

1-17. An 1890s trade card advertising the Blasius piano. In this instance, the scientific caché of the Phonograph was used to recommend another product. (Value code: F)

1-18. A turn of the twentieth century trade card from a piano dealer who also sold Edison Phonographs. *Courtesy of the Tom and Sandi McCarthy collection.* (Value code: G)

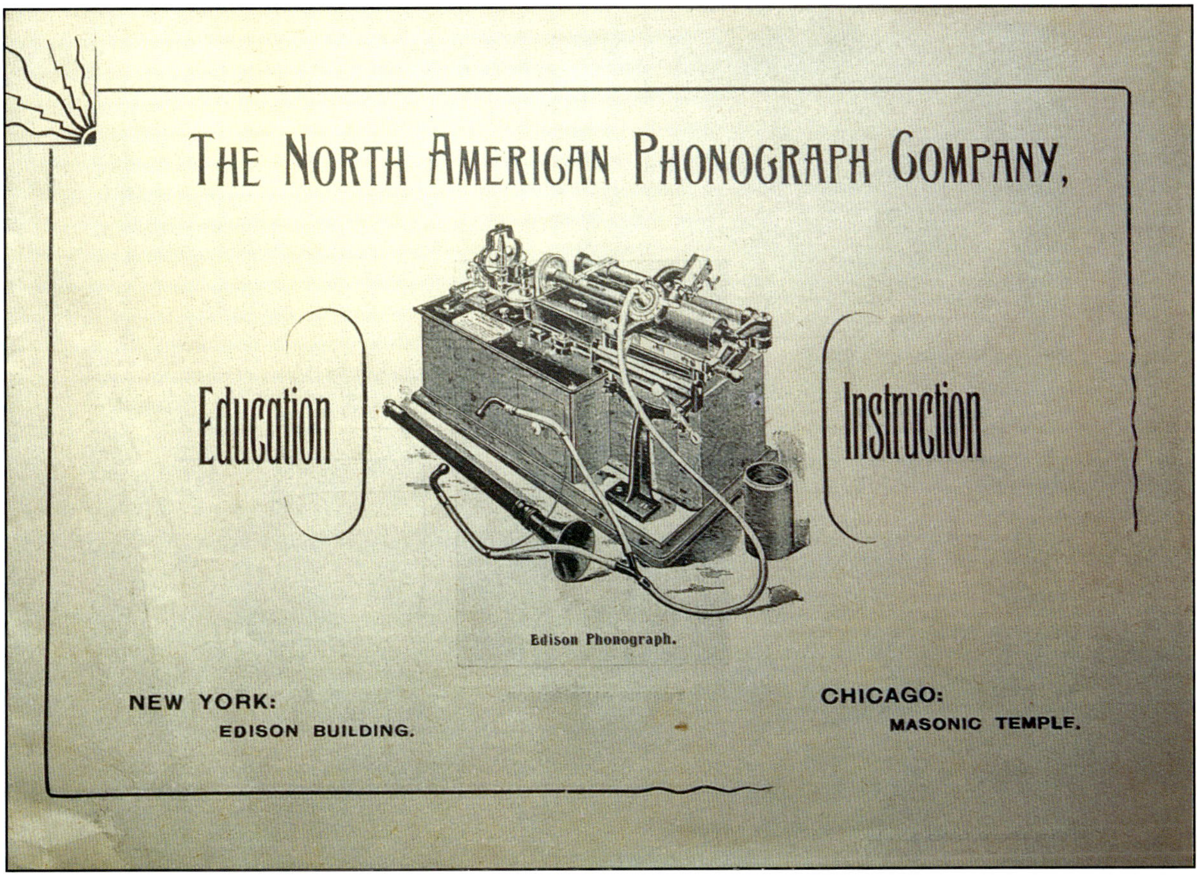

1-19. The cover of a booklet (5 1/4" x 7 3/4") from the North American Phonograph Company pointing out the educational and instructional benefits of the Edison Phonograph. Circa 1893. *Courtesy of Nina and Dave Heitz.* (Value code: VR)

1-20. Contained in the booklet are photographs such as this one, showing a class activity centered around an Edison Phonograph installed in a desk. *Courtesy of Nina and Dave Heitz.*

1-21. ...and pupils "declaiming" and "judging" by Phonograph. *Courtesy of Nina and Dave Heitz.*

1-22. The classical languages are included... *Courtesy of Nina and Dave Heitz.*

1-23. …as well as modern languages such as German, with an appropriately-Teutonic model. *Courtesy of Nina and Dave Heitz.*

1-24. This French student has really dressed the part. *Courtesy of Nina and Dave Heitz.*

1-25. Finally, the Phonograph demonstrates its instructional capacity to an immaculately-coiffed pupil. *Courtesy of Nina and Dave Heitz.*

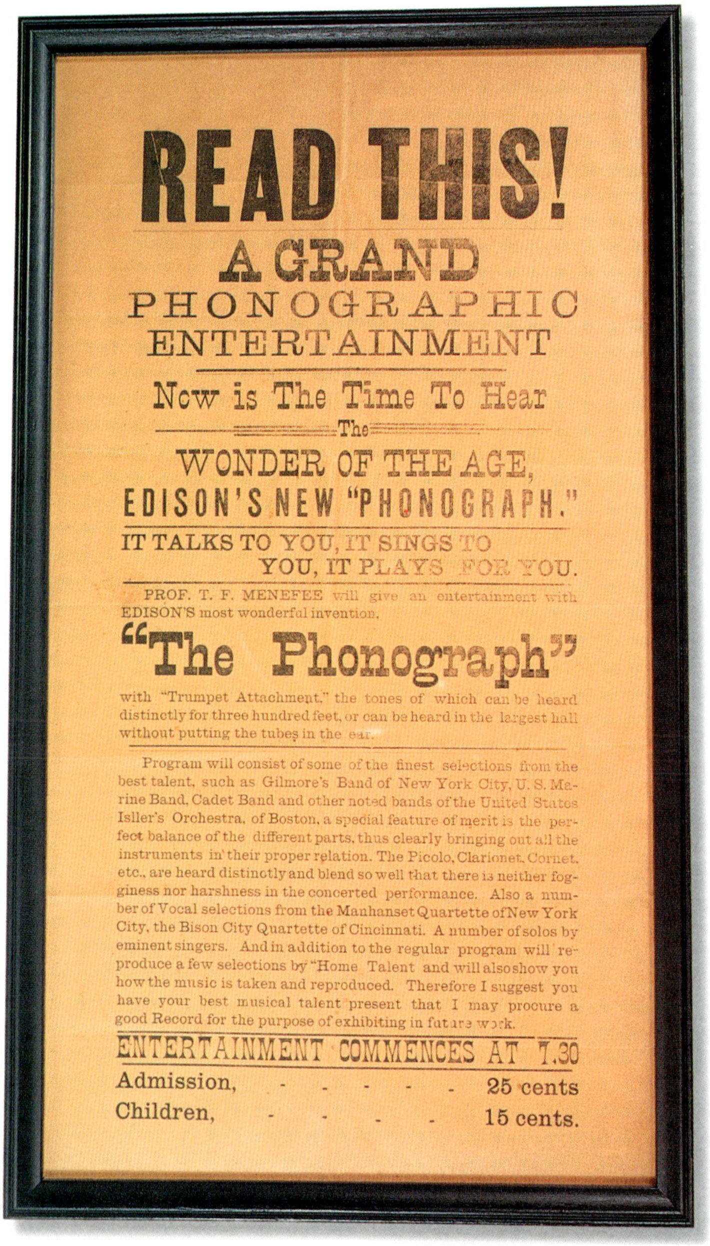

1-26. During the early-to-mid 1890s, phonograph exhibitions were revived as a popular form of entertainment. Showmen fanned out across the country with heavy Class "M" Edison electric Phonographs in tow, renting local halls and demonstrating "the wonder of the age" with plenty of trumped-up scientific hoopla. This 9 3/4" x 16 3/4" broadside included all the classic elements of such presentations. The "Trumpet Attachment, the tones of which can be heard distinctly for three hundred feet" obviated the more commonly-used ear-tubes. Furthermore, "Professor" Menefee's clever invitation to capture the performances of local talent not only stimulated business, but added to his repertoire of recordings. *Courtesy of Nina and Dave Heitz.* (Value code: E)

1-27. A 6 1/2" x 9 1/2" phonograph exhibition handbill from 1893, that laid important emphasis on the entertainment's suitability for ladies. *Courtesy of Nina and Dave Heitz.* (Value code: E)

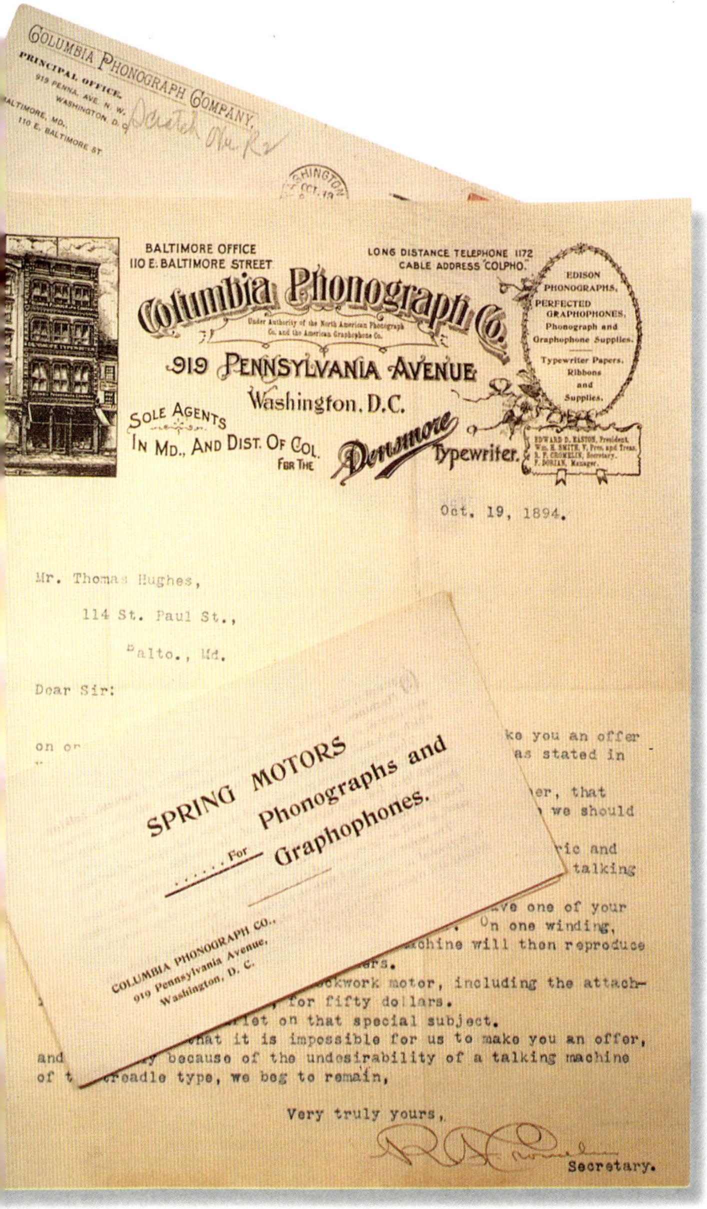

COLUMBIA PHONOGRAPH COMPANY,
PRINCIPAL OFFICE,
919 PENNA. AVE. N. W.
WASHINGTON, D. C.
BALTIMORE, MD.,
110 E. BALTIMORE ST.

BALTIMORE OFFICE
110 E. BALTIMORE STREET

LONG DISTANCE TELEPHONE 1172
CABLE ADDRESS "COLPHO."

Columbia Phonograph Co.
919 PENNSYLVANIA AVENUE
Washington, D.C.
SOLE AGENTS IN MD., AND DIST. OF COL. FOR THE Densmore Typewriter.

EDISON PHONOGRAPHS, PERFECTED GRAPHOPHONES, Phonograph and Graphophone Supplies. Typewriter Papers, Ribbons and Supplies.

Oct. 19, 1894.

Mr. Thomas Hughes,
114 St. Paul St.,
Balto., Md.

Dear Sir:

SPRING MOTORS For Phonographs and Graphophones.

COLUMBIA PHONOGRAPH CO., 919 Pennsylvania Avenue, Washington, D. C.

Very truly yours,

Secretary.

1-28. In 1894, the clockwork motor designed for the American Graphophone Company by Thomas Macdonald was one of the first alternatives to electric drive in Phonographs and Graphophones. At that time, the Columbia Phonograph Company of Washington, D.C. was on the verge of assuming control of American Graphophone, after which the Columbia Graphophone would become a formidable force in the talking machine industry. *Courtesy of Ray Phillips.* (Value code: VR)

The Edison
GRAND CONCERT
Machine.

WILL EXHIBIT AT

La Grand School House
Monday Night Sep 2d

This is the LARGEST and LATEST MACHINE out. It plays, talks, laughs and sings. Its music is loud, clear and sweet, and consists of VOCAL MUSIC, SOLOS, QUARTETS, BAND, VIOLIN, FIFE, DRUM, PICOLO, CORNET, ORCHESTRA, and other selections, We also have some comic talking records.

Come and Enjoy Yourselves.

ADMISSION--Adults 15 cents,
Children under 12 years 10 cents.

1-29. This 6" x 8" handbill advertised an exhibition of "The Edison Grand Concert Machine." Knowledgeable collectors might interpret this nomenclature literally, surmising that an Edison "Concert" Phonograph was employed. Since the "Concert" was introduced in February 1899, it is tempting to date this handbill no earlier. However, the style and content of this advertisement suggest an earlier date. Examining the calendar reveals only one viable possibility: Monday, September 2, 1895. Such individualistic language from talking machine exhibitors was common, and the historian must proceed with caution. In this case, the "Edison Grand Concert Machine" was undoubtedly an Edison Class "M" Phonograph. *Courtesy of Gilbert (Bert) Pasley.* (Value code: E)

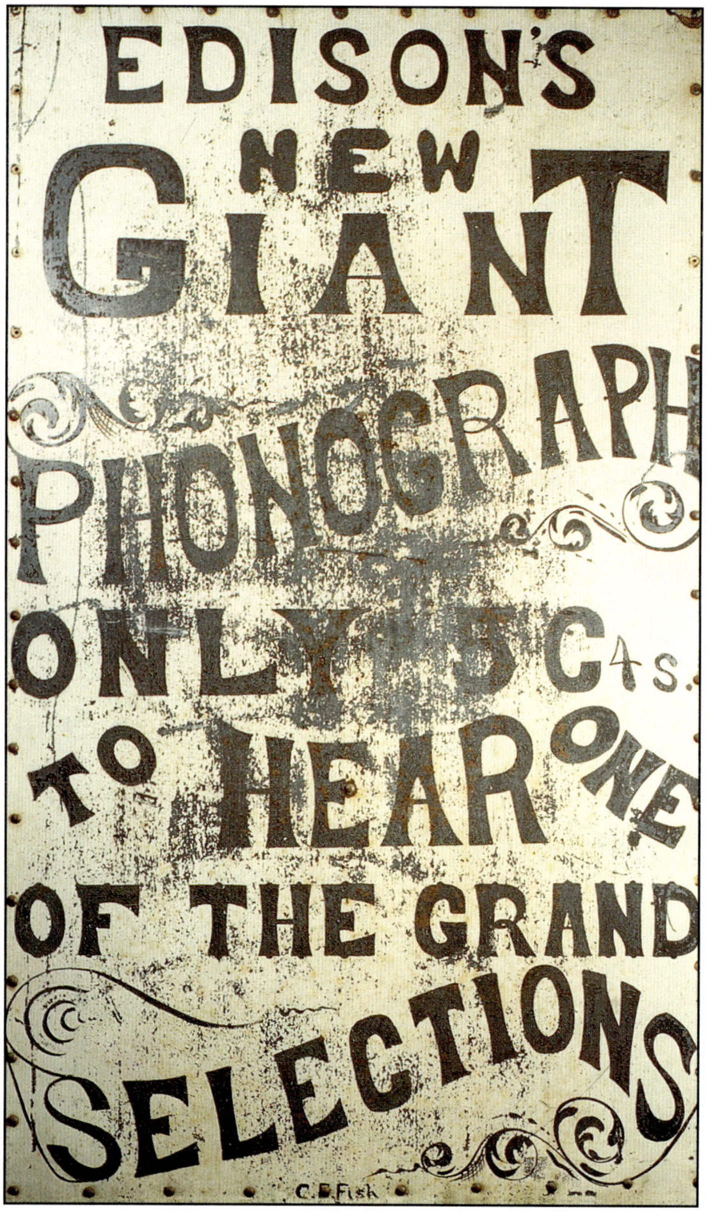

1-30. A locally made tin exhibition sign measuring 24" x 42", permanently mounted on a 72" tall easel. Again, the parlance of "Giant Phonograph" and especially "Grand Selections" might mislead one into believing that this artifact dates from 1899 or later. In this instance, the price of five cents for one selection implied that hearing tubes were employed, a practice not required with 5" talking machines because of greater volume they produced. More likely, this advertisement was rendered in the 1894-1898 period, and the terminology was simply part of the showmanship. The identity of "C.E. Fish" remains a mystery: perhaps the sign-painter or the exhibitor, or possibly both. *Courtesy of the Gfell family collection.* (Value code: VR)

1-31. This scrapbook contains a remarkable record of phonographic exhibitions presented from 1895 until 1898. Mr. H. Dannbury and Miss N. Dannbury (presumably his daughter or sister) traveled throughout southeast Asia with an Edison Class "M" Phonograph, presenting recorded entertainments. (Value code: VR)

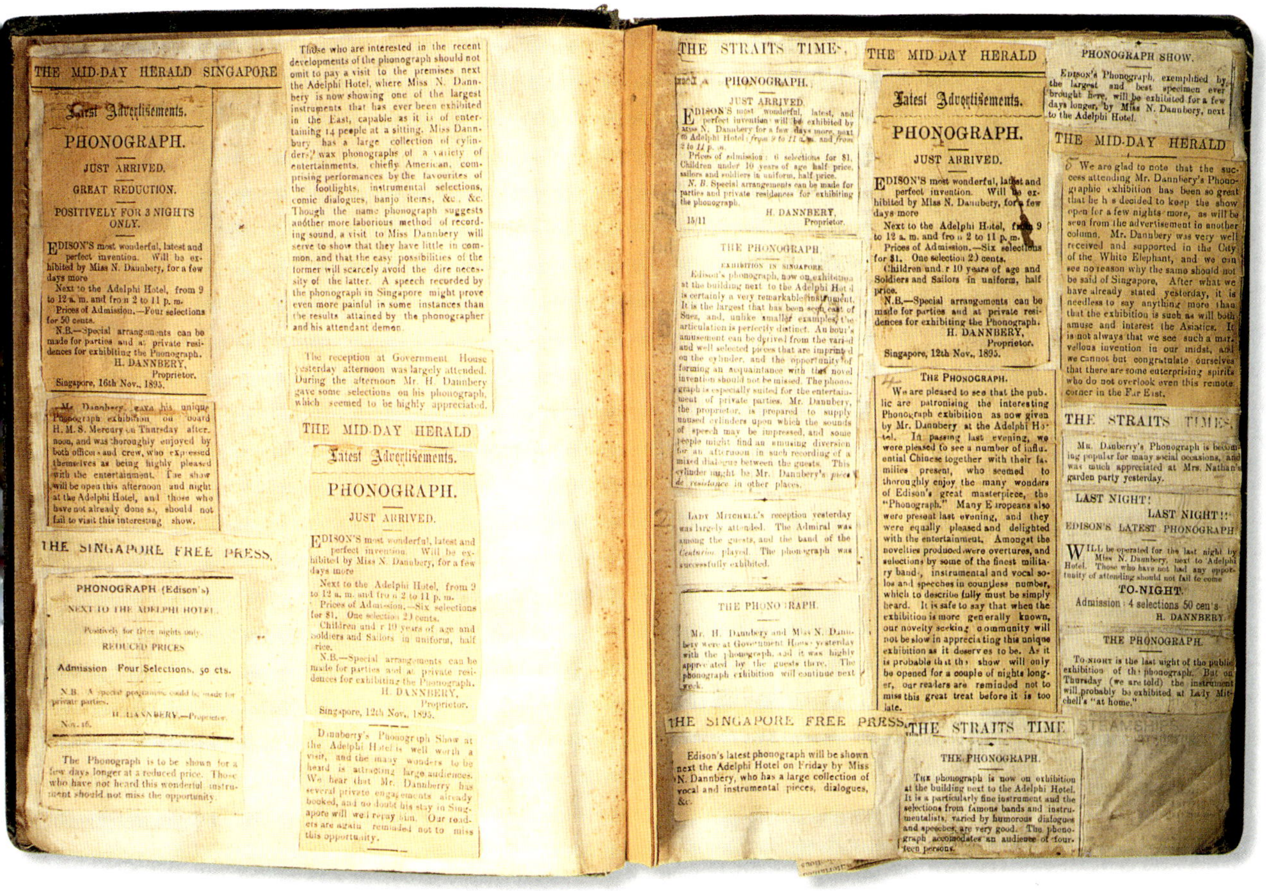

1-32. These press clippings were carefully collected and preserved by the Dannburys. They document the couple's travels from Singapore to Rangoon and southern India. Ceylon and Java are also mentioned in the news copy.

1-33. It becomes obvious from the identical wording of texts from various publications, that the Dannburys provided the copy to local newspapers, which printed these contributions verbatim.

EXPRESS.

MASONIC CLUB, SINGAPORE.

Saturday, 18th January, 1896.

Bro. H. Dannberg will give a performance with his fine new Edison's Latest Phonograph, in the Reading Room, on Saturday Night, commencing at 8-30 p.m., to which Members and their Friends (including Ladies), are invited.

Bro. Dannberg has a large number of Cylinders with the latest Songs and Music, Vocal and Instrumental, and can furnish an admirable evening's entertainment. He has fixed the low price of 50 cents for five selections.

THE MID-DAY HERALD

Mr. Dannbery's phonograph will be exhibited for the last time to-night next to Adelphi Hotel. It is being much admired by those who have witnessed it, and those who have not yet made themselves acquainted with this marvellous instrument should not lose the opportunity. We are glad to hear that the enterprising proprietor has secured an engagement at Government House on Thursday, when he will exhibit to Lady Mitchell's guests at the Reception.

THE STRAITS TIMES.

PHONOGRAPH.

JUST ARRIVED.
GREAT REDUCTION.

Positively for 3 nights only.

EDISON'S most wonderful, latest, and perfect invention will be exhibited by Miss N. Dannbery for a few days more, next to Adelphi Hotel: *from 2 to 11 p. m.*

Prices of admission: 4 selections for 50 cents. Children under 10 years of age half price, sailors and soldiers in uniform, half price.

N. B. Special arrangements can be made for parties and private residences for exhibiting the phonograph.

H. DANNBERY,
Proprietor.

THE phonograph is still on exhibition in the building next to the Adelphi Hotel. Yesterday, Mr. Dannbery gave a successful entertainment with Edison's invention on board H. M. S. *Mercury.*

1-34. Sometimes referred to as "Bro. Dannbury" (or even "Dannberg"!), and occasionally as "Professor," Mr. Dannbury adjusted his prices during the tour. In Singapore, the entertainment had cost $1.00 (local currency) for 6 selections, or 20 cents each. This charge was reduced to 5 selections for 50 cents. Eventually, the Dannburys settled on 4 selections for 50 cents. Children and military men in uniform were admitted for half price.

1-35. "Edison's Latest Phonograph" was the aging Class "M," a design which first appeared in 1888 and whose improvements ceased in 1891. An efficient, albeit complicated mechanism, the Dannburys' Class "M" was usually fitted with a rail of 14 listening tubes. The use of a "funnel" is also mentioned.

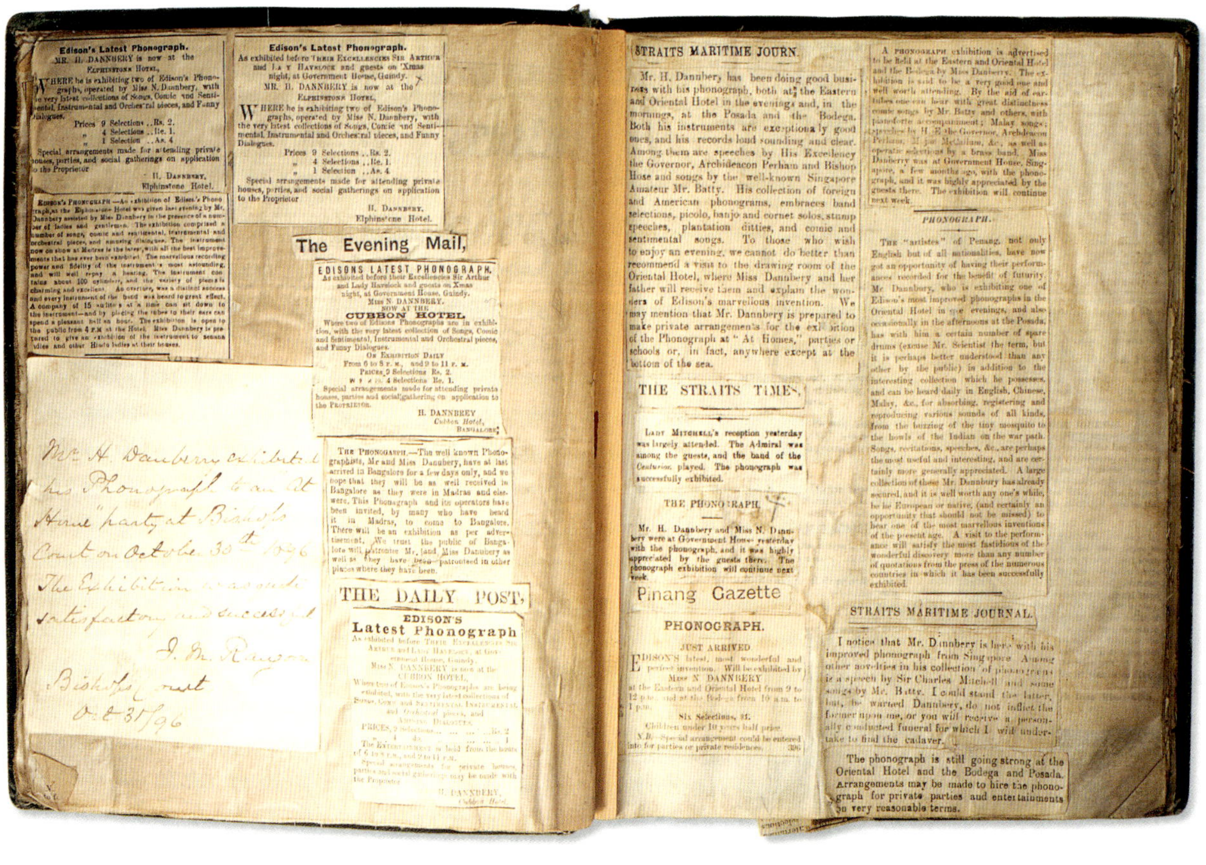

Edison's Latest Phonograph.

The Evening Mail.

Mr. H. Danbery exhibited his Phonograph to an At Home party at Bishop's Court on October 30th 1896. The Exhibition was most satisfactory and successful.

THE DAILY POST.

STRAITS MARITIME JOURN.

THE STRAITS TIMES.

Pinang Gazette

STRAITS MARITIME JOURNAL.

The phonograph is still going strong at the Oriental Hotel and the Bodega and Posada. Arrangements may be made to hire the phonograph for private parties and entertainments on very reasonable terms.

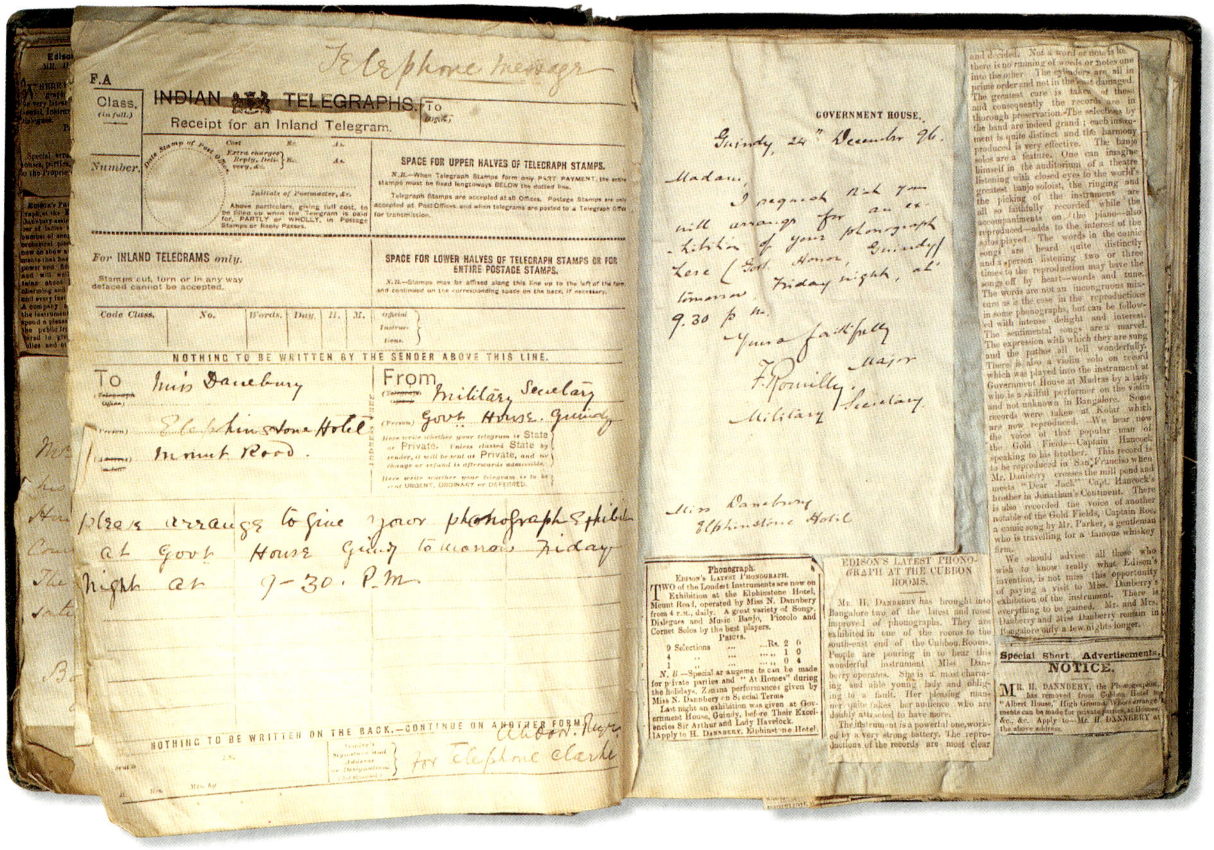

1-36. The Dannburys recorded the words of local dignitaries and ethnic pieces, including excerpts from the Koran to entertain Islamic patrons. Many of the clippings mention that entertainments were attended not only by Europeans, but also by members of the ethnic population.

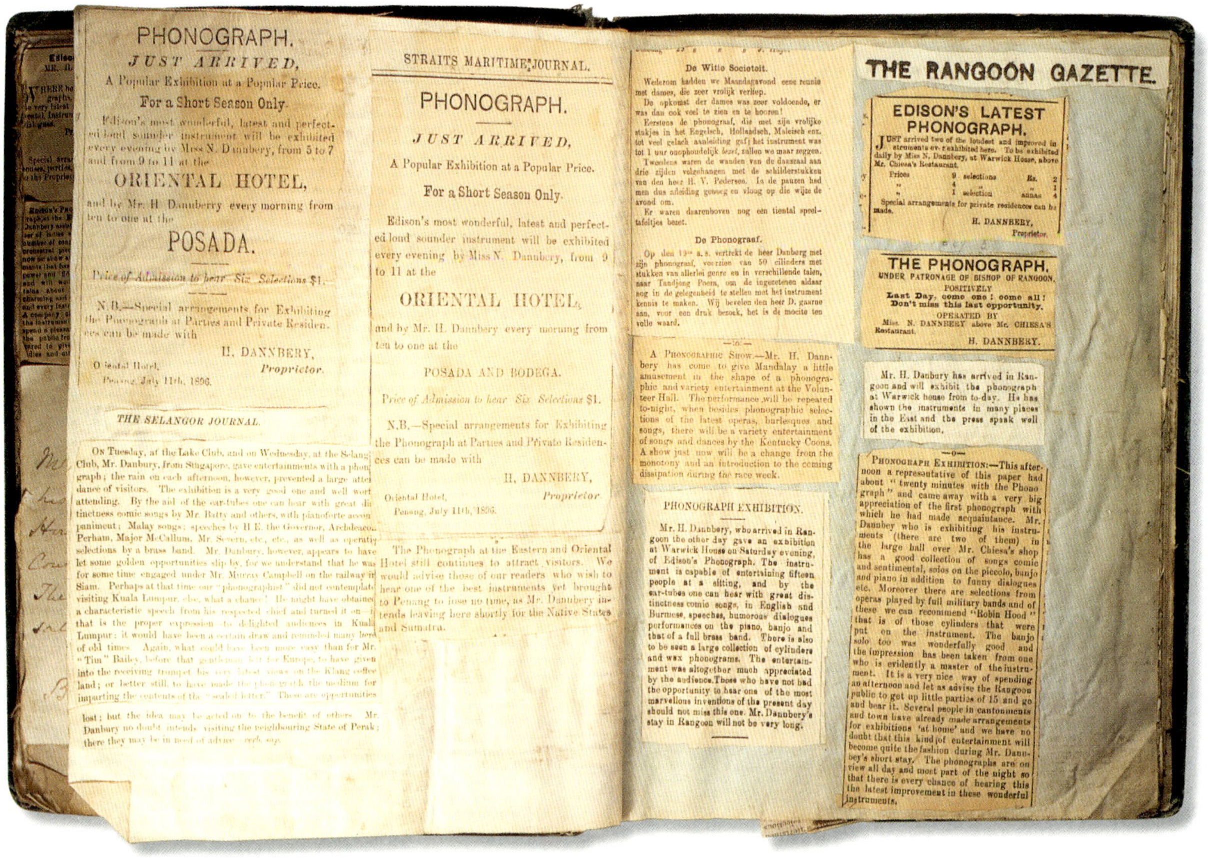

1-37. The clipping at the lower left makes it clear that not all of the Dannbury's publicity was written by them. In this instance, the writer laments not only the weather, but also the lost opportunities for recording during a rail trip.

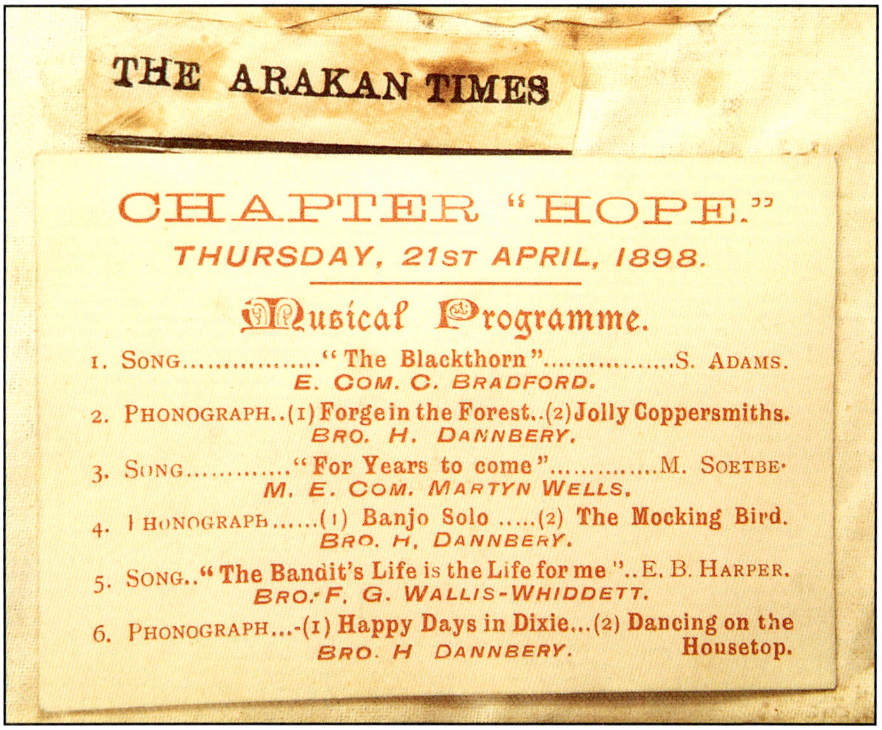
THE ARAKAN TIMES

CHAPTER "HOPE."

THURSDAY, 21ST APRIL, 1898.

Musical Programme.

1. SONG................."The Blackthorn"................S. ADAMS.
E. COM. C. BRADFORD.

2. PHONOGRAPH..(1) Forge in the Forest..(2) Jolly Coppersmiths.
BRO. H. DANNBERY.

3. SONG............"For Years to come"............M. SOETBE.
M. E. COM. MARTYN WELLS.

4. PHONOGRAPH......(1) Banjo Solo .....(2) The Mocking Bird.
BRO. H. DANNBERY.

5. SONG.."The Bandit's Life is the Life for me"..E. B. HARPER.
BRO. F. G. WALLIS-WHIDDETT.

6. PHONOGRAPH...-(1) Happy Days in Dixie...(2) Dancing on the Housetop.
BRO. H DANNBERY.

1-38. By the end of the Dannbury's three-year tour, "Bro. Dannbury" was sharing the stage with live performers. The scrapbook abruptly ends, with no clue given regarding the couple's plans, future venue, or activities. Whatever may have become of the Dannburys, this document is a noteworthy record of their phonographic sojourn, and the way in which it was publicized.

1-39. The French "Bébé Jumeau" phonograph doll incorporated a Lioret "Le Merveilleux" (the Marvelous) mechanism within the popular Jumeau doll. Seldom seen is the original box with its distinctive advertising label. The lid interior carried instructions and a list of celluloid cylinder records available for the doll (as seen in the foreground). Box measures 9 1/4" wide by 26 1/4" long. *Courtesy of the Tom and Sandi McCarthy collection*. (Value code: box is VR)

LE MERVEILLEUX

CATALOGUE DES CYLINDRES DE RECHANGE

CHANSONS	Chansons Enfantines
Allume, Allume	Polichinelle
Czarine	Ah mon beau château
Le clairon (Déroulède)	Nous n'irons plus au bois
Les Gardes Municipaux	Petit papa
Le Chat Noir (Bruant)	Petit poupon
A Ménilmontant	La mère Michel
Tararaboum	J'ai du bon tabac
La ronde des matelots	Cadet Rousselle
Tyrolienne. Ma Fernanda	Il pleut bergère
Auprès de ma blonde	Au clair de la lune
Tonton Tontaine	Fais dodo
Petit Faust	Le roi Dagobert
François les bas bleus	Il court le Furet
Les deux aveugles	Giroflée Girofla
Ousqu'est St-Nazaire	**PISTON**
Les bas noirs	Les gardes Municipaux
POTS POURRIS	La ronde des matelots
Il était un petit navire	Les bleus à Madagascar
Mlle Thérèse	Au clair de la Lune
Le Roi Dagobert (Duo)	Les petits bateaux
Sur le pont d'Avignon	La Marseillaise
Rachel (Parodie)	Marche Royale (Espagnol)
CLAIRON	Le sentier des Violettes etc., etc.
Toutes les marches de la 1re à la 10e	**TROMPETTE**
Réveil, Extinction, Arbi, Bugeaud, Aux Champs, etc.	Sonnerie de cavalerie: Duo Réveil, Extinction, Retraite etc.

MARQUE HL DÉPOSÉE

MARQUE HL DÉPOSÉE

PHONOGRAPHE SYSTÈME LIORET PARLANT A HAUTE VOIX
Reproductions en toutes langues
Demander le catalogue général

1-40. A flyer showing the Lioret "Le Merveilleux" phonograph and a catalogue of available celluloid cylinder records. Note the list of children's songs ("Chansons Enfantines") suitable for the "Bébé Jumeau" phonograph doll. Flyer measures 3 5/8" x 7 1/4". Courtesy of *René Rondeau.* (Value code: F)

1-41. The influential United States Phonograph Company of Newark, New Jersey, existed from 1893 through 1897. This firm acted as Edison's export agent, incubated several key men in the talking machine and recording industry, and was a major wholesaler and retailer of cylinder recordings. These cabinet photographs (4 1/2" x 6 1/2") of musical talent were intended to promote the sale of records. Popular vocalist Edward M. Favor, center, is flanked by bandleaders Edward Issler (left), and Patrick Gilmore (right). *Courtesy of the Charles Hummel collections.* (Value code: VR)

1-42. Gianni Bettini aspired to make his ingenious "Micro-Phonograph" an instrument of culture and refinement. Integral to this goal was the persuasion of first-rank performers to make recordings for him. In February 1896, the world-famous stage star Sarah Bernhardt visited the Bettini studio to make recordings. This coup warranted the presence of a photographer, and the resultant images saw service in Bettini publicity for several years. This mounted photograph is stamped, "Micro Phonograph Studio, 110 Fifth Avenue, New York," and was proudly inscribed and signed by Bettini himself. 12 1/2" x 14 3/4". *Courtesy of the Tom and Sandi McCarthy collection.* (Value code: VR)

CATALOGUE

• • OF • •

The Famous • • •

"Columbia

• • • Records,"

MANUFACTURED BY THE

Columbia

Phonograph Company,

PRINCIPAL OFFICE:

919 Pennsylvania Avenue,

WASHINGTON D. C.

CABLE ADDRESS, "COLPHO, WASHINGTON."

1-43. The Columbia Phonograph Company of Washington, D.C. had been a local subsidiary of the ill-fated North American Phonograph Company network, and one of the few to survive the 1894 collapse of the mother firm. While other North American branches foundered trying to market unreliable Phonographs and Graphophones, Columbia had prospered by recording, manufacturing, and selling entertainment cylinders (largely to support a burgeoning need in the coin-operated talking machine industry). This 3" x 9" catalogue from August, 1896 justifiably referred to "the famous Columbia records." *Courtesy of Ray Phillips.* (Value code: VR)

1-44. Just a year after its introduction, the Type "N" Graphophone was depicted in this typical line drawing. The advertisement, from the August 1896 issue of *Cosmopolitan*, also announced Columbia's innovative coin-operated Type "N." (Value code: H)

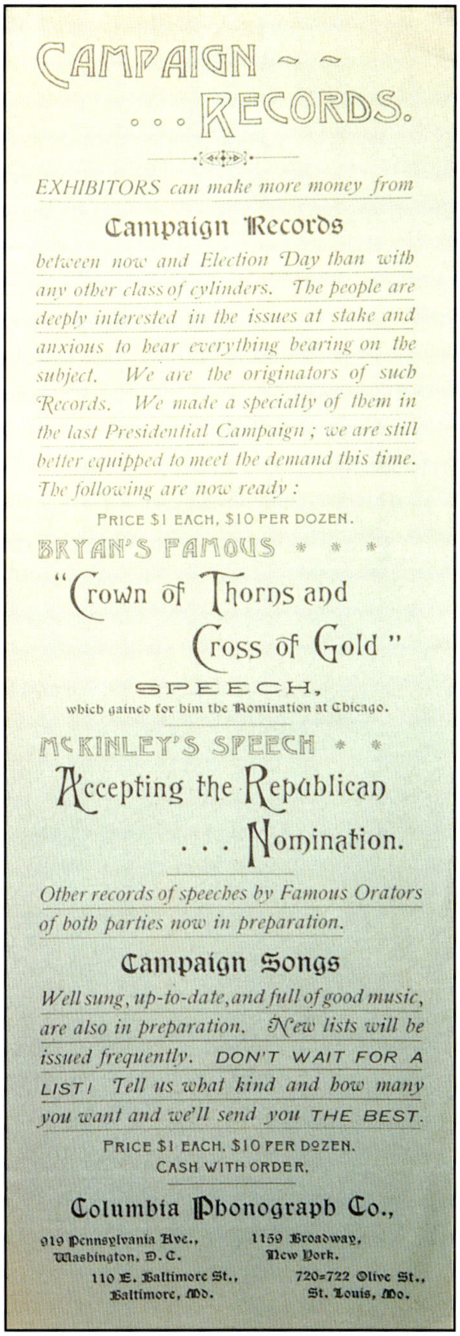

1-45. The role of the phonograph in Presidential campaigns was felt early and would increase with time. This 1896, 3" x 9" supplement intriguingly made mention of records from the 1892 campaign, when Grover Cleveland prevailed over Benjamin Harrison. It is also fascinating to note the emphasis on the sale of records to coin-slot exhibitors, which had been Columbia's salvation during the bleakest years of its existence. *Courtesy of Ray Phillips*. (Value code: VR)

GRAND OPERA HOUSE,
JOHNSON & RICHARDSON, Mgrs.

SATURDAY NIGHT, NOV. 21

Greatest Marvel of the Age

AN OPPORTUNITY TO SEE AND HEAR

EDISON'S

PHONOGRAPH

—OR—

TALKING MACHINE,

The wonderful mechanical invention which reproduces the Human Voice with correct accent, emphasis and tone. It also reproduces Instrumental Music with absolute distinctness and harmony, whether producing the tones of a Single Instrument or those of an Entire Brass Band.

The PHONOGRAPH USED ON THIS OCCASION

Is one of the best and has all the appliances and attachments necessary to give satisfactory results in public entertainments. There is a large horn attached to the Phonograph, so that all the audience can hear it without having tubes attached to their ears, as has been the custom heretofore.

PROGRAMME.

1. Fire Alarm, as played by Holding's Military Band.
2. Selections from Hoyt's Brass Monkey.
3. Farewell to Dresden, by U. S. Marine Band.
4. Slide, Kelly Slide, as sung by Geo. Jefferson Gaskin.
5. Famous Speech of Capt. Dempsey, Montgomery Guards.
6. Home, Sweet Home, with Variation. Clarionet Solo.
7. Going Back to Dixie. Vocal Quartette.
8. Operatic Selections, as played by Ishler's Orchestra.
9. The Day of Our Lord, by U. S. Marine Band.
10. Laughing Song. Vocal Solo by Geo. W. Johnson.
11. Pat Brady on a Spree. Comic Speech by Dan Kelley.
12. Old Simon. Vocal Solo.
13. Washington Guards Polka. Cornet Solo.
14. In Rapture Sweet, Waltz, by Ishler's Orchestra.
15. St. Patrick's Day. Speech by Dan Kelley.

Other reproductions of songs as rendered by the most noted singers. Band and Orchestra Music as played by the best musical organizations in the country.

WE GIVE A CORDIAL INVITATION

To any persons in the audience who desire to do so, to come up after the performance and sing or talk into the machine, when the same will be reproduced for the benefit of the audience.

Admission 15c. Children 10c. Reserved Seats 25c., at Carlton's Drug Store.

DEMOCRAT PRINT, BEDFORD.

1-46. This poster advertised "the opportunity to see and hear" an Edison Phonograph on Saturday, November 21, 1896. Note the provision of "…a large horn attached to the Phonograph, so that all the audience can hear it without having tubes attached to their ears, as has been the custom heretofore." Most unusual is the offering of "Reserved Seats" for 25 cents. Measures 4 3/4" x 12 3/4". *Courtesy of the Charles Hummel collections.*
(Value code: E)

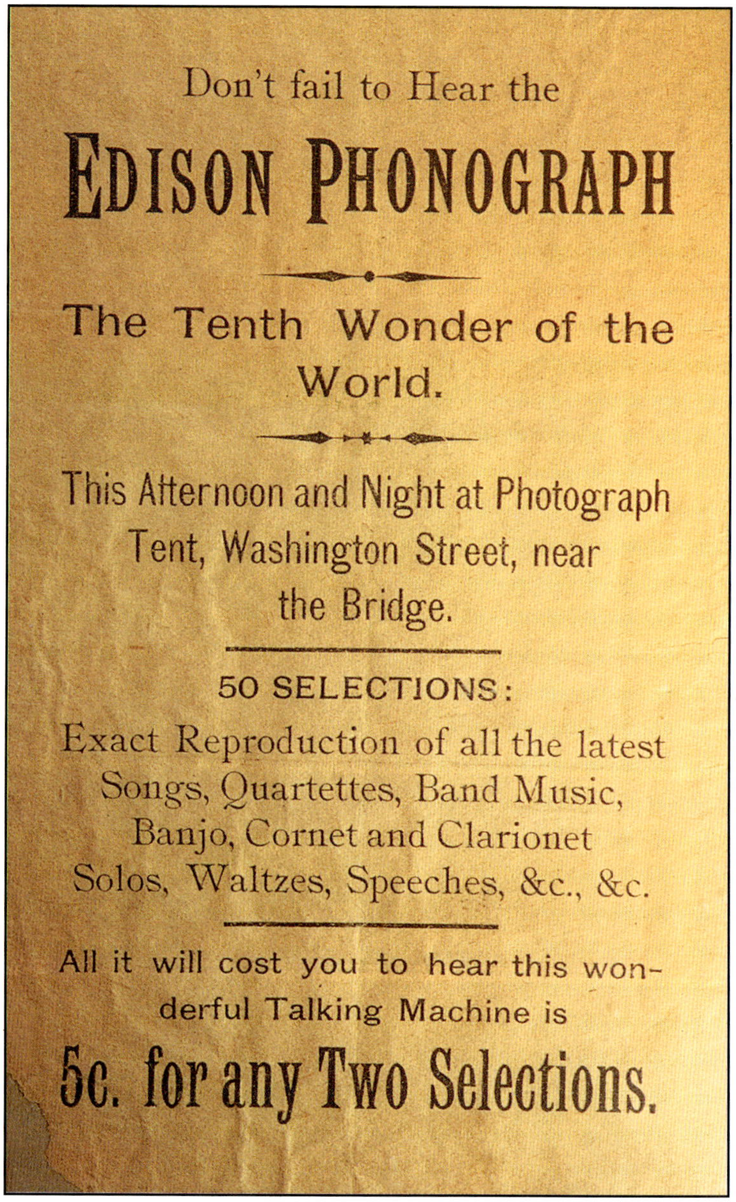

Don't fail to Hear the

EDISON PHONOGRAPH

The Tenth Wonder of the World.

This Afternoon and Night at Photograph Tent, Washington Street, near the Bridge.

50 SELECTIONS:

Exact Reproduction of all the latest Songs, Quartettes, Band Music, Banjo, Cornet and Clarionet Solos, Waltzes, Speeches, &c., &c.

All it will cost you to hear this wonderful Talking Machine is

5c. for any Two Selections.

1-47. A slightly later handbill promoting an Edison Phonograph ensconced in the "Photograph Tent" of a town social or fair. The charge of five cents for two selections suggests the use of ear tubes, and the fifty available selections would be an inducement for patrons to return and hear more. In this way, customers could listen when it was most convenient for them, and not be sequestered for large blocks of time. *Courtesy of the Charles Hummel collections.*
(Value code: E)

1-48. At the time this 6" x 9 1/4" catalogue was issued late in 1896, the Columbia Phonograph Company was on the threshold of greatness. The popular-priced ($25.00) Type "A" Graphophone had just been introduced, and this catalogue also featured the newly-sprouted Type "N" coin-slot Graphophone (one of the first of many widely distributed automatic models). *Courtesy of the Tom and Sandi McCarthy collection.* (Value code: E)

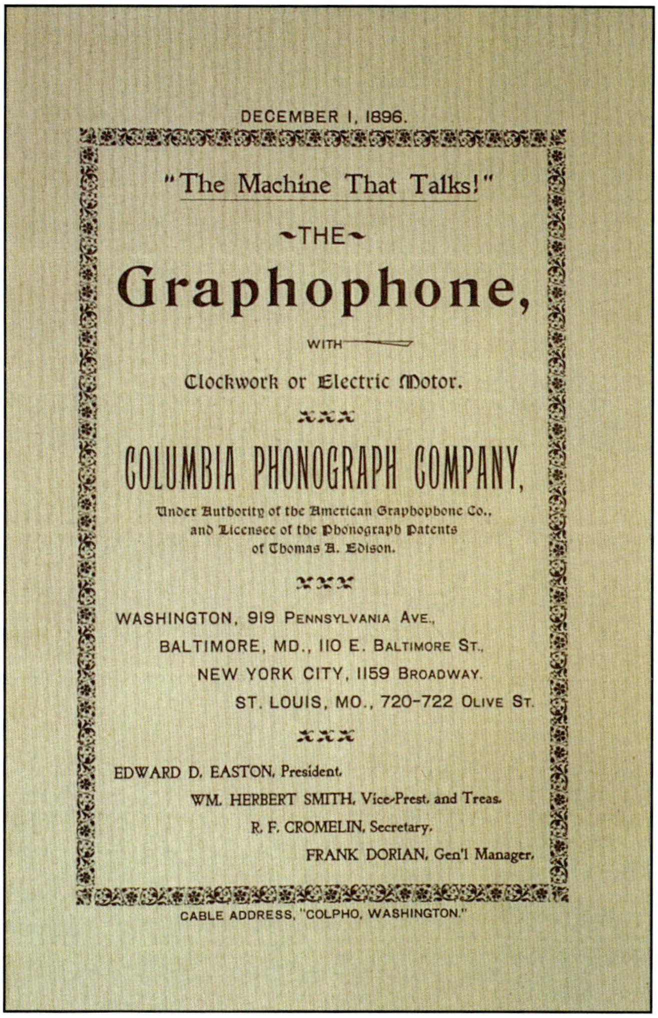

DECEMBER 1, 1896.

"The Machine That Talks!"

THE

Graphophone,

WITH

Clockwork or Electric Motor.

xxx

COLUMBIA PHONOGRAPH COMPANY,

Under Authority of the American Graphophone Co., and Licensee of the Phonograph Patents of Thomas A. Edison.

xxx

WASHINGTON, 919 PENNSYLVANIA AVE.,
BALTIMORE, MD., 110 E. BALTIMORE ST.,
NEW YORK CITY, 1159 BROADWAY.
ST. LOUIS, MO., 720-722 OLIVE ST.

xxx

EDWARD D. EASTON, President.
WM. HERBERT SMITH, Vice-Prest. and Treas.
R. F. CROMELIN, Secretary.
FRANK DORIAN, Gen'l Manager.

CABLE ADDRESS, "COLPHO, WASHINGTON."

AN IMPROVED about August 1897

Amplifying Reproducer

FOR GRAPHOPHONES.

Our latest and most substantial improvement is an AMPLIFYING REPRODUCER of aluminum, which greatly increases the volume of sound, imparts a remarkably pure, FIRM, sweet tone to both vocal and instrumental music, and reproduces the loudest records WITHOUT harshness or "blast."

The aluminum reproducer takes the place of the hard rubber reproducer, and fits all types of Graphophones. Exhibitors must have it to be up-to-date. In large halls or auditoriums the gain is striking and impressive. All users of Graphophones will find it greatly improves the quality of records and increases the attractiveness of the instrument. Price $5, cash with order. State serial number and type of Graphophone in ordering. An allowance of $1.50 each made for old reproducers (with sapphire point) in exchange, if in good order. New machines equipped with aluminum reproducers in place of the regular model at $3.50 extra.

Order from office nearest you.

COLUMBIA PHONOGRAPH COMPANY,

1155, 1157, 1159 BROADWAY, NEW YORK CITY.
919 PENNSYLVANIA AVENUE, WASHINGTON, D. C.
110 E. BALTIMORE STREET, BALTIMORE, MD.
720-722 OLIVE STREET, ST. LOUIS, MO.
1032 CHESTNUT STREET, PHILADELPHIA, PA.
BOARDWALK AND KENTUCKY AVE., ATLANTIC CITY, N. J.

1-49. A 5" x 8" flyer from August 1897 announcing the introduction of Columbia's aluminum-bodied reproducers. The earliest Graphophone reproducers had been molded from gutta percha (a tree-sap resin) or "hard rubber." The slightly heavier aluminum variety facilitated tracking, and also increased volume. *Courtesy of Ray Phillips.* (Value code: G)

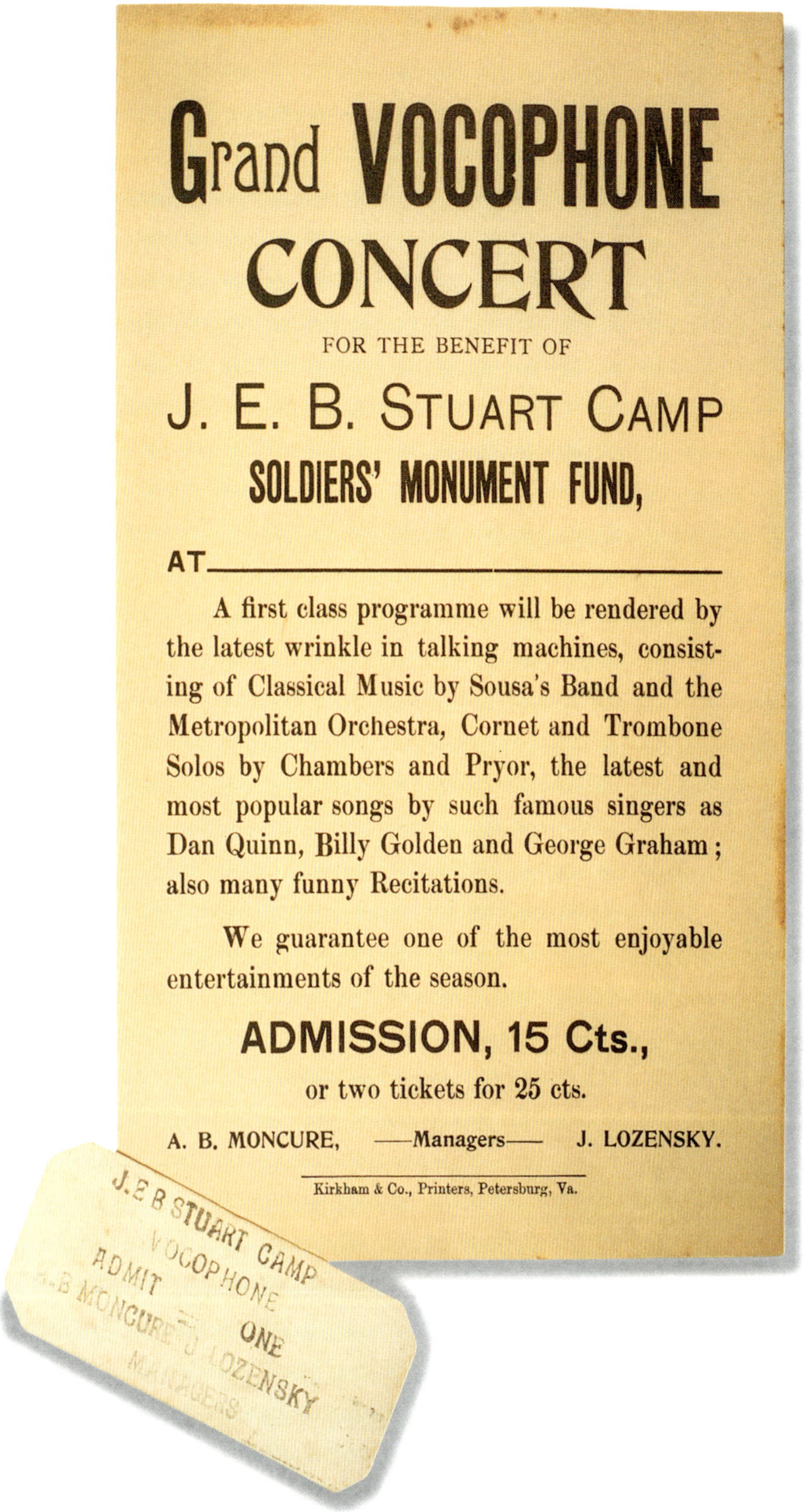

Grand VOCOPHONE CONCERT

FOR THE BENEFIT OF

J. E. B. STUART CAMP

SOLDIERS' MONUMENT FUND,

AT__________________________

A first class programme will be rendered by the latest wrinkle in talking machines, consisting of Classical Music by Sousa's Band and the Metropolitan Orchestra, Cornet and Trombone Solos by Chambers and Pryor, the latest and most popular songs by such famous singers as Dan Quinn, Billy Golden and George Graham; also many funny Recitations.

We guarantee one of the most enjoyable entertainments of the season.

ADMISSION, 15 Cts.,

or two tickets for 25 cts.

A. B. MONCURE, ——Managers—— J. LOZENSKY.

Kirkham & Co., Printers, Petersburg, Va.

1-50. The name of Emile Berliner's disc talking machine, the Gramophone, was often (and is still) confused with Columbia's cylinder-playing Graphophone. In an effort to avoid unintentionally advertising his cylinder-playing competition, Frank Seaman briefly marketed the Berliner "Improved Gramophone" using two different names from late 1897 through 1898. The better-known of these two was "Zonophone." Within two years, when he threw his support behind a new disc talking machine, Seaman would resurrect this moniker. The other term, "Vocophone," was a mere flash-in-the-pan, never to be heard from after 1897. The Berliner management took a dim view of these marketing experiments, and ordered Seaman to immediately cease the practice. This 5 3/4" x 9 1/4" handbill announcing a "Vocophone" exhibition, along with the stamped admission ticket, recalls Seaman's brief flirtation with alternative names for the Gramophone. *Courtesy of the Scott Malawski collection.* (Value code: VR)

1-51. This unknown showman exhibited his Berliner "Improved Gramophone" mounted atop a tripod originally intended for a box camera. The arrangement allowed for plenty of height (the better for the music to be heard), and was much easier to transport than a table. *Courtesy of the Charles Hummel collections.* (Value code: F)

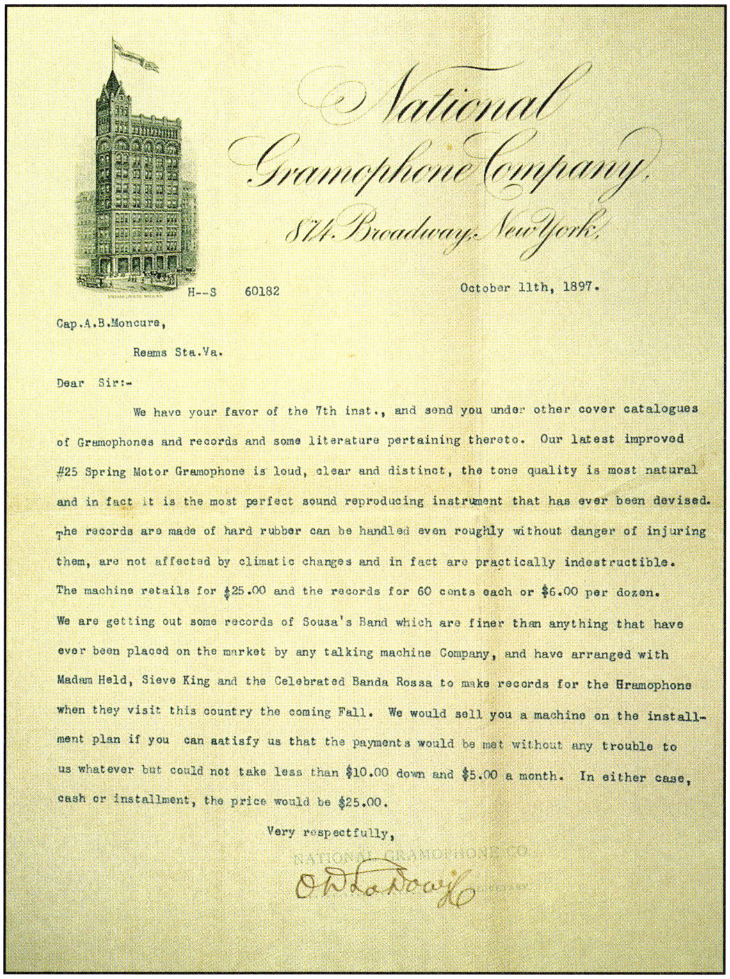

National Gramophone Company,
874 Broadway, New York.

H--S 60182 October 11th, 1897.

Cap. A. B. Moncure,

Reams Sta. Va.

Dear Sir:-

We have your favor of the 7th inst., and send you under other cover catalogues of Gramophones and records and some literature pertaining thereto. Our latest improved #25 Spring Motor Gramophone is loud, clear and distinct, the tone quality is most natural and in fact it is the most perfect sound reproducing instrument that has ever been devised. The records are made of hard rubber can be handled even roughly without danger of injuring them, are not affected by climatic changes and in fact are practically indestructible. The machine retails for $25.00 and the records for 60 cents each or $6.00 per dozen. We are getting out some records of Sousa's Band which are finer than anything that have ever been placed on the market by any talking machine Company, and have arranged with Madam Held, Sieve King and the Celebrated Banda Rossa to make records for the Gramophone when they visit this country the coming Fall. We would sell you a machine on the installment plan if you can satisfy us that the payments would be met without any trouble to us whatever but could not take less than $10.00 down and $5.00 a month. In either case, cash or installment, the price would be $25.00.

Very respectfully,

NATIONAL GRAMOPHONE CO.

O. W. LaDow

1-52. In October 1897, Cap. A.B. Moncure of Reams Station, Virginia, wrote to the National Gramophone Company for information regarding its products. Shown is the company's response on an attractive letterhead, signed by Orville LaDow, secretary of the company. Note the offer to sell the Gramophone on an installment plan. *Courtesy of the John and Nancy Duffy family*. (Value code: F)

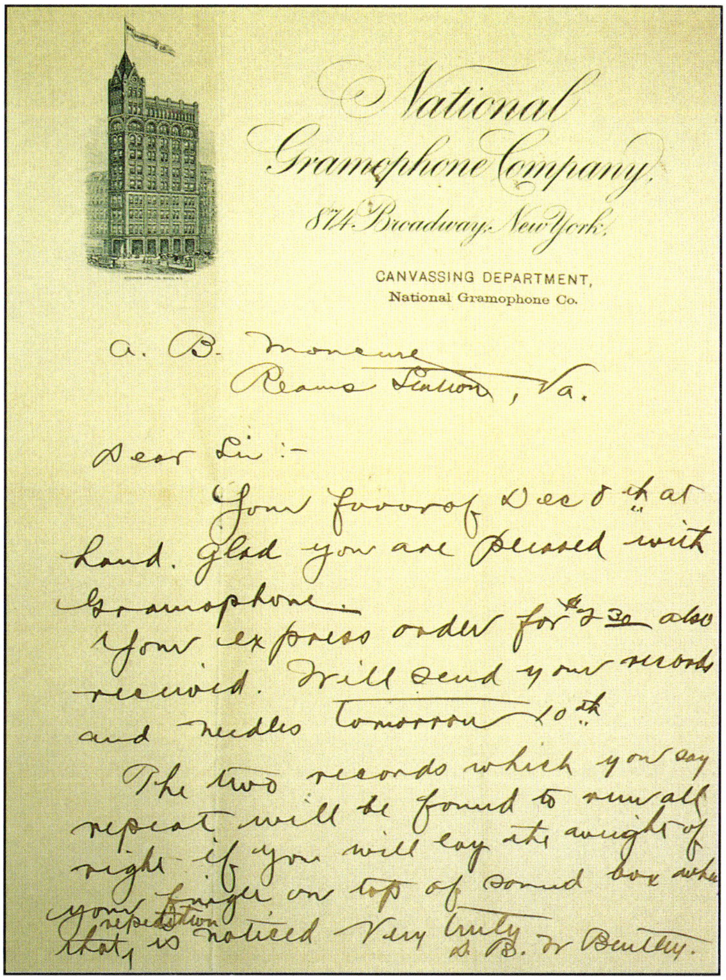

National Gramophone Company,
874 Broadway, New York.

CANVASSING DEPARTMENT,
National Gramophone Co.

A. B. Moncure
Reams Station, Va.

Dear Sir:-

Your favor of Dec 8th at hand. Glad you are pleased with Gramophone. Your express order for $2.30 also received. Will send your records and needles tomorrow 10th

The two records which you say repeat will be found to run all right if you will lay the weight of your finger on top of sound box when that repetition is noticed. Very truly

A. B. W. Bentley.

1-53. Two months later, Mr. Moncure, having purchased a Gramophone, ordered more records and needles. In response to a complaint of defective records, National Gramophone's Mr. Bentley offered this helpful advice: "The two records which you say repeat will be found to run all right if you will lay the weight of your finger on top of the sound box when that repetition is noticed." *Courtesy of the John and Nancy Duffy family*. (Value code: F)

1-54. In 1899, the National Gramophone Company lowered the price of the "Improved Gramophone" from $25.00 to $18.00. This 5 1/2" long advertising card announced the reduction. *Courtesy of Nina and Dave Heitz*. (Value code: F)

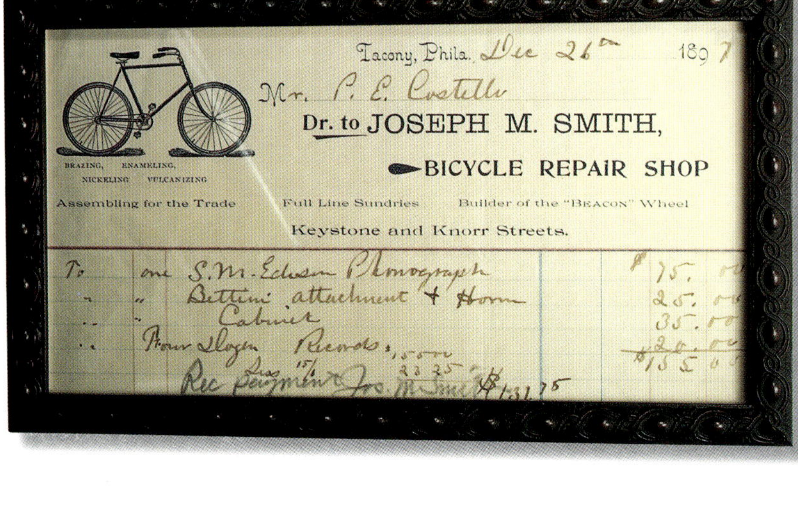
Tacony, Phila. Dec 26th 1897
Mr. P. E. Costello
Dr. to JOSEPH M. SMITH,
BICYCLE REPAIR SHOP
BRAZING, ENAMELING, NICKELING VULCANIZING
Assembling for the Trade Full Line Sundries Builder of the "BEACON" Wheel
Keystone and Knorr Streets.

To	one S. M. Edison Phonograph	75.00
"	" Bettini attachment + Horn	25.00
"	Cabinet	35.00
"	Four Dozen Records	20.00
		155.00

Rec Payment Jos. M. Smith

1-55. Mr. Costello must have used his Christmas money to buy what would today be considered an extreme object of desire. $155.00 may have been a small fortune in 1897, but that's what it took to procure a top-of-the-line Edison "Spring Motor" Phonograph equipped with Bettini's sophisticated Micro-Phonograph attachment. Gianni Bettini was a scientific dabbler who patented, manufactured and sold well-engineered recorded sound apparatus, and cylinder records. *Courtesy of Nina and Dave Heitz*. (Value code: F)

1-56. A 6" x 9 1/4" catalogue of the Michigan Electric Company from December, 1897. The cover's non-secular Christmas theme is a far cry from the obligatory Santas and tarted-up conifers that would dominate twentieth century Christmas advertising. *Courtesy of the Tom and Sandi McCarthy collection.* (Value code: VR)

1-57. This 12 1/2" x 26" brass-plated conical horn carried retailer advertising. The double-seamed body was stenciled: "Cleveland Graphophone Co., 227-229 Sheriff St., Cleveland." *Courtesy of the Gfell family collection.* (Value code: VR)

1-58. A close-up of the stenciled advertising. *Courtesy of the Gfell family collection.*

1-59. Sears, Roebuck & Company heavily marketed Graphophones with an eye toward customer exhibition of its machines. The Sears catalogue regularly offered "outfits" designed to allow the purchaser to embark on a new career of presenting recorded entertainment for a fee. These "outfits" (consisting of a Graphophone, horn, records, carrying case, and admission tickets), invariably included posters printed in black on white or tinted paper to be used for publicizing such events. Shown is a rare example of a Sears poster printed in black plus three colors. *Courtesy of the collection of Howard Hazelcorn*. (Value code: E)

Opposite page: 1-60. Another Sears, Roebuck & Company exhibition poster, this one intended to advertise an illustrated lecture on the worsening Cuban situation, including the destruction of the battleship *Maine*. In one of the first chilling examples of the power of mass media, newspaper tycoon William Randolph Hearst virtually orchestrated what would become the Spanish-American War. Despite Spain having granted Cuba partial autonomy in 1897, and having abolished its notorious prison camps, Cuban insurgents demanded full independence. A virtual civil war ensued in Cuba, and the United States battleship *Maine* was sent to protect American citizens and property. On February 15, 1898, while anchored in the Port of Havana, a massive explosion of unknown origin destroyed the *Maine*. Hearst's newspapers immediately indicted Spain for sabotage, whipping up American public sentiment. It was at this juncture that this 20" x 26 1/4" (framed) poster was supplied by Sears, Roebuck & Company to accompany one of its illustrated lecture outfits. Note the inflammatory rhetoric borrowed from Hearst: "...the impositions, cruel and inhuman treatment which has been imposed upon the inhabitants by the Spanish Government; their heroic struggle for liberty, extending over a period of three years; their awful suffering from want of food, clothing and shelter; the explosion of the United States Battleship Maine, and what this Government proposes to do and is doing to assist in a worthy cause." War was soon declared. On May 1, 1898, American naval forces destroyed the Spanish fleet anchored in Manila Bay, the Philippines. By July 1, United States troops were assailing Santiago, Cuba. Two days later, a Spanish naval squadron was annihilated while attempting to break the American blockade of Santiago Harbor. On July 18, 1898, Spain asked for a settlement, which ultimately ceded the Philippines, Guam, and Puerto Rico to the United States, and ended Spanish rule of Cuba. Significant numbers of Americans died of wounds, malaria, and dysentery in their quest to avenge the treacherous destruction of the Maine. In 1969, it was determined that the battleship had exploded due to a defective boiler. (Value code: F)

CUBA
THE MAINE THE CUBAN WAR
AND THE
Wonderful Talking Machine
AN ILLUSTRATED LECTURE.... AND MUSICAL ENTERTAINMENT
EXPLOSION OF THE MAINE.
SHOOTING PRISONERS.
IT TALKS LAUGHS PLAYS SINGS....
The Talking Machine is truly one of the ....MOST WONDERFUL OF INVENTIONS....
Copyrighted, Feb. 1898.
A most interesting and instructive lecture will be given describing the immense natural resources of the Island of Cuba; the impositions, cruel and inhuman treatment which has been imposed upon the inhabitants by the Spanish Government; their heroic struggle for liberty, extending over a period of three years; their awful suffering from want of food, clothing and shelter; the explosion of the United States Battleship Maine, and what this Government proposes to do and is doing to assist in a worthy cause.
The Lecture will be illustrated throughout with... 50 MAGNIFICENT VIEWS Projected from the MAGIC LANTERN
The views will include a correct map of Cuba; views of the most important places and events of interest, such as Havana, Matanzas, Morro Castle, the execution of Cuban prisoners, the starving reconcentrados, the odd customs of the people, the Captain-General's Residence, General Fitzhugh Lee, Rear Admirals Dewey and Sampson, General Gomez and other officers of the Cuban and Spanish Governments, the Battleship Maine before and after the explosion, the Cuban flag, etc.
THE VIEWS WILL BE ILLUMINATED by an intense light, magnified by powerful lenses and projected onto an immense screen with 100 square feet of surface, making them so large that everyone can see while comfortably seated in any part of the hall. There has been a large amount of money spent in collecting authentic and reliable information and in securing the
MAGNIFICENT :: PHOTOGRAPHIC :: VIEWS
We will also render a high-class MUSICAL PROGRAMME, consisting of THE LATEST MUSICAL SELECTIONS, as played by the best bands and orchestras of this country, VOCAL SELECTIONS, as sung by the most noted comic and sentimental singers, SPEECHES of our most noted men, DANCES WITH CALLS, ETC.
The Reproduction of the VOICE in either Song or Speech is so natural and the articulation so distinct that anyone would believe it a human being except that they knew the difference, and its Reproduction of Instrumental Music is Phenomenal.
Special arrangements have been made for magnifying the sound, so that all may hear the entire concert while comfortably seated in any part of the Hall.
We promise a Royal Entertainment. DON'T FAIL TO COME AND BRING YOUR FRIENDS, AND ESPECIALLY THE CHILDREN.
THE LECTURE AND ENTERTAINMENT WILL BE GIVEN AT
PRICES OF ADMISSION: Adults ______ Cents. Children ______ Cents.
ENTERTAINMENT BEGINS AT 8 P. M. ______

1-61. At the turn of the twentieth century, independent talking machine exhibitors abounded. Many of these showmen dispensed "generic" tickets, so it is unusual to find the names of the promoters printed as shown here. (Value code: H)

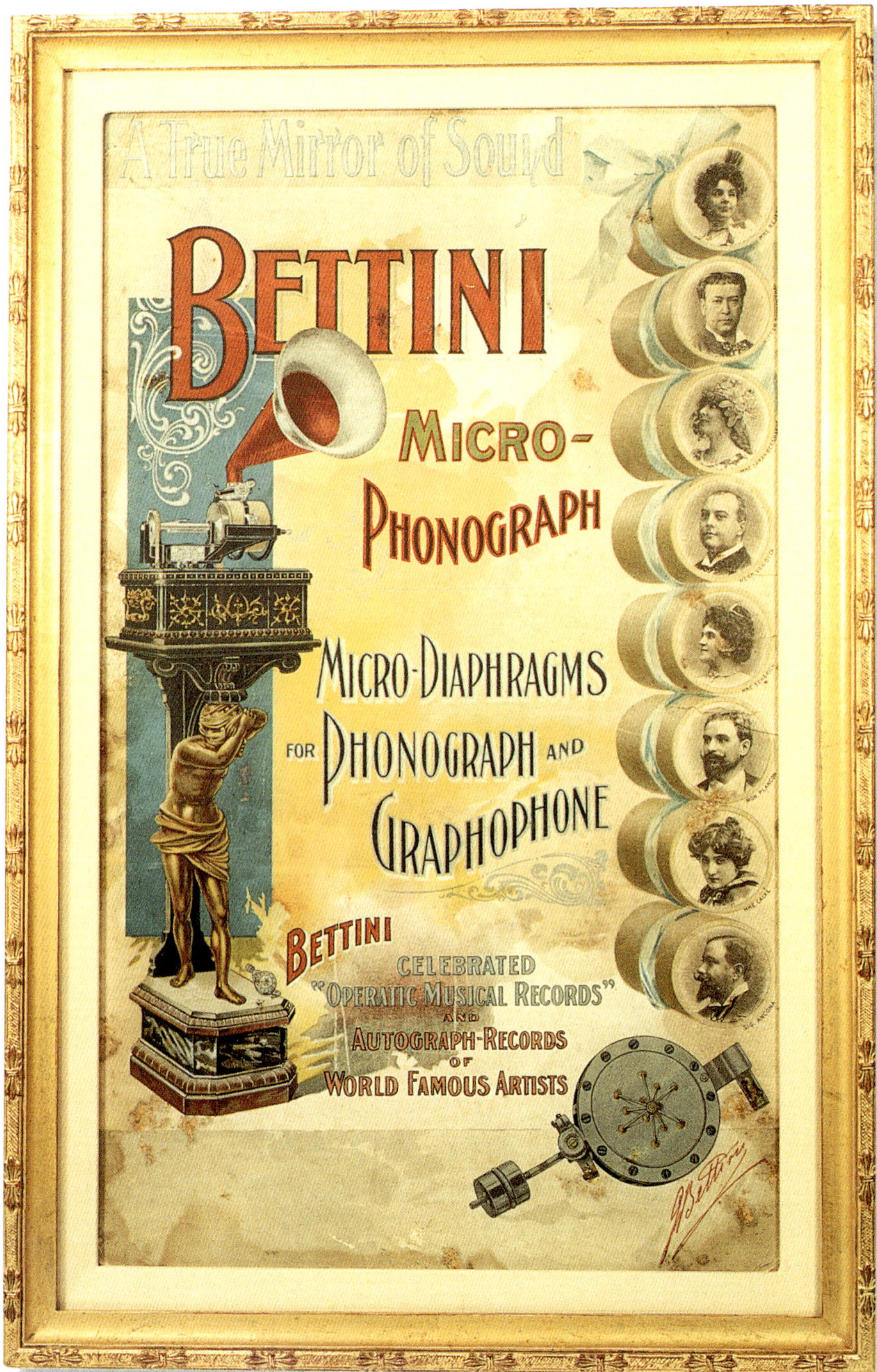

1-62. Gianni Bettini's beautifully designed reproducer ("Micro-Diaphragm") and a bevy of operatic luminaries are shown in this colorful poster, circa 1899. However impressive the custom-cased, Bettini-equipped Edison "Concert" Phonograph may be, it is Bettini's recorded legacy that makes the onetime Italian cavalry officer's name magic among collectors today. At a time when no one else was recording serious opera, Bettini was encapsulating legendary voices in wax. Although extremely rare, Bettini recordings offer a unique glimpse of several performers in their prime, and others unavailable anywhere else. Certain documented recordings, including one by Mark Twain, have never been found. This 14 1/4" x 22 3/4" poster from Bettini's heyday aptly illustrates the enduring romance of his brief phonographic endeavor. (Value code: VR)

1-63. Cylinder record boxes were widely used for company advertising. Of this representative group, all but the two Lambert examples (at the lower right) display dealer advertising. Some dealers such as Burke & Rous, Bacigalupi, Eastern Talking Machine Company, and possibly the Cleveland Graphophone Company, made their own recordings on blank cylinders supplied by other firms. With rare exceptions (such as Burke & Rous), this small, back-room industry virtually ceased after 1902. However, dealer advertising labels on cylinder record boxes persisted for many years. (Value code: F)

1-64. Dealer advertising labels on cylinder record boxes are sometimes seen, but promotional labels on disc records are a rarity. What this Brooklyn Novelty Company label lacked in aesthetics was compensated for by the originality of its location: attached to the back of an 1899, 7" diameter Berliner record. Until 1908, when double-faced disc records came into general use, the blank reverse side of these objects offered a good place for advertising, yet very few firms availed themselves of the opportunity. (Value code: G)

1-65. Dealer advertising is occasionally found on early talking machines. Although anxious to promote itself, Sears, Roebuck & Company exercised restraint in the marking of this Type "A" Graphophone. Interestingly, the otherwise conventional cabinet decal appears to have been specially designed to allow for an ink-stamped attribution. (Value code: machine, so marked, C)

1-66. "In happier times," before being blacklisted by Edison, Hawthorne and Sheble emblazoned the Edison instruments they sold with this distinctive decal. Here, it is used on the rear panel of a "Home" Phonograph Model "A," circa 1900. *Courtesy of Pat and Jamie Jones*. (Value code: machine, so marked, C)

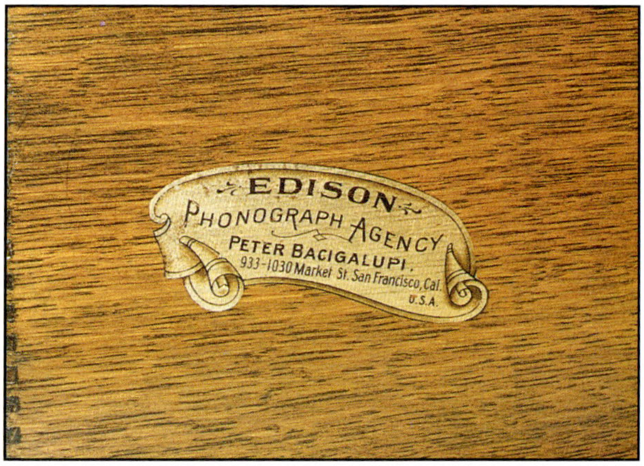

1-67. Prominent San Francisco distributor and retailer Peter Bacigalupi sold this Edison "Concert" Phonograph with a none-too-subtle decal proclaiming its origin. *Courtesy of the Babcock House Museum, John H. Perschbacher*. (Value code: VR)

1-68. This 4 1/4" tall oil bottle carries Peter Bacigalupi's advertisement cast into the glass. The 933 Market Street address was occupied by Bacigalupi from November 1898 until the great San Francisco earthquake of April 18, 1906. *Courtesy of René Rondeau.* (Value code: F)

1-69. William F. Nye was a well-known maker of lubricants for a variety of household machinery. In this unusual instance, Nye adorned the bottle with an illustration of the 1898 model Edison "Standard" Phonograph, and the claim of a special formulation "*Expressly for use on PHONOGRAPHS*." 4 5/8" tall. *Courtesy of René Rondeau.* (Value code: F)

1-70. This fascinating trade card, circa 1899, incorporated a genuine frame of celluloid movie film. Prizefighting was a popular subject for the early motion picture camera, and some events were faked to quench public demand. Bacigalupi's Talking Machine Agency was, in the parlance of the times, a live wire outfit. It distributed and sold a wide variety of phonographic products for over 20 years. *Courtesy of Gilbert (Bert) Pasley.* (Value code: VR)

1-71. A flyer from retailer A.C. Becken of Chicago, showing the Edison "Standard" and "Home" Phonographs. The "Polyphone" attachment is shown on the Edison "Standard" at the bottom of the page. The "Polyphone" utilized two separate reproducers with their styli riding in the same record groove, approximately 1 1/2" apart. Although resulting in a slight "echo" the apparatus was claimed to make the performance, "...more than twice as loud and many times more musical than any other Talking Machine..." *Courtesy of the Tom and Sandi McCarthy collection.* (Value code: F)

1-72. Edison cylinder record lists and the envelope in which they were mailed in 1899. The yellow notice at the right referred to a price reduction aimed at stimulating sales of the costly "Concert" Phonograph and records. The previous year, Columbia had outflanked Edison with a risky maneuver. Columbia had introduced the "Graphophone Grand" (Type "GG"), a cylinder talking machine designed to play records the diameter of which was more than twice that of conventional cylinders. The "GG" was stratospherically priced at $300.00, and the 5" diameter "Grand" records cost a princely $5.00 each. Yet, the gamble paid off. The public accepted the 5" diameter format, Columbia introduced lesser-priced models, and Edison scrambled to design a competing machine – the "Concert," released at $125.00 in February 1899. By November 1st, Edison instituted the price reduction seen here. Edison "Concert" cylinders were lowered from $4.00 to $2.50 each, to reflect the descending prices of comparable Columbia products. *Courtesy of Michael F. Khanchalian.* (Value code: VR)

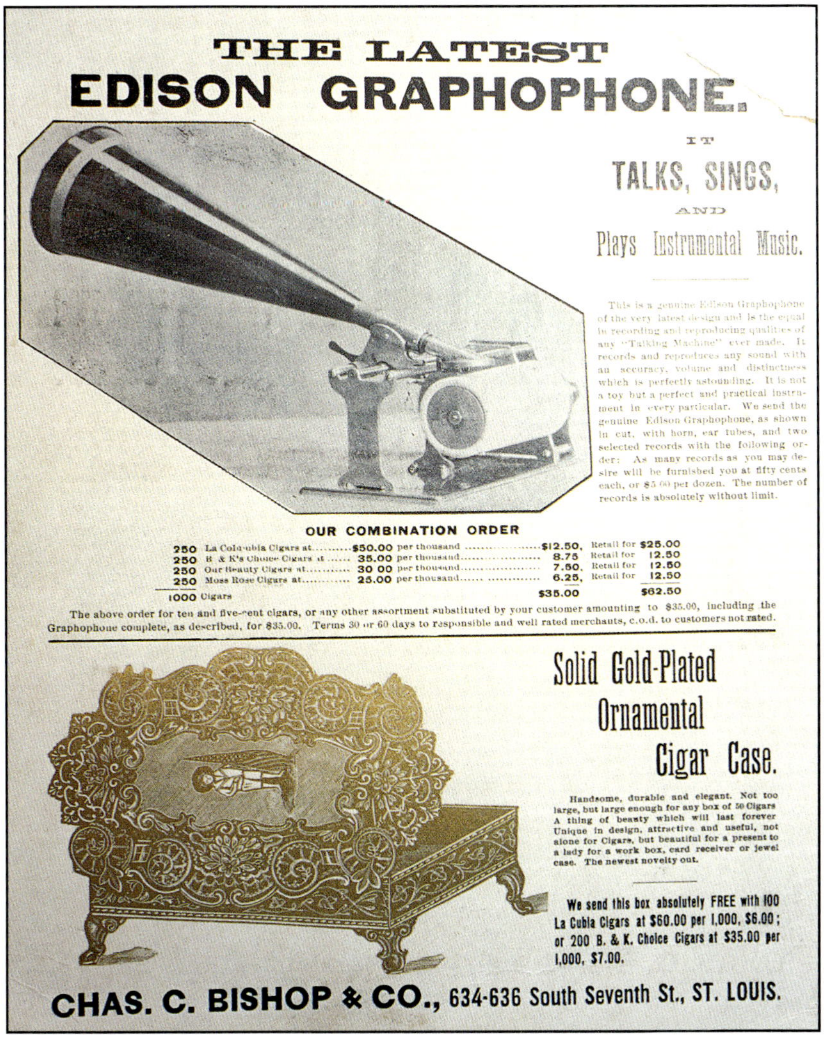

1-73. The popular $5.00 Type "Q" Graphophone was used as a sales premium by the St. Louis cigar purveyor, Charles C. Bishop & Company. Note the incorrect (and illegal) use of Edison's name in promoting the rival Graphophone product. Edison's fame made such "borrowing" of his imprimatur all too commonplace. *Courtesy of the collection of Howard Hazelcorn.* (Value code: G)

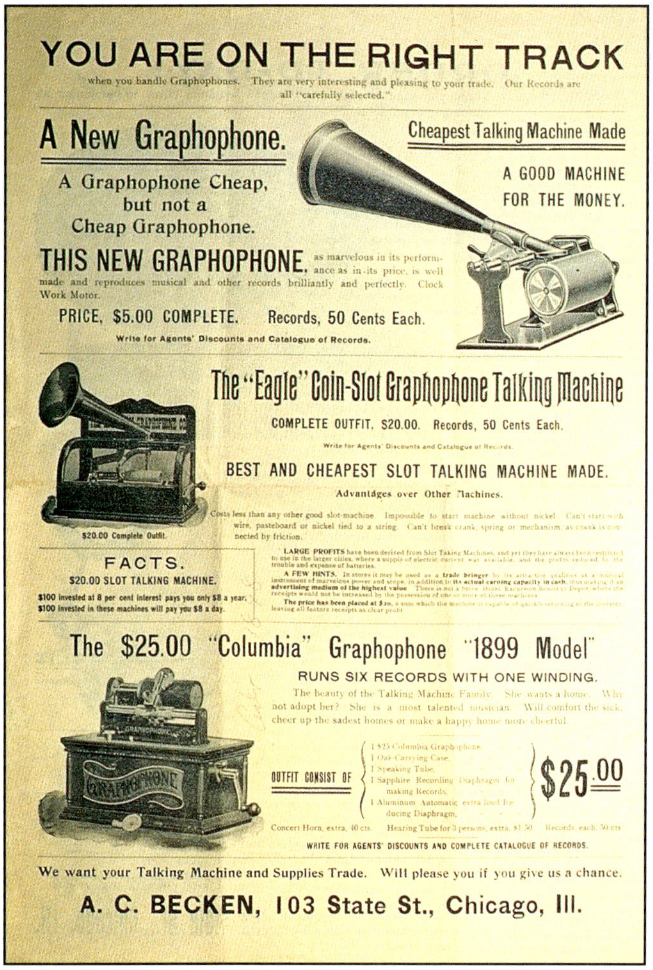

1-74. A flyer advertising Graphophones from late 1898. The "1899 Model" Graphophone "AT" was introduced to (eventually) replace the popular but less decorative Type "A." *Courtesy of the Tom and Sandi McCarthy collection.* (Value code: F)

1-75. As talking machines proliferated in the late 1890s and early 1900s, information on them slowly became available in a more permanent, compendious format (as opposed to company catalogues). The two books in the foreground were meant to provide the public with "generalized" information on the subject. From the left, George Tewksbury's *Complete Manual of the Edison Phonograph* (1897) outlined all of the Edison models then extant, along with tips on home recording. Thomas Edison himself provided the forward to this book. To the right, a similar work entitled *The CWN Handbook of the Phonograph* by C.W. Noyes was published in 1901. In the center is a slim volume for Victor dealers, *How to sell Victors on instalments* [sic]. Published in 1907, it explained the mechanics of time-payments and the advantages of this method of selling. *Courtesy of the Tom and Sandi McCarthy collection.* (Value code: VR)

1-76. With his stable of noteworthy inventions and worldwide fame, Thomas Edison was by far the best chronicled of the talking machine developers. Shown are the 1891 and 1896 editions of *Edison and his Inventions*, edited by J.B. McClure. The 1900 work entitled *The Phonograph and How to Use It* was published by Edison's sales organization, the National Phonograph Company, and gave descriptions of all the Edison Phonograph models, along with folksy treatises such as *How We Gave a Phonograph Party* and *What Mr. Openeer Heard*. (Value code: G)

1-77. A selection of Berliner Gramophone catalogues. The distribution of such booklets to American homes, along with eye-catching magazine advertising, insured that the Gramophone would become a success in the closing years of the nineteenth century. The back cover of the booklet at upper right shows the "Improved Gramophone" which, when later paired with a little white dog named Nipper, would become the most famous trade-mark in the world. (Value code: VR)

1-78. Rival companies advertising similar technology. In the late 1890s, the Berliner Gramophone Company continued to sell certain hand-powered models even after it had introduced a successful spring motor. Above, a Zonophone catalogue from 1900 featured the unknown Type "E" "For the Children," also hand-propelled. The inescapable similarity of the soundboxes illustrates how Zonophone borrowed from (and in some cases improved upon) the Gramophone. (Value code: E)

1-79. This 18" x 11" single-faced placard advertised Columbia standard size and 5" "Grand" cylinder records, circa 1899. As has been mentioned earlier, the "Grand" cylinders were designed to deliver increased volume and fidelity from greater surface speed. By 1902, the 5" cylinders would be rendered obsolescent by a new cylinder molding process that improved the quality of the standard size cylinders. At the time this placard was issued, however, Columbia cylinders of either size were considered state-of-the-art. Note the patriotic eagle in addition to red, white, and blue accents that give the appearance of the Fourth of July. The embossing and bold use of color are unusual for the period. The two small holes at the top center were used for hanging the placard with a string. *Courtesy of the Gfell family collection.* (Value code: VR)

1-80. Two rare Graphophones illustrated in Columbia catalogues. In the background is a December 1, 1896 catalogue showing the Type "K" or "Standard" Graphophone, which would be discontinued eight months later. In the foreground is a late 1899-early 1900 catalogue showing the "Toy Graphophone" at its initial $3.00 price, soon to be lowered to $1.50. Note the diminutive size of this machine as seen in the photograph to the right. Yet, in the artist's rendition to the left, the same machine has taken on more substantial (and imaginary) proportions. (Value code: VR)

1-81. During the late 1890s, the Columbia Phonograph Company had attempted to break into the disc talking machine business several times by backing small firms, whose life or death would have no negative effect on Columbia. By the end of 1899, Columbia was prepared to try a different course. Offering a small toy disc talking machine for $3.00 seemed an expedient way to test the strength of rival patents without incurring much risk of damages. Unfortunately, the scheme was more suited as a legal trial balloon than as effective merchandising. The little "Toy Graphophone" sold poorly, even after the price was lowered to only $1.50. Shown is a shipping box with colorful advertising label, a rare survivor of this unsuccessful promotion. *Courtesy of the Domenic DiBernardo collection.* (Value code: VR)

1-82. Three of the rarest record catalogues. Consolidated, of Newark, New Jersey, produced non-molded cylinder records for a short period, circa 1898. The United States Phonograph Company, also of Newark, had an interesting history. It was associated with Edison during the 1890s, when it manufactured the earliest examples of the "Triton," the first factory-supplied spring motor to power an Edison Phonograph. United States also produced non-molded cylinders during the 1894-1897 period. The Lambert Company of Chicago was a pioneer in the manufacture of celluloid (non-breakable) cylinder records. Lambert's process created the first molded, mass-producible cylinders in America, beginning in 1900. Although Edison and Columbia were not far behind in the manufacture of molded cylinders, neither succeeded in marketing a celluloid cylinder for years (Columbia in 1908, and Edison not until 1912). Lambert's distinctive records (dyed bright fuchsia during the first years of production) enjoyed as much success as could be harvested by an independent firm with limited capital and distribution, consistently harassed by Edison's richly funded legal department. Despite its enviable position as the only American manufacturer of celluloid cylinders during the period 1900-1905, the Lambert Company soon thereafter foundered and died. *Courtesy of Michael F. Khanchalian.* (Value code: VR)

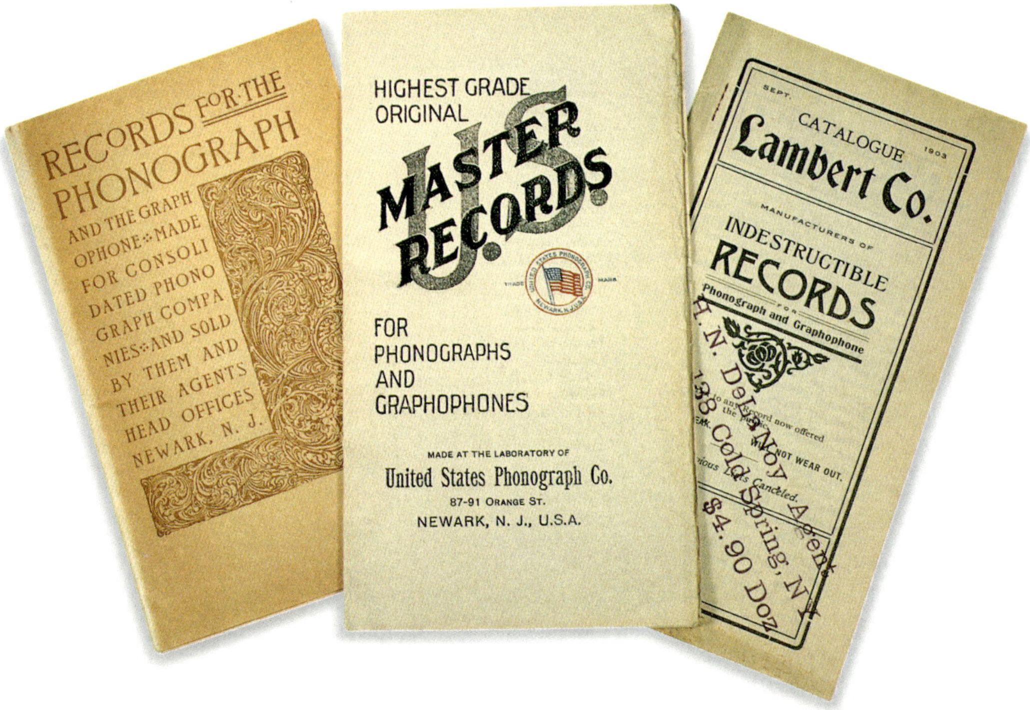

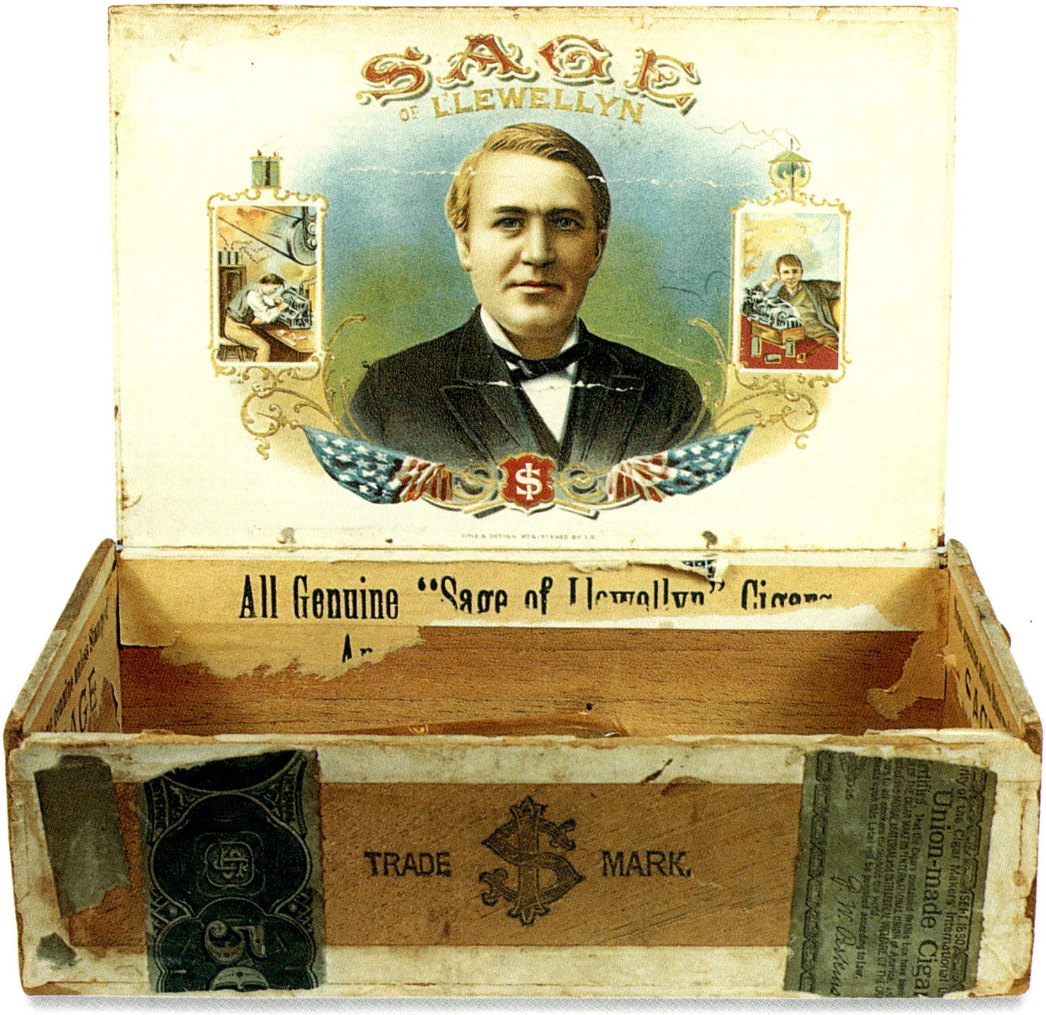

1-83. Cigar manufacturers vied with one another to produce the most unusual and beautifully lithographed labels to adorn the boxes in which their products were sold. Tobacco stores became veritable galleries of kitsch art. This example, circa 1900, featured an inset of Mr. Edison with his 1888 "Perfected Phonograph." The nomenclature referred to Llewellyn Park, where Edison's residence was located. Though not rightly advertising for Edison's Phonograph, peripheral imagery such as this was effective in creating public recognition of the product. *Courtesy of the Charles Hummel collections.* (Value code: VR)

1-84. Newspapers used copper dies, or "electrotypes" to print line-cut images. The copper reverse image was mounted to a block of wood that fit into the composition of a page. Shown here are electrotypes of two Columbia machines: a Type "AT" cylinder Graphophone (circa 1900), and a Disc Graphophone Type "AJ" (circa 1902). The largest, the "AT," is 2" x 2 1/8". *Courtesy of Mr. R. Chase.* (Value code: H)

1-85. Aside from the well-known Sears, Roebuck examples, posters advertising talking machine concerts were seldom adorned with illustrations, especially when commissioned by independent exhibitors. Even more unusual were instances when half-tone photographs were incorporated into the poster. A.W. Luce, who lived near Lilydale, New York, was an exhibitor of talking machines and moving pictures. In 1900, Luce had a nine-foot long phonograph horn built by Hawthorne & Sheble of Philadelphia (which H&S put in its catalogue for $150.00). He mounted this huge horn to his Type "GG" Graphophone Grand (which also retailed for $150.00), and proceeded to exploit his investment by offering "Grand Concerts." This 16"x 22" canvas-backed advertising poster featured not one or two, but three photographs of Luce, his Type "GG" Graphophone Grand, its mammoth horn, an assistant, and a small boy. Aside from the misspelled and untrue assertion that he was operating under the auspices of "The Columbia Graphaphone [sic] Company" (an as yet nonexistent entity), Luce nevertheless managed to accurately employ the Columbia marketing terminology, "Grand." (Value code: VR)

Chapter Two

THE GOLDEN AGE OF ANTIQUE PHONOGRAPH ADVERTISING, 1901~1913

Communication. It would be one of the defining currents of the twentieth century; a century of invention and discovery which would witness, more than any preceding period, profound changes in the way humanity interacted and communicated.

The broad popularization of the telephone, phonograph and, later, radio and television would create an everyday reality that previously could be only imagined in the fantasies of writers and visionaries such as Jules Verne. Each of these technological marvels was marketed with hoopla and ballyhoo. Yet, each would be itself a medium of advertising. As they matured, the telephone, radio and TV would become increasingly more important as agents of advertising. We do not, however, commonly view the phonograph in that same light. The phonograph is more frequently associated with entertainment.

It's true that in the arena of advertising the phonograph lacked the significance of radio, for example. Yet, in this chapter we will explore the ways in which the phonograph promoted itself, as well as the methods by which it was marketed through other media.

Berliner Began the Ballyhoo

In the blush of its discovery, the phonograph suggested vast possibilities to an eager world. Among these were talking clocks, spoken correspondence and pre-recorded advertising. In the twenty years following its 1877 birth, the phonograph struggled with growing pains. The initial public enthusiasm waned, the nascent phonograph drifted into obscurity, competitive research brought revitalization, new but flawed models were introduced which failed in the marketplace, retrenchment followed, and, finally the surviving phonograph manufacturing companies slowly began to build an industry.

It was after two decades of the talking machine's bumps and false starts that the first widely circulated advertising record appeared ("On the Gramophone" by George Graham, 1896). As discussed in the first chapter of this book, Berliner was the first to employ recorded advertising on a popular scale, and also the first to satirize the subject by presenting a flimflam man's overblown testimonial for a fictitious product ("Oven Rising Plant's Baking Powder," also by Graham).

By the end of the 1890s, the concept of recorded advertising had been fully contemplated and formatively initiated by the Berliner Gramophone Company. In a peculiar prolepsis, both the novelty impact of a recorded sales-pitch, and the comic consequences of over-doing it had been explored.

2-1. Cylinder phonographs pervaded the imagery of turn of the twentieth century advertising, before disc-playing instruments had become familiar to the public. It is unusual, therefore, to see this spool of thread decorated with the stylized depiction of a Berliner "Improved Gramophone" (note the vertical winding handle). *Courtesy of Walter and Carol Myers.* (Value code: G)

The Phonograph as Salesman Finds Its Feet

Pre-recorded advertising was slow to mature. During the first two decades of the twentieth century, it remained largely the province of self-promotion by talking machine companies.

In 1901, Eldridge R. Johnson, a former talking machine parts manufacturer who now controlled the patents of the Berliner Gramophone Company, issued a 3" diameter single-faced disc to promote his new line of "Victor" talking machines. The record was distributed as a premium at the Pan American Exposition held in Buffalo, New York, (where President McKinley was assassinated), and was labeled "Ask your nearest Music Dealer to let you hear what this Record has to say on the Victor Talking Machine."

2-2. Even the lowliest packing crate could convey an important marketing message. *Courtesy of the Scott and Denise Corbett collection.* (Value code: F)

At the turn of the twentieth century, cylinder phonograph manufacturers were reluctant to follow the lead of the Gramophone, and the reason was lodged in the evolution of cylinder technology. Multiple copies of a Berliner disc such as "On the Gramophone" could be pressed from the initial master. However, cylinder duplication was impeded throughout the 1890s, and during the first two years of the twentieth century, by the lack of a practical system of mass production. While discs were conveniently being turned out in hundreds, cylinder record companies were mechanically pantographing or aurally dubbing copies of cylinder performances in small batches.

In 1901, Edison and Columbia adopted a cylinder record molding process. The stage was set for a cylinder demonstration record that could be produced in significant numbers. Several years later, Edison released its two-minute wax "Advertising Record." This selection was intended for dealer use, and it was marked on the lid of the box "not to be sold." Although some copies undoubtedly found their way into the homes of customers, the text of the record makes it clear that it was to be played for new clients. In a stentorian voice, recording artist Len Spencer intoned a paean to the Edison Phonograph:

I am the Edison Phonograph, created by the great wizard of the New World to delight those who will have melody or be amused. I can sing you tender songs of love. I can give you merry tales, and joy and laughter. I can transport you to the realms of music. I can call you to join in the rhythmic dance. I can lull the babe to sweet repose, or waken in the aged heart soft memories of youthful days. No matter what may be your mood, I am always ready to entertain you. When your day's work is done, I can bring the theatre or the opera to your home. I can give you Grand Opera, comic opera or vaudeville. I can give you sacred or popular music, band, orchestra or instrumental music. I can render solos, duets, trios, quartets. I can aid in entertaining your guests. When your wife is worried after the cares of the day, and the children are boisterous, I can rest the one and quiet the other. I never get tired and you will never tire of me, for I always have something new to offer. I give pleasure to all, young and old. I will go wherever you want me: in the parlor, in the sickroom, on the porch, in the camp or to your summer home. If you sing or talk to me, I will retain your songs or words, and repeat them to you at your pleasure. I can enable you to always hear the voices of your loved ones, even though they are far away. I talk in every language. I can help you to learn other languages. I am made with the highest degree of mechanical skill. My voice is the clearest, smoothest and most natural of any talking machine. The name of my famous master is on my body, and tells you that I am a genuine Edison Phonograph. The more you become acquainted with me, the better you will like me. Ask the dealer.

2-3. The Edison "Advertising Record," that declaimed the merits of the cylinder Phonograph. *Courtesy of the Scott and Denise Corbett collection.* (Value code: in original carton, E)

2-4. This good quality 6 3/8" x 9 1/8" lithograph of the Victor trademark was circulated in magazines of the 1905 period. The colorful reproduction, on heavy stock, stood out among the pages of publications such as *Munsey's*. (Value code: G)

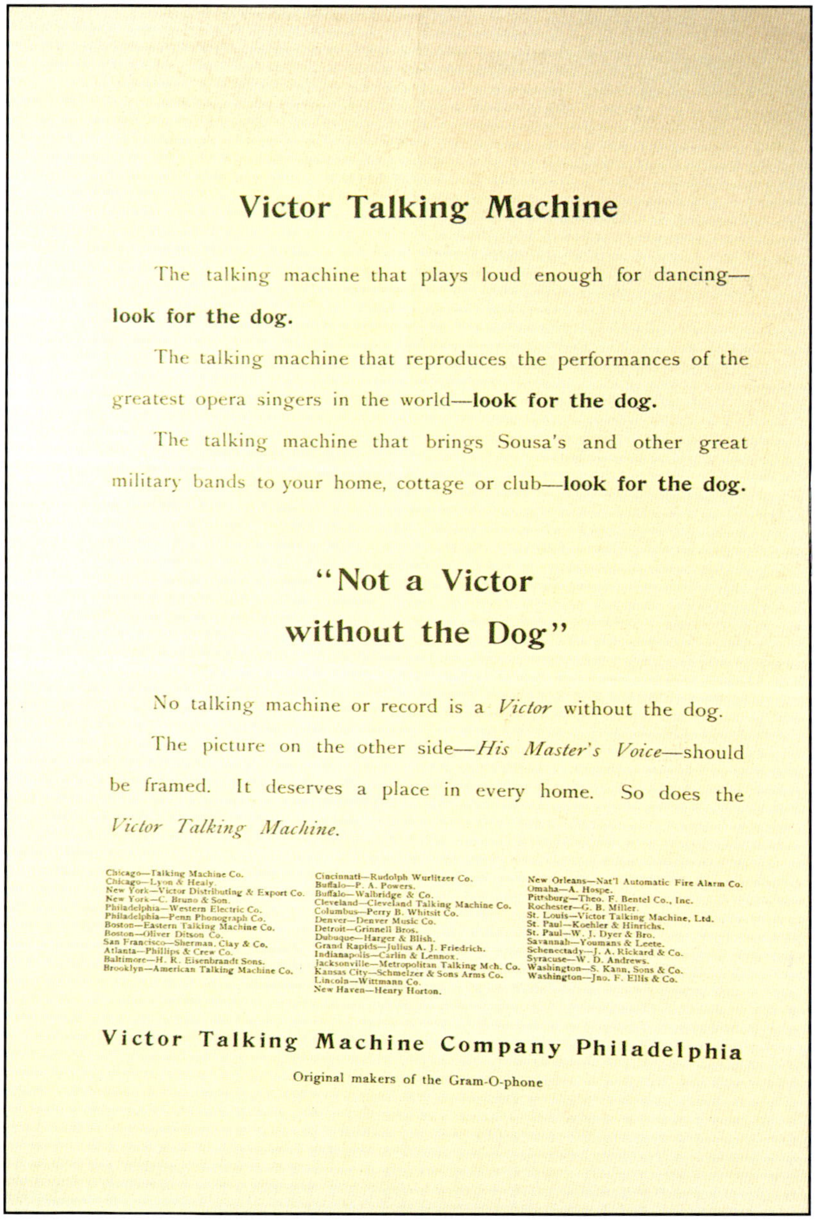

Victor Talking Machine

The talking machine that plays loud enough for dancing—**look for the dog.**

The talking machine that reproduces the performances of the greatest opera singers in the world—**look for the dog.**

The talking machine that brings Sousa's and other great military bands to your home, cottage or club—**look for the dog.**

"Not a Victor without the Dog"

No talking machine or record is a *Victor* without the dog.

The picture on the other side—*His Master's Voice*—should be framed. It deserves a place in every home. So does the *Victor Talking Machine.*

Chicago—Talking Machine Co.
Chicago—Lyon & Healy.
New York—Victor Distributing & Export Co.
New York—C. Bruno & Son.
Philadelphia—Western Electric Co.
Philadelphia—Penn Phonograph Co.
Boston—Eastern Talking Machine Co.
Boston—Oliver Ditson Co.
San Francisco—Sherman, Clay & Co.
Atlanta—Phillips & Crew Co.
Baltimore—H. R. Eisenbrandt Sons.
Brooklyn—American Talking Machine Co.
Cincinnati—Rudolph Wurlitzer Co.
Buffalo—P. A. Powers.
Buffalo—Walbridge & Co.
Cleveland—Cleveland Talking Machine Co.
Columbus—Perry B. Whitsit Co.
Denver—Denver Music Co.
Detroit—Grinnell Bros.
Dubuque—Harger & Blish.
Grand Rapids—Julius A. J. Friedrich.
Indianapolis—Carlin & Lennox.
Jacksonville—Metropolitan Talking Mch. Co.
Kansas City—Schmelzer & Sons Arms Co.
Lincoln—Wittmann Co.
New Haven—Henry Horton.
New Orleans—Nat'l Automatic Fire Alarm Co.
Omaha—A. Hospe.
Pittsburg—Theo. F. Bentel Co., Inc.
Rochester—G. B. Miller.
St. Louis—Victor Talking Machine, Ltd.
St. Paul—Koehler & Hinrichs.
St. Paul—W. J. Dyer & Bro.
Savannah—Youmans & Leete.
Schenectady—J. A. Rickard & Co.
Syracuse—W. D. Andrews.
Washington—S. Kann, Sons & Co.
Washington—Jno. F. Ellis & Co.

Victor Talking Machine Company Philadelphia

Original makers of the Gram-O-phone

2-5. The reverse of the Victor lithograph. Along with the suggestion that the picture should be removed from the magazine and framed, note that the slogan "look for the dog" is repeated three times, whereas the far more enduring "His Master's Voice" is mentioned only once.

In December 1905 Victor recorded a 10" disc entitled "Hints to Victor Salesmen." Distributed to Victor dealers, the record was double-faced, about two years before Victor (rather begrudgingly) began issuing double-faced discs to the public. This dealer record was backed with a recorded talk to children. "Hints to Victor Salesmen" was not only promotional, but also experimental.

Columbia, which was the rival of both Edison and Victor, and a company well-known for its innovative thinking, oddly never offered a cylinder record to promote its line of Graphophones. However, in 1910, by which time Columbia's emphasis had shifted to the manufacture of Disc Graphophones, the company released a 10" doubled-faced 78 entitled "Special Demonstration Double-Disc." As already noted, Columbia and Victor had begun producing double-faced records at the end of 1908. The "Demonstration Double-Disc" spoke of the quality and advantages of the new style of record:

> *The purpose of this record is to demonstrate the Columbia Double Disc record. It is not offered for sale. Columbia Double Disc records - music on both sides; a different selection on each side; two records at a few cents above the price of one. They may be played on any disc machine, the Columbia Graphophone or the Victor Talking Machine, and they give you double value for your money, plain as daylight. The music of Columbia Double Disc records is the music itself, not merely our idea of what we can make the people think music ought to be* [this was aimed at Victor's highfalutin catalogue of long-hair music]. *You are assured of as perfect a record on each side of the disc as you ever bought before under any name at any price. Perfect in surface, perfect in tone and extraordinary in durability. The Columbia Double Disc record will unfailingly outwear any other disc record. This statement has been proved over and over again, and it is easy enough for you to prove it for yourself. The Columbia process of recording, as developed especially during the last two years, produces a naturalness and roundness and perfection of tone that is positively unequalled in any other. The singing voice, as recorded in the Columbia laboratory is the living voice of the artist - clear, flawless and natural - and from the simple brassy note of the bugle to the delicate shading of the violin, Columbia recording of instrumental music is marvelously true. Note the ringing clarity of the orchestra bells, the pure, golden tone of the cornet, the dulcet blending of the flute and violin, the birdlike warble of the piccolo, the stately sonority of the trombone, the reedy sweetness of the clarinet, and, now, the splendid ensemble of the full orchestra. Columbia Double Disc records – double discs, double value, double wear, double everything except price. Don't put your record money into any other.*

"NOT for sale" was clearly marked on the label of the "Demonstration Double-Disc." However, Columbia allowed its dealers, who had to purchase the records, to charge 10 cents to return their investment. The intent was to promote Columbia records in homes already equipped with a talking machine, of which there were millions. In 1913, Columbia issued another, similar demonstration disc. The later version was sold to customers for 25 cents.

> [Trumpet fanfare] *The other side of this type of Columbia record affords the best possible evidence of the quality of Columbia recording. It demonstrates the faithfulness of our reproduction of the singing voice, and is typical of the quality of every record in the entire Columbia list. The standard price of 10" Columbia Double Disc records is 65 cents. As an interesting experiment, as well as a demonstration of the Columbia process of recording instrumental music, you will now hear some of the instruments of the Columbia Orchestra commencing with the first violin and adding, successively, the second violin, the viola, cello, flute, bass, oboe, clarinet, bassoon, French horn, bells, cornet and trombone. Listen carefully and see if you can detect the exact moment at which each instrument is introduced.* [The orchestra plays "Home Sweet Home."] *A point to remember: Columbia Double Disc records may be played on either Columbia or Victor machines, and they will unfailingly outwear any other record.*

2-6. You've heard of "a play within a play" – well, how about a brochure advertising advertising? Circa 1909. *Courtesy of Tom and Joanna Broome.* (Value code: H)

2-7. Columbia advertised its second version of the promotional disc, calling it "a novel musical experiment." (Value code: H)

50,000 Frenchmen Can't Be Wrong

Pathé was a French firm that had begun selling cylinder phonographs in the late 1890s, and, afterward, disc talking machines. Pathé disc machines and records enjoyed considerable success in France, Great Britain and various European countries. In 1913, an American relative of the company was unveiled, with the intent of assembling Pathé instruments and pressing records in the United States. Pathé discs were "vertically" recorded (also called "hill and dale" recording) and were reproduced by a sapphire ball stylus. Conventional "lateral cut" 78s, which had been produced since the 1890s by firms such as Victor, Columbia, and most other American and foreign record companies, were played by a steel needle. Lateral records used up enormous numbers of needles, which generally wore out after one playing. A Pathé stylus was permanent. During the mid-teens, the vertical system was in the ascendant, with a number of firms about to join its ranks.

The vertical cut process used by Pathé could only benefit from comparisons to rival lateral cut technology ("No Needles to Change"), and Pathé recordings rose to the challenge with a distinctive crispness that merited attention. Pathé "Demonstration Record No.2 " (No.1 featured two selections from Gounod's *Romeo and Juliette*), "Exhibiting the superiority of tone of Pathé recording," embraced the familiar expository format:

> [Bugle call] *I am a Pathé record, guaranteed to play 1000 times - and, with care, I will live to speak to your grandchildren when they are as old as you are. I differ from other makes of record because I am played with a sapphire ball instead of a needle. The sapphire ball is round, smooth and permanent, thus eliminating the trouble of changing sharp, pointed metal needles which cut and rip the record. The Pathé repertoire of recordings is acknowledged to be the finest in the world. Pathé reproduces each and every tone faithfully. Hark to the delicate tones of the Hawaiian guitars and ukulele played by Louise and Ferrera. And now, to the rich, resonant tones of the trombone. Now listen to Miss Grace Hoffman modulate her voice so that it can hardly be distinguished from the flute. Mr. Winsch will now sing the chorus of "A Hot Time In the Old Town Tonight."* [Song, followed by a band playing "Columbia, the Gem of the Ocean."]

By the time the United States entered World War I, a great many disc talking machines were being sold with "convertible" tone arms, adaptable to either the lateral or vertical cut system. Customers could purchase the Pathé "Demonstration Record No.2" for 25 cents (later 50 cents, depending at which point in the inflationary teens it was pressed) to play at home on a Pathéphone, or one of many other talking machine brands. Of course, Victor and Columbia, which had the most to lose, refused to participate in the modification of their instruments to play vertical cut discs. For this reason, an aftermarket industry in conversion attachments emerged.

2-8. The teens would be the heyday of the vertical cut disc in America. Topping the list of vertical brands was Pathé, with ten years of experience in the field. This colorfully enameled sign with mounting flange, prominently displayed Pathé's mascot, the strutting red rooster – like the French, proud and pugnacious. Manufactured by the Metallograph Corporation, overall size 13 1/2" x 18 1/4". *Courtesy of the Tom and Sandi McCarthy collection.* (Value code: C)

Hole-ier Than Thou

Columbia was also responsible for a demonstration record that its client, the Standard Talking Machine Company of Chicago, distributed to stores that sold the distinctive Standard disc instruments, circa 1910. Standard enforced the sale of its own brand of record by equipping its machines with a turntable spindle of approximately ½" diameter (conventional talking machines used a ¼" diameter spindle). The records, of course, had an aperture of corresponding size, and dealers thus had the confidence that customers would return to their stores to purchase discs.

There was a further gimmick: Standard talking machines were what was then known as "scheme goods." Typically, the outlets that handled Standard products were not music stores or other traditional sellers of phonographs. Department stores, general merchandise stores, as well as various shops-around-the-corner eagerly promoted the medium-quality Standard goods, with their promise of creating regular cash customers.

Cash-paying customers (or those who paid off their accounts in cash) were given coupons by the dealer every time a purchase was made. When the patron had amassed enough, these tickets could be exchanged for a Standard talking machine and a set of records. Standard machines and records were manufactured by Columbia, which maintained a full stable of such "client" brands.

2-9. The rough-and-ready staff of this bucolic furniture store looked prepared to *move* merchandise. What better way to improve turn-over than to offer "free talking machines." Two 1911-style Model "A" Standard disc talking machines sit in the foreground, next to descriptive handbills. The setting suggests just the kind of small-town market in which the Standard instruments and records thrived. *Courtesy of Dennis Peterson.* (Value code: G)

The text of the following letter, dated "6.29.09," from the Standard Talking Machine Company to a store in Retsof, New York, clearly described Standard's manner of doing business:

There's an old story told – you've heard it before – about a farmer who put a pair of your customers through "green spectacles" – it is exactly what it seems to be, a clean, liberal proposition, there is no "scheme" or "catch" about it – your customer knows that after making certain purchases at your store [allowing the proprietor some latitude to decide what purchases would qualify] *a high grade Standard Talking Machine is given absolutely free and all that you ask in return, is that the records be purchased from you – that's all there is to it.*

Occasionally a dealer will say – "but they wont [sic] *buy enough records". Do you keep your record stock up to date? Do you take advantage of the new lists we mail to you month after month? If you do not, that explains why they don't buy more records...*

Begin with this latest July list – one of the best selections of records ever offered to you. We wrote several days ago and submitted our new MODEL "A" machine – here is an opportunity for you to order several of the new instruments and select your records from this newest July list...

Thanking you in advance for your order...

Standard had its own version of the demonstration disc to draw passersby into a shop offering a "free" talking machine. This record was created around 1910, before the Standard Talking Machine Company's final epoch, which began in 1911 and ended with the firm's absorption by the Consolidated Talking Machine Company in late 1915. (In its last years, Standard reorganized, and for the first time sold machines directly to the public.)

The demonstration disc took the form of a then popular "rube sketch," with comedy artist Len Spencer playing a smooth pitchman who matches wits with a clever yokel. Columbia, which recorded and pressed the disc, employed its customary language of self-appraisal. Spencer remarked of the "free" Standard talking machine (probably the Model "A"), "This Graphophone represents one of the greatest achievements of the largest and best talking machine industry in the world." The record commenced in the same fashion as the two demonstration discs Columbia produced under its own name:

[Bugle sounds the familiar cavalry charge.]
Pitchman: Don't miss it – it's free!
Country Bumpkin: Say, what's free?
Pitchman: Why, this machine you're listening to.
Bumpkin: Please, do tell. Say...
Pitchman [interrupting]: *Yes sir, it's absolutely free to all customers of this store! Did you ever have a talking machine?*
Bumpkin: Well, not exactly, but, say – I got a wife! And I tell ya it's got to be a pretty good machine to beat Betsy Ann a-talkin'! [The crowd laughs.]
Pitchman: Well, this IS a good machine – it not only talks, but it can sing as well and play all the latest popular music of the day.
Bumpkin: [Whistles] *Do tell. Say, kin it whistle?*
Pitchman: Whistle? Well I should say so! You just listen.
[A piccolo performs "The Wearing of the Green" to applause and cheers from the crowd.]
Bumpkin: Well, gosh all hemlock! That's pretty slick! Hey, kin you tell a story?
Pitchman: Why, certainly. I suppose you've heard the story about the 900 foot well?
Bumpkin: Well, not yet – it's too deep! [Crowd laughs.]
Pitchman: And, ah, you've heard the story about the three eggs...?
Bumpkin: What about the three eggs?
Pitchman: Two bad! [He and everyone else laughs.]
Bumpkin: Say, you're so smart, I just reckon you never heard the story about the little red apple.
Pitchman: Well, I can't say that I have.
Bumpkin [laughing]: *Well, say, that's where you bite!* [Crowd laughs.]
Pitchman: Say, lookit, isn't that story rather far-fetched?
Bumpkin: Well, I should say so! I fetched it all the way from Skowhegan [Maine]*!* [Laughter]
Pitchman: Hey, you're quite an old joker.

Bumpkin: Yas, I'm a regular cut-up!
Pitchman: Well, you remind me of a banana skin.
Bumpkin: Why? What about the banana skin?
Pitchman: Why, you're ON....
Bumpkin: I'm ON...???
Pitchman: Yes, you're standing on!
A member of the crowd: Look out! Look out, Reuben! [A crash]
Bumpkin [getting up]*: Well, by jiminy!*
Pitchman: Hope you didn't hurt yourself.
Bumpkin: Hey, you didn't catch me that time!
Pitchman [breaking into laughter]*: No, but you tumbled just the same!* [Crowd laughs.] *Say, tell us another one of your funny stories.*
Bumpkin: Well, I can't – when I slipped on that banana skin, I broke my funny bone! [All laugh.]
Pitchman: Say, you remind me of a fella that fell out of a ten story window.
Bumpkin: Awww, that ain't nothin', I fell out of one eleven stories....
Pitchman [breaking into laughter]*: But, say, that's another story!* [All laugh.]
Bumpkin: Say, I'm jest about tuckered out.
Pitchman: Well, come inside, rest awhile – it's free... And, say, folks ALL of you come in and hear our Standard high-class talking machine. This machine is given absolutely free to all customers of our store. Step inside and ask to hear the specially-prepared records of bands and other instrumental music, songs, stories, recitations and so forth. This Graphophone represents one of the greatest achievements of the largest and best talking machine industry in the world, and is given free to customers of this store. Save your cash tickets – the machine is free – ask for full particulars, and get a Standard talking machine!

Edison Announces a Disc

While the sales of its cylinder Phonographs were still strong, the Edison company began experimenting with disc talking machines. The road, which was to culminate with the introduction of the Edison Disc Phonographs and records late in 1912, was littered with the patents of other firms, most notably the Victor Talking Machine Company. Even with considerable design constraints, Edison managed to create a finely engineered system, employing a permanent diamond stylus that reproduced a micro-groove record. Edison's new disc products were indeed revolutionary. However, the bulky mechanics required to circumvent rival-owned patents, and to support the close tolerances of a micro-groove format, would eventually prove disastrous. Edison Disc Phonographs and records (to which the name "Diamond Disc" was applied beginning in 1914) would never crack the lucrative low-to-mid price range. They would survive, and finally perish, for the amusement of the upper middle class and the wealthy. A special 10" advertising record, declaimed by elocutionist Harry E. Humphrey, bespoke the Edison company's earliest aspirations for the Disc Phonograph, though with a patronizing ring unfortunately common to Edison marketing:

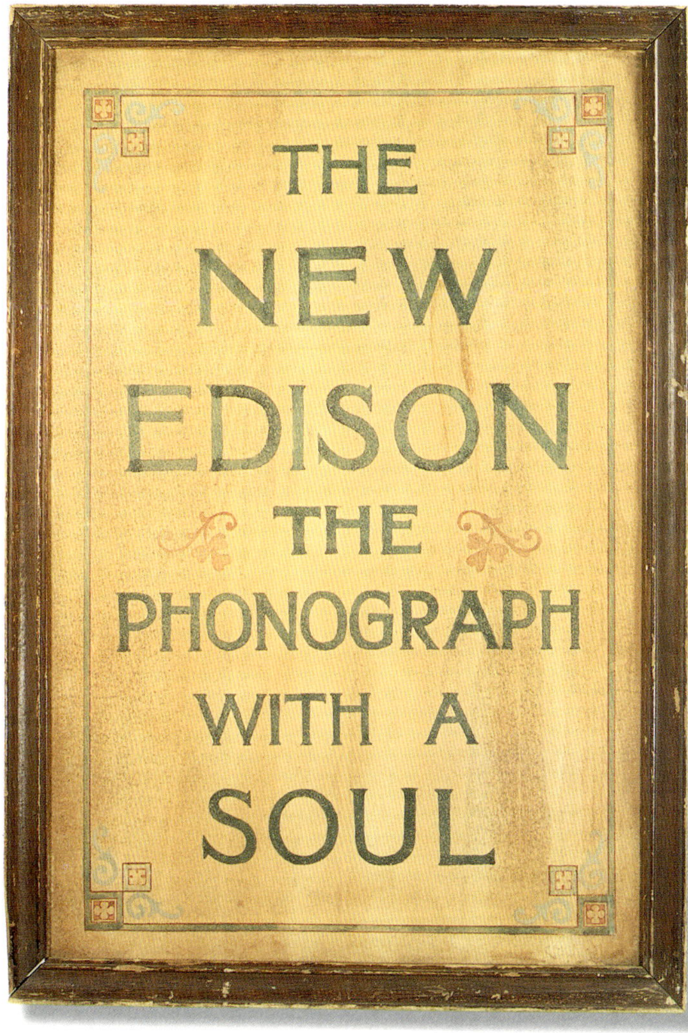

2-10. An Edison dealer displayed this sign to advertise the Edison Diamond Disc Phonograph, "The Phonograph With A Soul." Made of pasteboard on a wooden frame, the sign measures 16 3/4" x 23 3/4". *Courtesy of the Gfell family collection.* (Value code: F)

If you are a close observer, you have already noticed that the Edison Disc Phonograph requires no change of needles. The reproducer point is a genuine diamond, carefully selected, polished and fitted. It is never changed. In 1878, Mr. Edison invented and patented the first disc phonograph ever made – but this instrument before you is the first disc phonograph he has permitted to be offered to the public in his name. It represents 34 years of personal investigation and experimentation by Mr. Edison, and probably marks the limit of human achievement in recording and reproducing sound.

In designing the reproducer for this instrument, Mr. Edison constructed and tested over 2000 different models. The material used in the records was selected with equal care. It is an entirely new material, possessing properties which have a very great part in the excellence of the reproduction. The motor is many times stronger and more costly than any other motor – with the result that the beautiful tone qualities of the instrument are perfectly sustained at all times. Mr. Edison has conducted a series of exhaustive acoustical experiments which have resulted in new methods of sound recording, entirely unknown to other manufacturers, and very much superior to their methods. As you listen to the reproduction of music by this instrument, you will notice that all of the overtones, or tone colors, are recorded and faithfully reproduced. Other sound reproducing instruments are not capable of this – with the result that their reproduction consists of the fundamental tone, and a more or less distorted and intermittent reproduction of merely one or two of the overtones. Other records, compared with Edison records, are like an outline drawing without color, shading or detail – compared to a finished painting with all the feeling, tone, colors and perspective. For the first time, there is a sound reproducing instrument which truly reproduces music, and does not distort it. The musical volume of this instrument is many times greater than that of any other. The so-called volume of other talking machines is a series of loud, false vibrations produced by improper methods of recording and reproduction.

Inasmuch as this instrument is capable of a real interpretation of music, Mr. Edison intends to make it the means of offering all of the world's finest music to the American people. From month to month, he will present purposeful programs of music, including the works of the great composers, a revival of English and ballad opera and historic lyrics, a review of the music of the nation, gems from Grand Opera, the fine old songs so aptly called "heart songs," the best musical numbers from modern light opera successes, and all of the contemporary popular music. The artists who make records for the Edison Disc Phonograph are chosen with the greatest care. They are judged by the standards that prevail in the musical centers of Europe, and include the finest voices in the world. In selecting artists, we disregard the bombastic claims of hired press agents, the illusions of stage settings, and the trapperies [sic] *or the charm of stage presence. We select only those singers whose art is so great that the full measure of their power is felt without seeing them; artists whose voices abound in a wealth of color, feeling and expression.* [Edison, like Columbia, had been frozen out of the Grand Opera star race by Victor, and thus turned to denigrating the competition.]

Realizing that the Edison Disc Phonograph is an instrument that will appeal to the most highly cultured people, we offer in the design of our instruments pure types of the following schools of furniture: Adam, Jacobean, Sheraton, Louis XV and Louis XVI, in addition to a well considered type of Modern Renaissance suited to a mixed scheme of furnishings. Now, if you will permit this instrument to play a record selected by you, it will more than prove statements I have made.

Advertising In the Eye Of the Beholder

Traditional printed advertising continued to evolve during the first decade of the twentieth century. This included everything from slap-dash handbills on newsprint to beautifully lithographed trade cards and posters. Local shops most often advertised in newspapers, while talking machine manufacturers commonly promoted their products in national magazines such as *Munsey's*, *Everybody's*, *McClure's*, and the *Saturday Evening Post*.

Beyond this, a whole universe of practical items began to be emblazoned with phonograph brand names, as well as the names and addresses of dealers. The advertising calendar was just coming into its own, but there were also pocket mirrors, rulers, paperweights, tip trays, watch fobs, blotters, framed lithographs for the home, and cardboard hand fans. Further afield were some rather unusual objects of talking machine advertising, including ladies' compacts, tea strainers, and parlor game scorecards.

Numerous effigies of Nipper, the little fox terrier of "His Master's Voice" fame would eventually be produced and distributed under the vigilant eye of the Victor Talking Machine Company, the trademark holder. Commencing in the teens and continuing for decades, there were plush Nippers for the nursery, life-sized papier mâché likenesses for the parlor, three-foot high versions for shop windows, and miniature ceramic doggy salt and pepper shakers for the dinner table.

The beginning of the twentieth century saw an explosion of marketing possibilities, and a continual refinement of the means by which the message was communicated. 1914 would be a year of world cataclysm – the beginning of a period when flags, insignia, uniforms, and scenes of sad departure and fond reunion would pervade record and phonograph advertising.

2-11. This Edison poster, measuring 19" x 26", with its beaming schoolboy and accurately-depicted 1901 model "Home" Phonograph, is a sheer delight. Printed by J. Ottmann, New York. *Courtesy of Nina and Dave Heitz.* (Value code: VR)

2-12. An Edison novelty trade card measuring 3 1/8" x 5 3/4", with the admonition, "figure it out." *Courtesy of the Tom and Sandi McCarthy collection.* (Value code: VR)

2-13. As the cardboard slide is withdrawn, Edison's portrait gives way to another image. The engineering of this piece is more complicated than might be immediately apparent. The transformation is graduated, as the central band descends. *Courtesy of the Tom and Sandi McCarthy collection.*

2-14. Pulling the slide all the way reveals a well-starched but slightly psychopathic little brat about to make mincemeat out of an Edison Phonograph. This humorous image was frequently exploited by Edison, circa 1904. *Courtesy of the Tom and Sandi McCarthy collection.*

2-15. Dealer advertising transfers were very seldom applied to talking machine horns. However, in the instance of this 1901 Victor "A," Chicago merchandiser Lyon & Healy attached a distinctive paper sticker. (Value code: VR)

2-16. A year or two later, a similar label was affixed to the cabinet of a Victor "Monarch Jr." *Courtesy of Steve and Ellie Saccente.* (Value code: machine, so marked, A)

2-17. This 10" conical horn was stenciled with advertising for the Columbia Phonograph Company of 88 Wabash Avenue, city unknown. Both "Disc and Cylinder Graphophones" were offered, dating this horn no earlier than October 1901. The bottom line reads, "An 'Ideal' Christmas Gift," suggesting that this may have been part of a dealer's display, rather than generalized dealer advertising. In any event, by late 1901 this horn was out-of-date due to its small size and primitive design. Exchanging its modest potential sales profit for use as an advertising novelty was clever marketing. *Courtesy of the collection of Howard Hazelcorn.* (Value code: VR)

2-18. Prior to 1908, disc records were single-faced. An enterprising Buffalo, New York dealer took advantage of the unused reverse surface to remind customers where more discs could be purchased. (Value code: H)

2-19. A clever dealer from Elmira, New York affixed this identifying label to the backs of Victor discs. (Value code: H)

2-20.A fanciful German advertising label. A delicate variation of "His Master's Voice." *Courtesy of the Babcock House Museum, John H. Perschbacher.* (Value code: G)

2-21. A Chinese red Edison Chinese record box, shown with a related Edison catalogue listing. *Courtesy of the Babcock House Museum, John H. Perschbacher.* (Value code: VR)

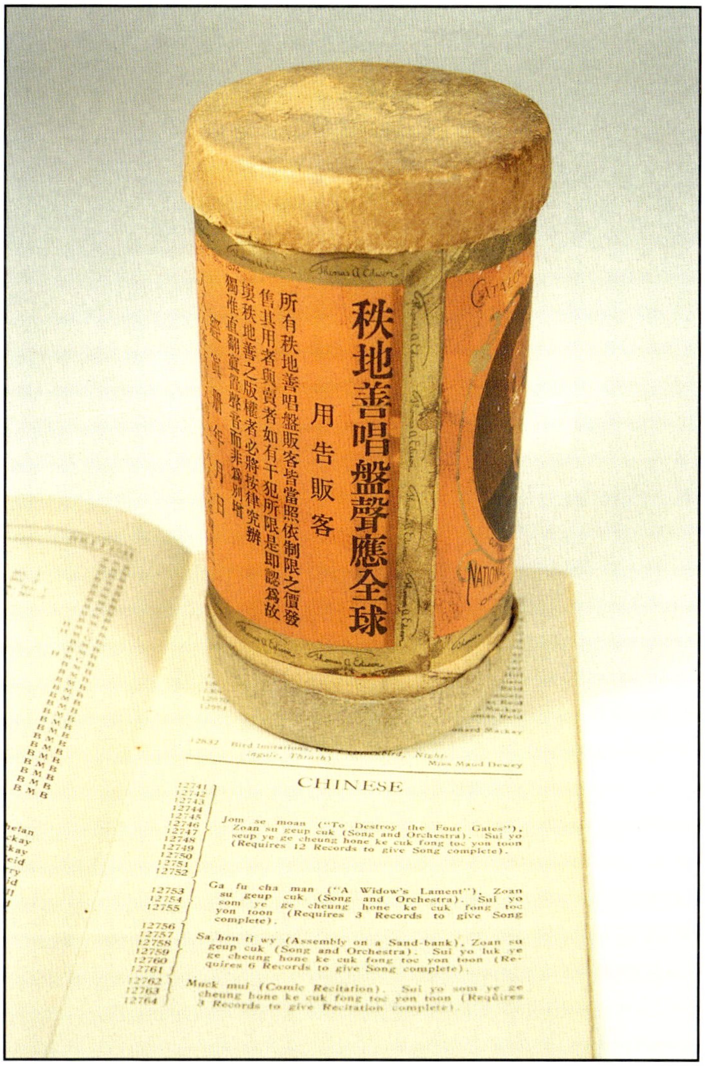

2-22. Another view of the Edison Chinese record box. *Courtesy of the Babcock House Museum, John H. Perschbacher.*

2-23. At the time that Gianni Bettini left his established digs in New York City and ensconced himself in France, this dual-language trade card was produced. Reference was still made to the "Autograph Records of World-famed Artists" that had distinguished Bettini among the cognoscenti of the 1890s. This elevated path eventually would be abandoned in favor of the low road to commercial survival. Bettini's French products would veer toward the ordinary as his business prospects faltered. 3 7/8" x 5 1/2". *Courtesy of the Charles Hummel collections.* (Value code: VR)

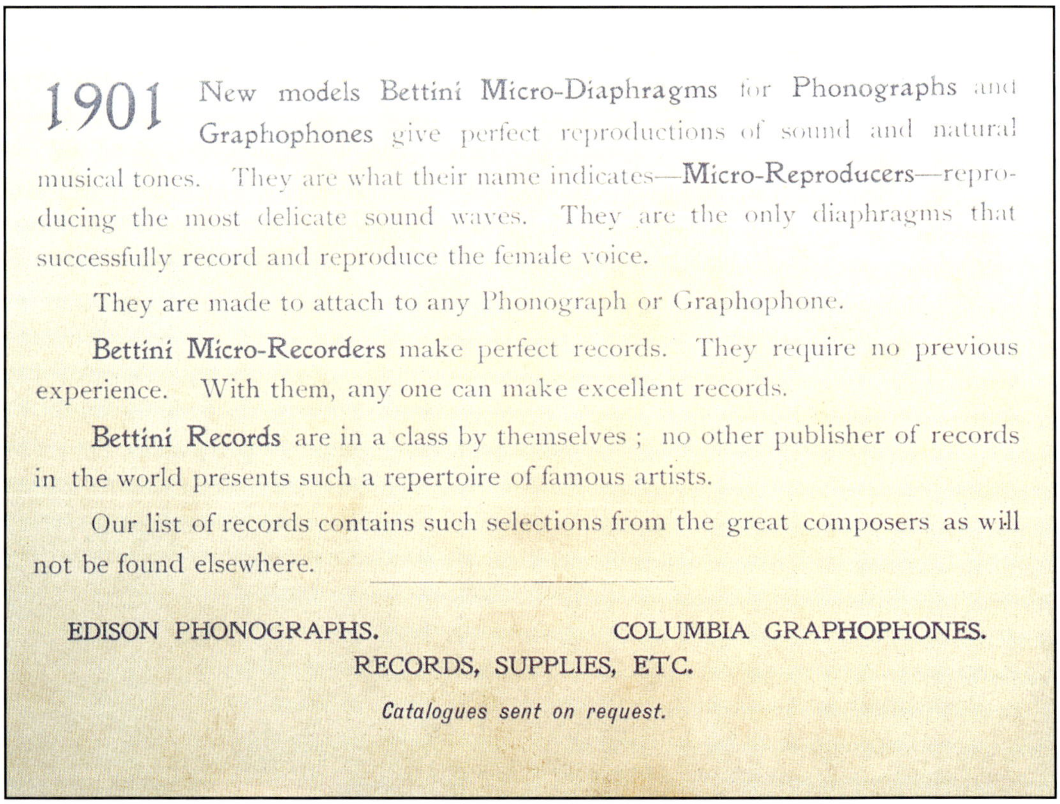

1901 New models Bettini Micro-Diaphragms for Phonographs and Graphophones give perfect reproductions of sound and natural musical tones. They are what their name indicates—Micro-Reproducers—reproducing the most delicate sound waves. They are the only diaphragms that successfully record and reproduce the female voice.

They are made to attach to any Phonograph or Graphophone.

Bettini Micro-Recorders make perfect records. They require no previous experience. With them, any one can make excellent records.

Bettini Records are in a class by themselves ; no other publisher of records in the world presents such a repertoire of famous artists.

Our list of records contains such selections from the great composers as will not be found elsewhere.

EDISON PHONOGRAPHS. COLUMBIA GRAPHOPHONES.
RECORDS, SUPPLIES, ETC.

Catalogues sent on request.

2-24. The reverse of the Bettini card. Here, Bettini's traditional marketing language was still employed. The date, however, was the frontier between Bettini's operations in the United States and France. *Courtesy of the Charles Hummel collections.*

2-25. This charming gilded statuette, in textbook turn-of the-twentieth-century style, was catalogued by Bettini for patrons who might like to add a little subtle advertising to their home décor. 10 1/2" high, signed on the base "J. Merculiano," and marked "Société des Micro Phonographes Bettini, 23 Bd des Capucines, Paris." (Value code: VR)

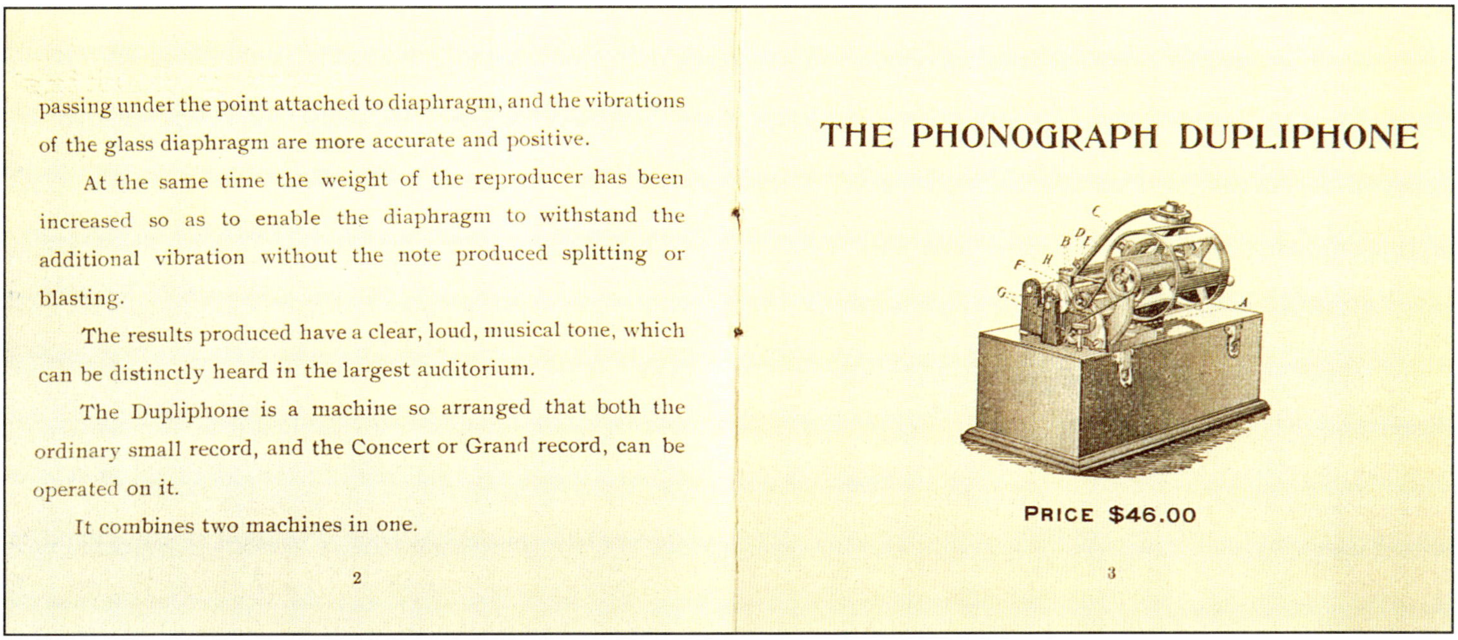

passing under the point attached to diaphragm, and the vibrations of the glass diaphragm are more accurate and positive.

At the same time the weight of the reproducer has been increased so as to enable the diaphragm to withstand the additional vibration without the note produced splitting or blasting.

The results produced have a clear, loud, musical tone, which can be distinctly heard in the largest auditorium.

The Dupliphone is a machine so arranged that both the ordinary small record, and the Concert or Grand record, can be operated on it.

It combines two machines in one.

2

THE PHONOGRAPH DUPLIPHONE

PRICE $46.00

3

2-26. Hawthorne & Sheble, like all independent talking machine enterprises, survived by its wits. The company contrived a wide variety of clever accessories and attachments, not the least of which was the "Dupliphone." This apparatus allowed a conventional two-minute Graphophone or Phonograph to play, in addition, the 5" diameter "Grand" or "Concert" cylinders. The clap-trap necessary to convert the Graphophone was nothing compared to the complicated mechanics of the "Phonograph Dupliphone" (shown here cantilevered to a "Home"). A "Dupliphone" catalogue, 3" x 3 5/8". *Courtesy of the Charles Hummel collections.* (Value code: VR)

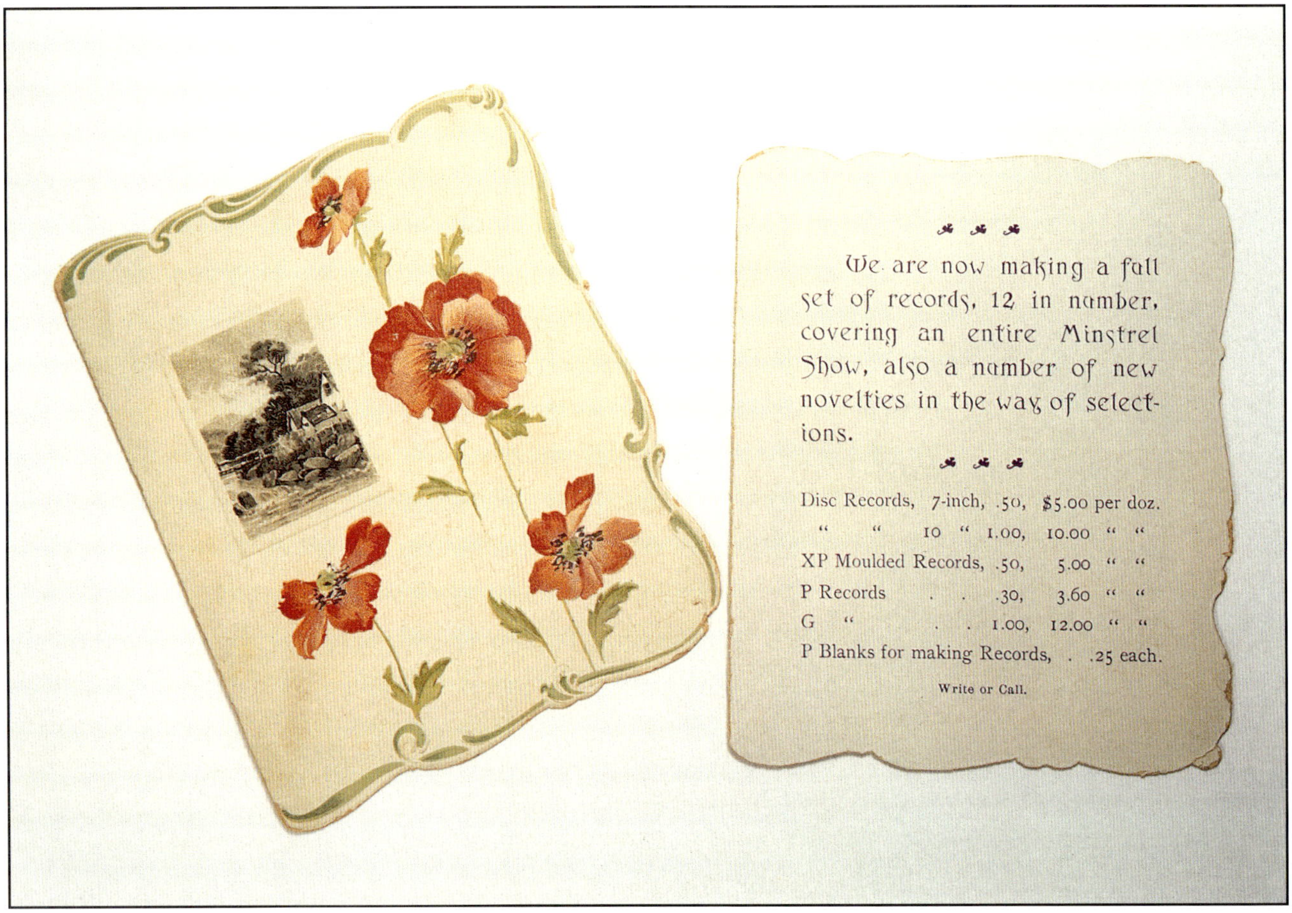

2-27. This delightful, 3 3/4" x 4 1/2" embossed Valentine's Day card from 1902 listed the prices of Columbia discs and cylinders, including the non-molded, brown wax "P" records that had recently been superceded by the mass-produced "XP" cylinders. The card has separated at the folded seam, allowing the face to be displayed next to the interior message. On the reverse, the advertising continued, "Valentine's Day, Columbia Phonograph Co., 164 Tremont Street, Boston, Mass... Have you heard the Marvelous XP Records?" (Value code: H)

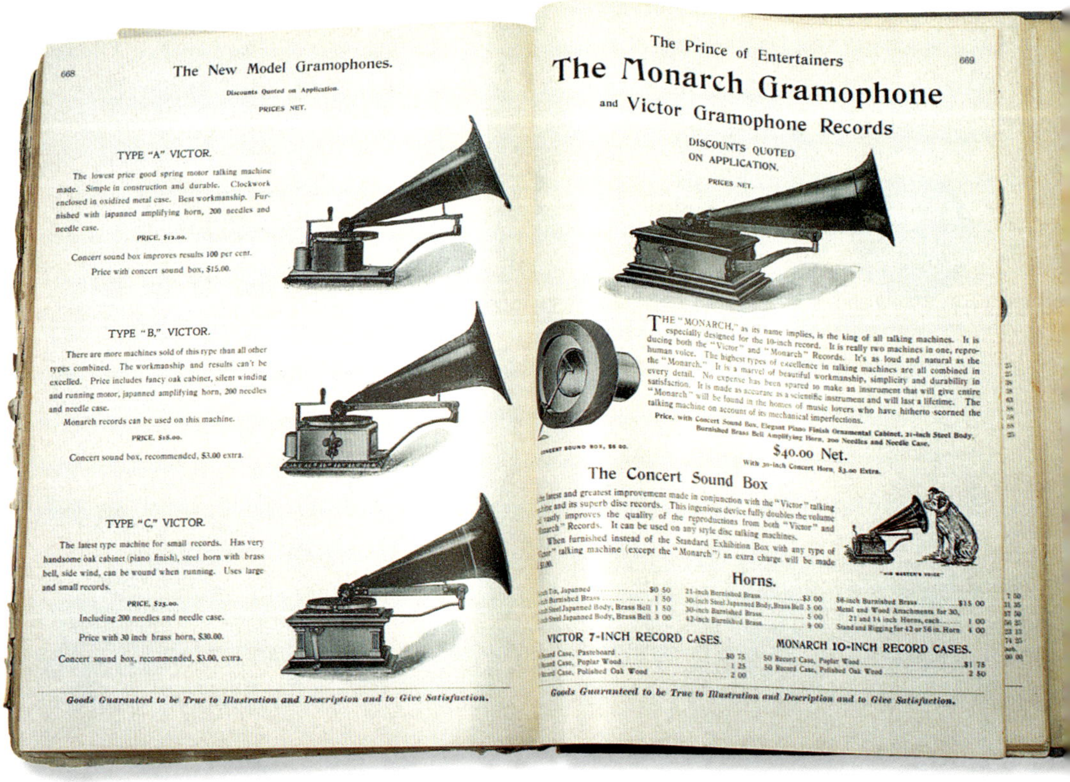

2-28. From a 1902 wholesale catalogue of the Equitable Manufacturing Company, an extremely rare double-page spread advertising Eldridge R. Johnson's disc machines. Note that the terminology reflected the turmoil that had only just subsided in the industry. The name "gramophone," although it is used here, was about to become extinct in the United States, though the rest of the world continued to recognize it to denote a disc-playing instrument. In America, Johnson chose to distance himself from the legal vagaries of the Berliner Gramophone Company, by adopting the more general term "talking machine." The instrument at the right was called a "Monarch" to indicate its superiority over the modestly-priced "Victor" line. However, Johnson rapidly abandoned this distinction of nomenclature, and christened his firm the Victor Talking Machine Company. *Courtesy of Michael F. Khanchalian.* (Value code: VR)

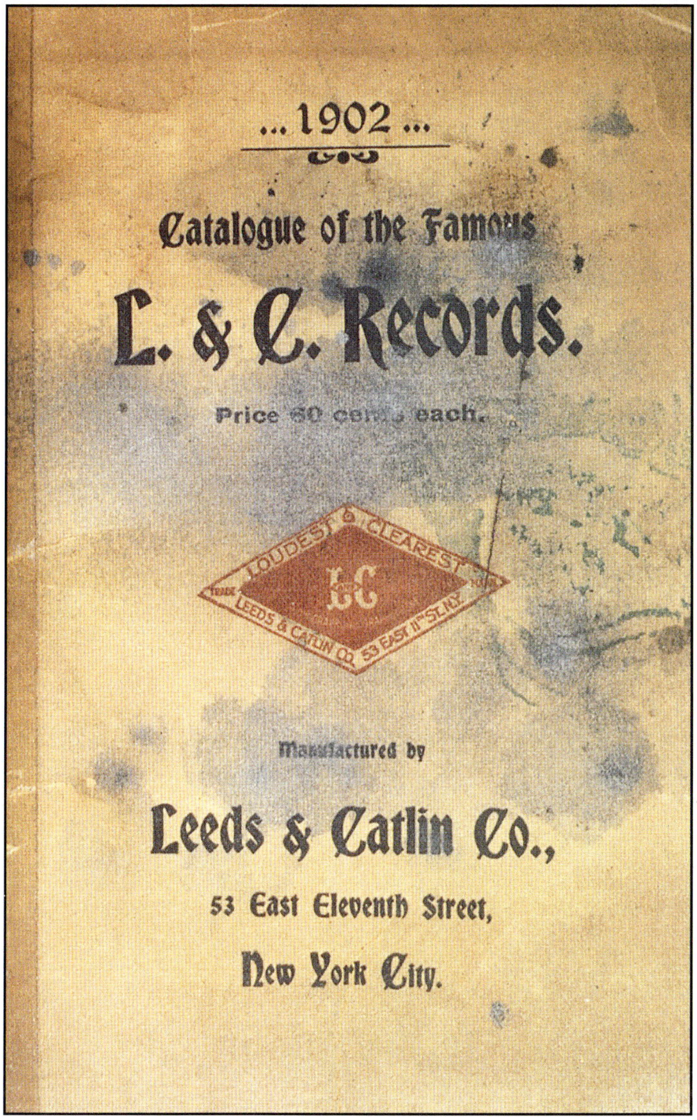

2-29. This rare 1902 Leeds & Catlin cylinder record catalogue shows signs of having been "conveniently" stored in the oily interior of a phonograph cabinet. The Leeds family was influential in the talking machine industry from the 1890s through 1908. In January 1907 Leeds & Catlin announced with great fanfare a new line of cylinders under the "Radium" brand name. A full-page advertisement appeared in the trade publication *Talking Machine World*, after which nothing was forthcoming. Although the "Radium" records were stillborn, L & C continued to produce disc records for about a year. (Value code: F)

2-30. Based on the Victor label illustrated, this advertising postcard was probably distributed during late 1901 or early 1902. Record "exchange" programs such as the one described here regularly emerged among dealers. These promotions were a sure way to achieve inventory reduction. Yet, one puzzles about the large-scale consequences for the dealer of accepting worn records, unless some form of recycling was in place. Manufacturers, in an extremely paternal business environment, strictly forbade the sale of "used" records. *Courtesy of Fred Guenther.* (Value code: H)

2-31. A delightful die-cut trade card, featuring the stylized image of a Zonophone, 12" x 17". *Courtesy of the Tom and Sandi McCarthy collection.* (Value code: F)

2-32. A 23 1/4" x 31 3/4" poster from Victor's French cousin, La Compaignie Française du Gramophone, circa 1903. The image of the dog Nipper listening to a Berliner Gramophone enjoyed worldwide popularity. "His Master's Voice" was translated into many languages. Here, the passerby is admonished to listen to the everlasting disc records of the famous talking machine, on sale HERE. *Courtesy of the Charles Hummel collections.* (Value code: VR)

2-33. A Columbia cylinder record box over-pasted by a dealer with Victor advertising. Note the reference to "easy payments." The catch phrase "a dollar down and a dollar a week" would enter the American argot as the quintessential expression of the "square deal." *Courtesy of Gilbert (Bert) Pasley.* (Value code: G)

2-34. An Edison Phonograph catalogue, circa 1903, with inset showing wholesale merchant discounts. In general, the dealer margins, never exceeding 40%, were not extraordinary – especially since freight was paid by the dealer. Edison and other industrial firms carefully cultured a stranglehold on the business practices of their dealers. Retail prices were set by the manufacturer, and could not be altered a penny. Second-hand machines could not be resold except by special license, and violators of any rule were blackballed. *Courtesy of Sam Sheena.* (Value code: F)

2-35. Noted operatic star Francesco Tamango was the first recording artist to receive a royalty contract. Victor's affiliate in Europe, Gramophone & Typewriter, Limited persuaded the great tenor to sign an exclusive contract in 1903. This was a year before Caruso's services were acquired, and the Victor/Gramophone companies were struggling to rise above the common vaudeville sketches, "coon songs," and band numbers that populated their record catalogues. In order to gain the imprimatur of an artist on the scale of Tamango, the companies offered substantial enticements. The eventual agreement included an advance of £ 2,000 (the equivalent of $10,000 at the time), 10% of the retail sales of his records, and unique packaging. Shown is No.95002, "Death of Otello," with its illustrated sleeve which revealed Tamango's photograph when the record was withdrawn. Tamango's records were released with much fanfare, and the sleeve served to advertise the fact that the Victor/Gramophone companies had achieved something special. Tamango died August 31, 1905, but his nineteen recordings would endure in the catalogues until the mid-1920s (without the distinctive sleeves). Royalty recording contracts would soon become commonplace, but Tamango's was the first. *Courtesy of H. Duane Goldman.* (Value code: F)

2-36. To facilitate the sale of Columbia machines on the installment plan, one dealer dispensed this handy booklet to customers. A collection agent was employed to call at the homes of the clients, who had already taken possession of the equipment. Front and back covers are shown to illustrate that both cylinder and disc Graphophones were being promoted. *Courtesy of the Babcock House Museum, John H. Perschbacher.* (Value code: G)

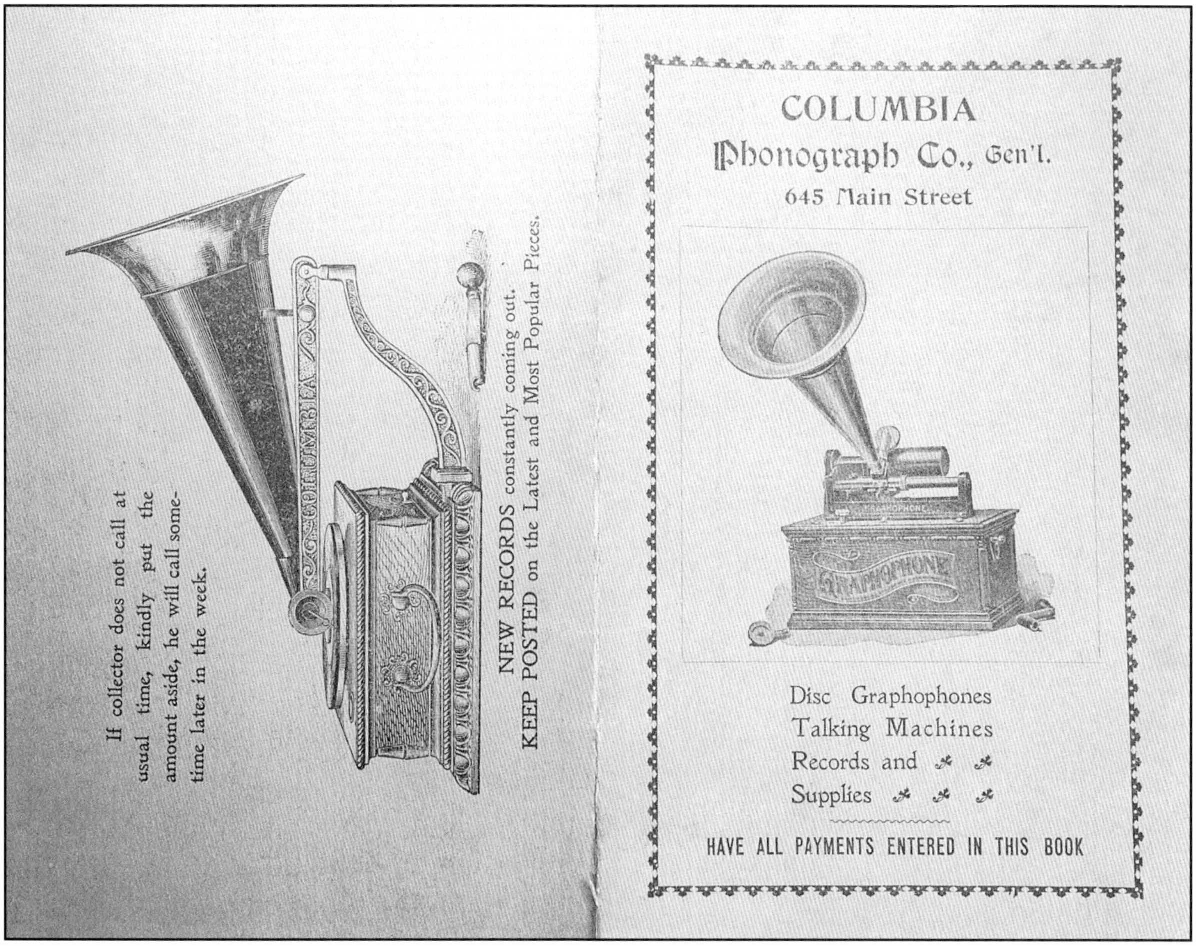

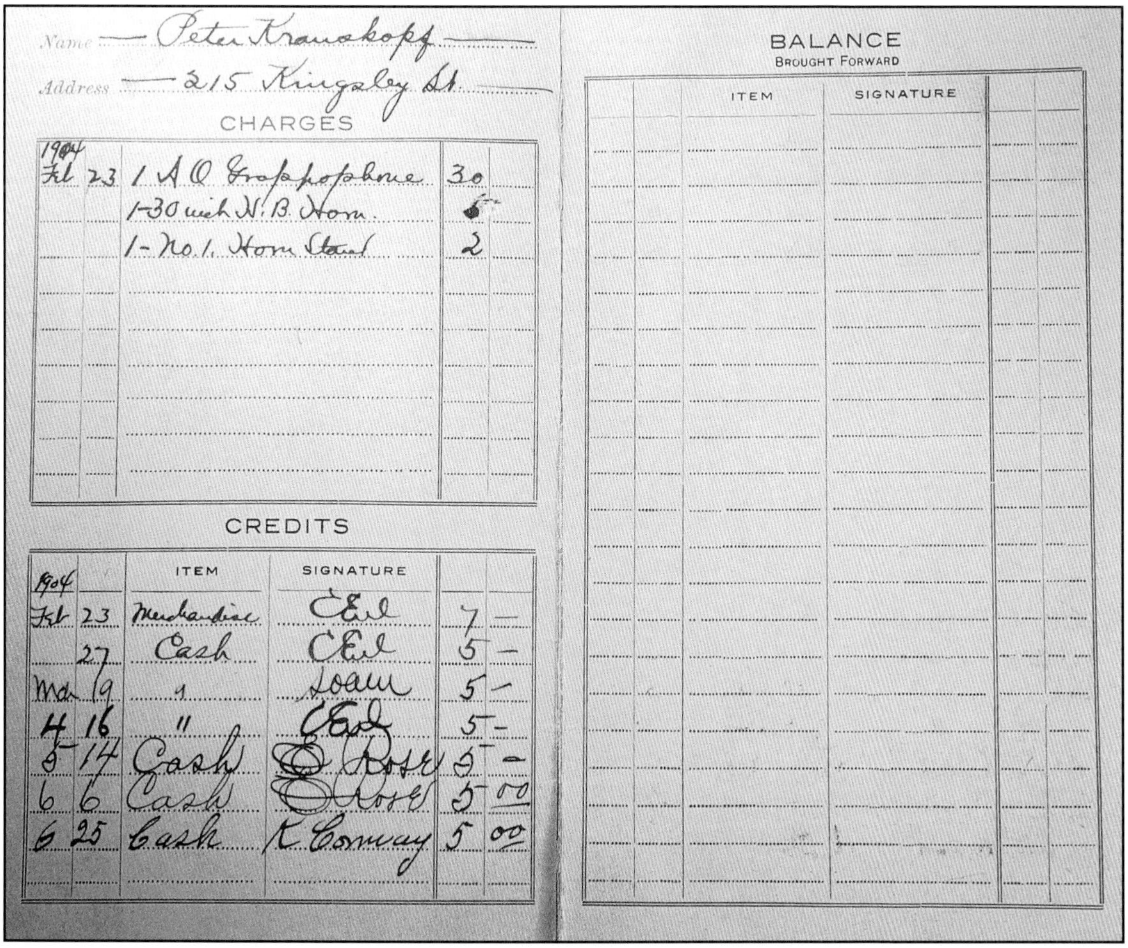

2-37. The interior of the Columbia time payment booklet indicated that this particular customer was paying off a Type "AO" Graphophone fitted with a 30" long horn and support stand. The first payment was indicated as $7.00 in "merchandise" – eggs, perhaps? 6 1/2" x 8 1/2" unfolded. *Courtesy of the Babcock House Museum, John H. Perschbacher.*

2-38. Following the election of Theodore Roosevelt and Charles W. Fairbanks in 1904, Columbia appropriately embellished its November record supplement. (Value code: H)

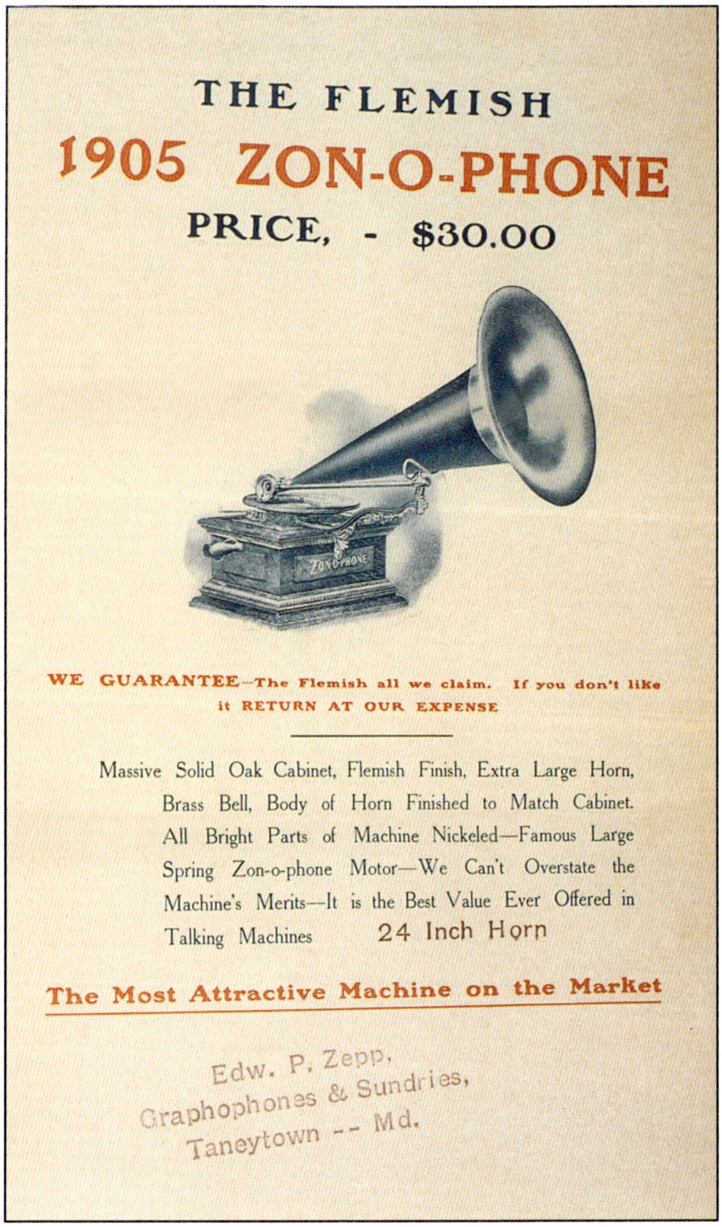

2-39. A Zonophone flyer, probably distributed late in 1904, promoting the "Flemish" finish. This term denoted a fad in home decorating, characterized by dark-toned oak. Of special note is the line, "Body of Horn Finished to Match Cabinet." This is one of the only known references to the wood-graining of the conical steel body of a talking machine horn (which customarily would have been painted black). (Value code: H)

2-40. Three talking machine advertising envelopes. Although Columbia never developed a novel image to rival Victor's wildly successful "His Master's Voice" (as Edison attempted with the jocular "old couple" logo), here we can detect Victor's influence in the girl auditioning a Columbia "AR" Disc Graphophone (1904). (Value code: H)

2-41. In the realm of peripheral promotion, what could be more unusual than this Edison cylinder record box affixed by a dealer with a label advertising a horse harness? *Courtesy of Nina and Dave Heitz.* (Value code: F)

2-42. A "Tiz-It" metal horn connector with an explanatory advertising flyer. The "new style 'Columbia'" of the text referred to the "Lyric" reproducer, introduced in 1905. *Courtesy of the Scott and Denise Corbett collection.* (Value code: flyer only, H)

2-43. Après moi, le déluge! Following Sig. Bettini's departure for France, his name continued to be associated with a (relocated) talking machine firm in New York City. Note that the old imagery of an embellished Edison "Concert" Phonograph with "Micro-Phonograph" attachment is employed, though Victor talking machines have been added to the list of wares. Inside this 3 1/4" x 6 1/4" catalogue is a list of "Philharmonic" single-faced 10" disc records (50 cents each) from the 1904-05 period. *Courtesy of the Charles Hummel collections.* (Value code: VR)

2-44. Cylinder phonographs displayed in a store window. It is interesting to note that the horns have been suspended on string from the ceiling. Every collector who has happened upon some "old fellow" who hanged his horn from the ceiling after misplacing the support crane, has probably winced. Here, however, is evidence that this is not a modern practice. *Courtesy of Dennis Peterson.* (Value code: H)

2-45. This 14" x 19 3/4" double-sided lithographed metal sign identified a dealer selling the disc machines and records of Victor's French relative. The trade name "Gramophone" fell out of use in the United States after 1900, but continued to be used (eventually with a lower case "g") to denote any disc-playing instrument by the rest of the world. *Courtesy of the Charles Hummel collections.* (Value code: A)

2-46. A rarely seen Edison poster, 16 1/4" x 23 1/4", emphasizing the middle-priced "Home" Phonograph, circa 1905. *Courtesy of Nina and Dave Heitz.* (Value code: VR)

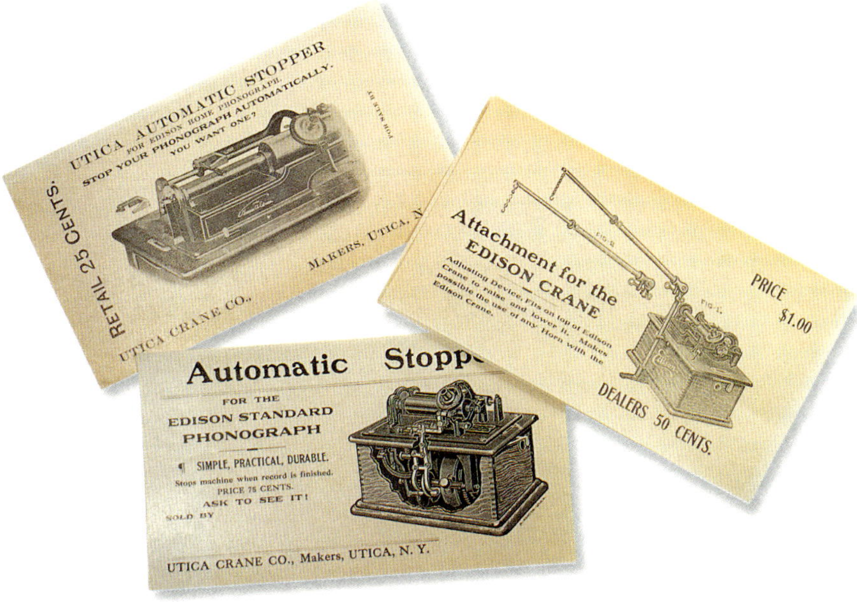

2-47. Three cards advertising optional attachments for Edison Phonographs. *Courtesy of Tom and Joanna Broome.* (Value code: H)

2-48. Brightly colored record labels, or those with black backgrounds (such as Victor and Columbia both employed) discouraged dealers from rubber stamping labels with their individual identification. In this instance, the white background of the American Record Company's "Indian" label afforded Burke & Rous the opportunity to use a specially-prepared stamp. Rous was Samuel Holland Rous, long associated with Victor, and known as singer S.H. Dudley. (Value code: H)

2-49. In a day when smokestacks belching unfiltered emissions were admired as signs of prosperity, Columbia proudly depicted its Bridgeport, Connecticut factory on this postcard. Similar imagery was used on catalogues, letterheads and even the backs of single-faced disc records. *Courtesy of the collection of Howard Hazelcorn.* (Value code: H)

2-50. A comic advertising postcard, circa 1905. (Value code: H)

2-51. A 22" long felt pennant from the Phono Cycle Company, circa 1905. *Courtesy of the Charles Hummel collections.* (Value code: F)

2-52. A porcelain enamel sign measuring 20" x 28". *Courtesy of the Charles Hummel collections.* (Value code: A)

2-53. Disc record sleeves became an important avenue of advertising as the twentieth century progressed. This practical marketing concept was exploited by both dealers and the record companies. In this instance, a store used the envelopes in which it sold Victor discs to promote wares that included Edison cylinder Phonographs and Kodak cameras. (Value code: H)

2-54. The Pathé company of France manufactured a highly original line of cylinder phonographs during the first decade of the twentieth century. The postcards shown here were used to promote Pathé products. Note the glass horns pictured in the lower two cards. Pathé equipped some of its machines with these lustrous, fragile artifacts, but not many have survived. (Value code: H)

2-55. Lyon & Healy of Chicago was one of the foremost sellers and distributors of talking machines in the Midwest. Nearly all Victor models were identified by a stamped metal plate affixed to the cabinet. As may be seen on this Victor "I," circa 1905, a specially-printed celluloid Lyon & Healy dealer tag, mimicking the conventional Victor ID plate, has been tacked in place. (Value code: machine, so marked, B)

2-56. The Holmes Music Company applied this decal to its products - in this instance, the rear cabinet panel of a 1905 Edison "Home" Phonograph. At this time, virtually all Edison Phonographs carried large "banner" decals on the fronts of their cabinets reading "Edison Home Phonograph," "Edison Standard Phonograph," and a few others. Within a year of this machine's manufacture, the Edison Phonograph Works, in response to customer demand, replaced its ostentatious "banner" decals with a small, understated one that read simply, "Edison." One wonders what customer reaction was to dealer decals such as this one.

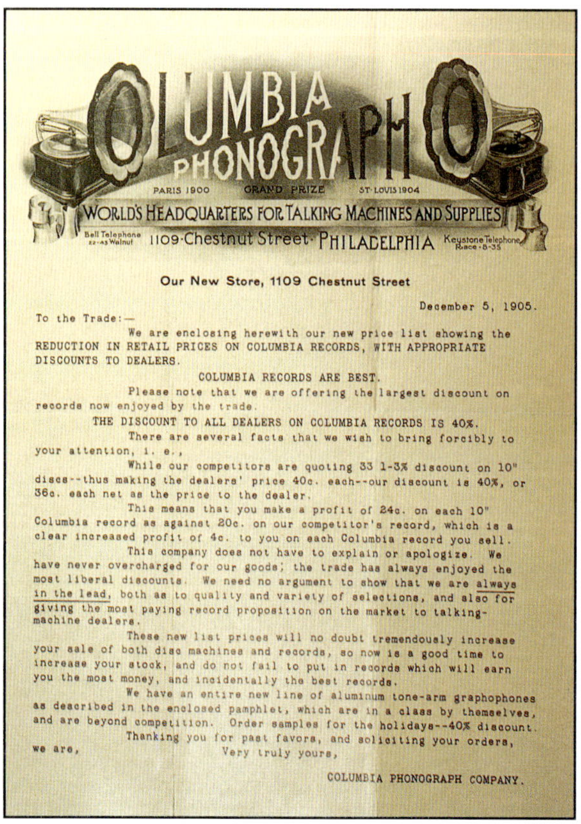

COLUMBIA PHONOGRAPH

PARIS 1900 GRAND PRIZE ST. LOUIS 1904

WORLD'S HEADQUARTERS FOR TALKING MACHINES AND SUPPLIES

Bell Telephone 22-43 Walnut 1109 Chestnut Street · PHILADELPHIA Keystone Telephone Race-8-35

Our New Store, 1109 Chestnut Street

December 5, 1905.

To the Trade:—

We are enclosing herewith our new price list showing the REDUCTION IN RETAIL PRICES ON COLUMBIA RECORDS, WITH APPROPRIATE DISCOUNTS TO DEALERS.

COLUMBIA RECORDS ARE BEST.

Please note that we are offering the largest discount on records now enjoyed by the trade.

THE DISCOUNT TO ALL DEALERS ON COLUMBIA RECORDS IS 40%.

There are several facts that we wish to bring forcibly to your attention, i. e.,

While our competitors are quoting 33 1-3% discount on 10" discs--thus making the dealers' price 40c. each--our discount is 40%, or 36c. each net as the price to the dealer.

This means that you make a profit of 24c. on each 10" Columbia record as against 20c. on our competitor's record, which is a clear increased profit of 4c. to you on each Columbia record you sell.

This company does not have to explain or apologize. We have never overcharged for our goods; the trade has always enjoyed the most liberal discounts. We need no argument to show that we are always in the lead, both as to quality and variety of selections, and also for giving the most paying record proposition on the market to talking-machine dealers.

These new list prices will no doubt tremendously increase your sale of both disc machines and records, so now is a good time to increase your stock, and do not fail to put in records which will earn you the most money, and incidentally the best records.

We have an entire new line of aluminum tone-arm graphophones as described in the enclosed pamphlet, which are in a class by themselves, and are beyond competition. Order samples for the holidays--40% discount.

Thanking you for past favors, and soliciting your orders, we are,

Very truly yours,

COLUMBIA PHONOGRAPH COMPANY.

2-57. The imaginative letterhead of this notice to dealers featured twin "BD" Disc Graphophones, the contours of which were incorporated into the lettering. The text is also of note. In December 1905, Victor rather suddenly reduced the price of its 10" popular disc records (single-faced at that time) from $1.00 to 60 cents. Columbia, usually the initiator in price wars, reacted immediately, and its January 1906 record supplements were rubber stamped to indicate an identical price reduction. The speed with which Columbia jumped may be gleaned from this letter dated December 5, 1905. The December Victor record supplement, with news of the price change, had just been issued. Late in 1908, both firms announced double-faced records, with Columbia's retailing at 65 cents each. Victor, which had not been sanguine about the shift to double-faced records in the first place, continued to concurrently produce discs in the old single-faced format until 1913. *Courtesy of Tom and Joanna Broome.* (Value code: H)

2-58. Postcards were commonly used for simple business correspondence at the turn of the twentieth century. This one, with its prominent Victor logo, is unusual for the quality and rich color of the printing. *Courtesy of Fred Guenther.* (Value code: H)

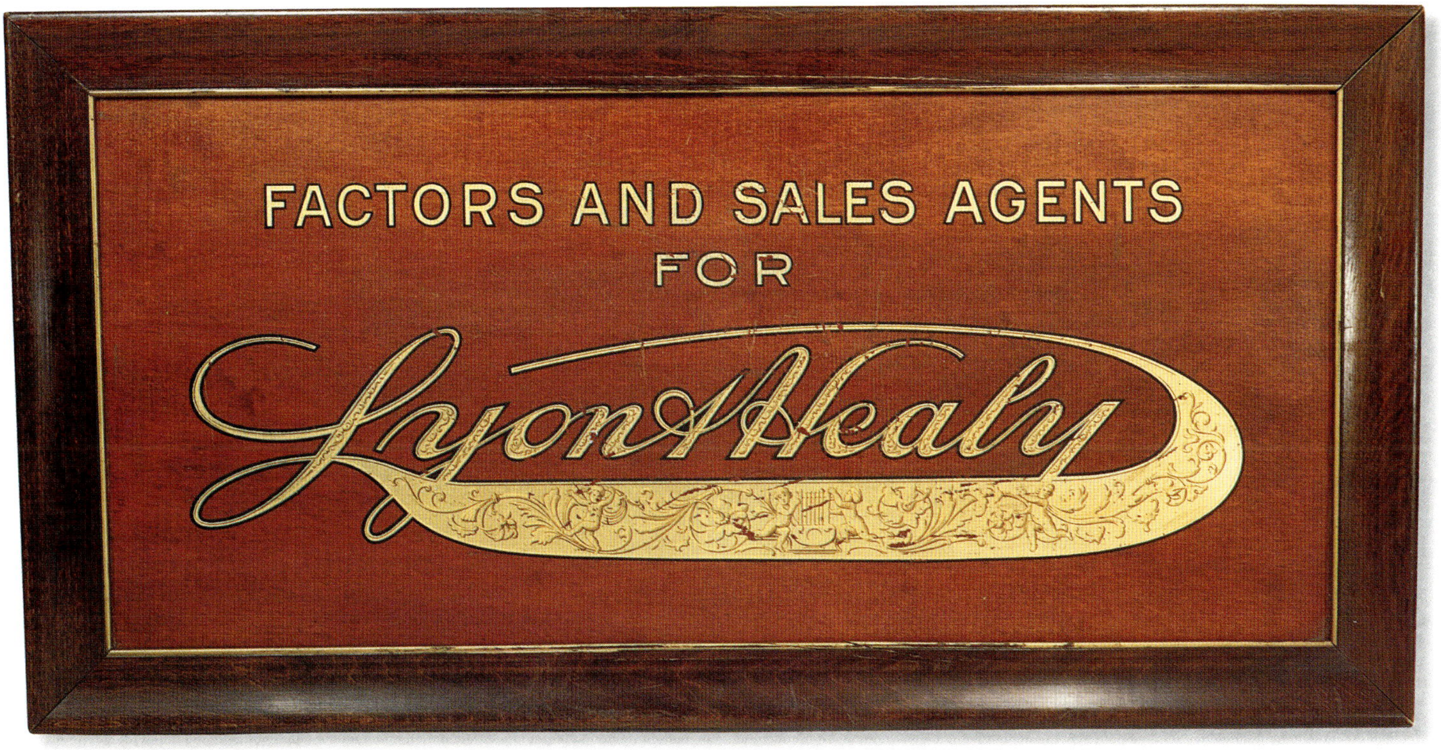

2-59. Lyon & Healy supplied many dealers with talking machines and accessories. Here, an eye-catching 12 1/2" x 24 1/2" metal sign identified a client dealer. *Courtesy of Pat and Jamie Jones.* (Value code: B)

2-60. As the first decade of the twentieth century reached midpoint, Columbia's venerable cylinder record was in transition. The 5" Columbia "Grand" records (left), introduced with much fanfare in 1898 for $5.00 apiece, had been rendered obsolescent and were offered for only 75 cents. Columbia's hard wax "moulded" cylinder records still merited their own separate listings in 1906 (center). Very soon, however, Columbia's disc records and talking machines would assume prominence in the company's advertising (right). By the end of 1909, Columbia's once-preeminent cylinder record business would be only a memory. (Value code: G)

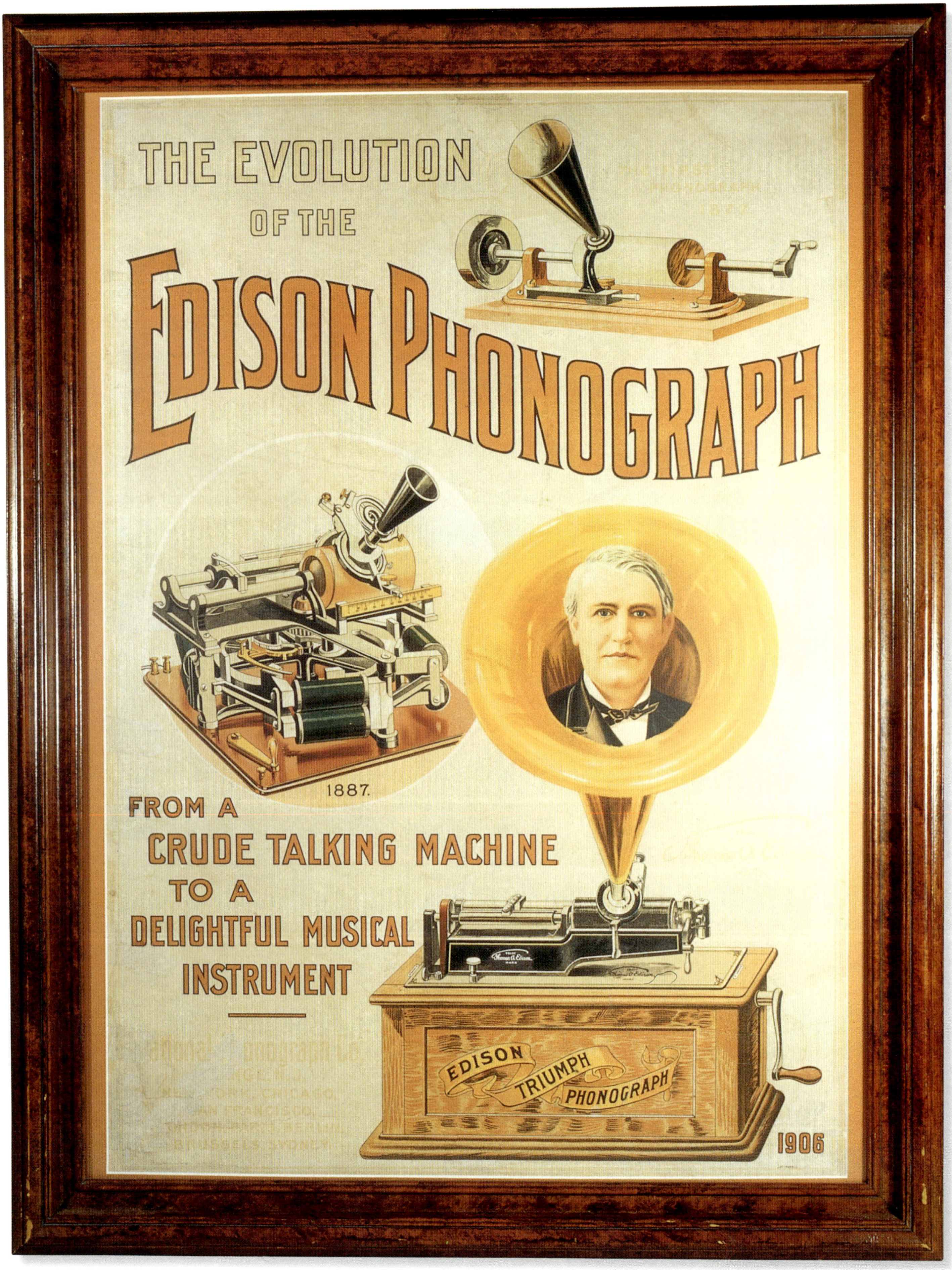
THE EVOLUTION
OF THE
EDISON PHONOGRAPH
1887.
FROM A
CRUDE TALKING MACHINE
TO A
DELIGHTFUL MUSICAL
INSTRUMENT
EDISON
TRIUMPH
PHONOGRAPH
1906

2-62. Contests and drawings have been marketing gimmicks for a long time. This 9" x 12" placard advertised "$2000 in Prizes" in a promotion sponsored by an Edison dealer. *Courtesy of the Charles Hummel collections.* (Value code: F)

2-63. A celluloid dealer tag from the Douglas Phonograph Company of New York City. Douglas embraced many aspects of the talking machine business during the first decade of the twentieth century. It sold Victor and Edison instruments, but also adapted Victor mechanisms to fit custom-designed cabinets. Some of these specialty cabinets were floor-standing, containing space in the lower half for record storage, with the motor, back-bracket, tone arm and horn of a conventional Victor "V" or "VI" mounted above. In 1907, the firm morphed into the General Phonograph Supply Company, under which name it sold a line of talking machine supplies and accessories including "Eureka" record cabinets and "Truetone" paneled wooden horns.

Opposite page: 2-61. Even in 1906, the Edison Phonograph had a 29-year heritage to show in its advertising. Illustrated are an 1878 "Second Model" Tinfoil Phonograph, an 1887 "New" Phonograph, and a "modern" 1906 Edison "Triumph" Phonograph. This was an odd departure from colorful depictions of good-looking young ladies and children enjoying the Phonograph. Measures 21" x 27" framed. *Courtesy of the Charles Hummel collections.* (Value code: VR)

2-64. The Victor company was eating everyone's lunch when it came to the high-toned music market. Victor's "Red Seal" discs, introduced in 1903, brought serious music and Grand Opera into the homes of millions. Columbia tried to compete by offering a disc series of classical vocal and instrumental music, but was forced to make do with lesser talent than Victor had already enlisted. Edison made several forays into the lucrative operatic market, the first of which was the two minute Grand Opera cylinders of 1906. Edison, like Columbia, could not retain singers of equal renown to Victor's Caruso and his Metropolitan Opera confreres. Consequently, each of Edison's several operatic series proved pale by comparison to Victor's glittering galaxy of recordings. *Courtesy of Ray Phillips.* (Value code: G)

2-65. The hayseed comedy character of "Uncle Josh (Whitcomb)" first appeared in the 1886 stage play *The Old Homestead*, portrayed by Denman Thompson. The play and the character became well known over the next ten years through tours and revivals. In 1897, comedian Cal Stewart (who had been an understudy to Thompson) began a series of "Uncle Josh" (now called Weathersby) country bumpkin monologues on both cylinder and disc records. Stewart's fame as an artist primarily known through the phonograph lasted for decades. This unusual 3 1/8" x 6" flyer, circa 1908, advertised Columbia "Uncle Josh" recordings by Cal Stewart. *Courtesy of Tom and Joanna Broome.* (Value code: G)

2-66. To employ the phonograph in the teaching and development of personal language skills was self-evident from the first. However, home study courses were not practical until after the introduction of molded, mass-produced cylinders in 1901. The Lewis Phono-metric Institute of Detroit, a client firm of Columbia, offered a therapeutic course for stammerers on two-minute cylinder records. This 10 1/2" x 14" brochure, circa 1906, illustrates Mr. Lewis himself creating a record with a Columbia Type "C" ("Universal") Graphophone. The ability of most cylinder machines to accept an incising head for home recording gave the cylinder format an important advantage over the disc. Lessons could be practiced, or even mailed to the school for review. (Value code: F)

2-67. These photos of Mr. Lewis' office (above) and "home laboratory" (below) were staged to indicate as much activity, and as wide a variety of equipment, as possible. The cylinders in the wooden caddy on the desk at the top center are 6" long "commercial" records, intended exclusively for office dictating machines. Dictating records and office machines no doubt were used in perfecting the content of the Lewis cylinder series that Columbia pressed. However, the Lewis Institute distributed to its mail-order students the diminutive but robust Type "Q" Graphophone, known primarily as a home entertainment device (such as the gentleman seated at the desk in the top photo is operating). Also worthy of note in the lower illustration is the treadle shaving machine to the right, and the idle Disc Graphophone.

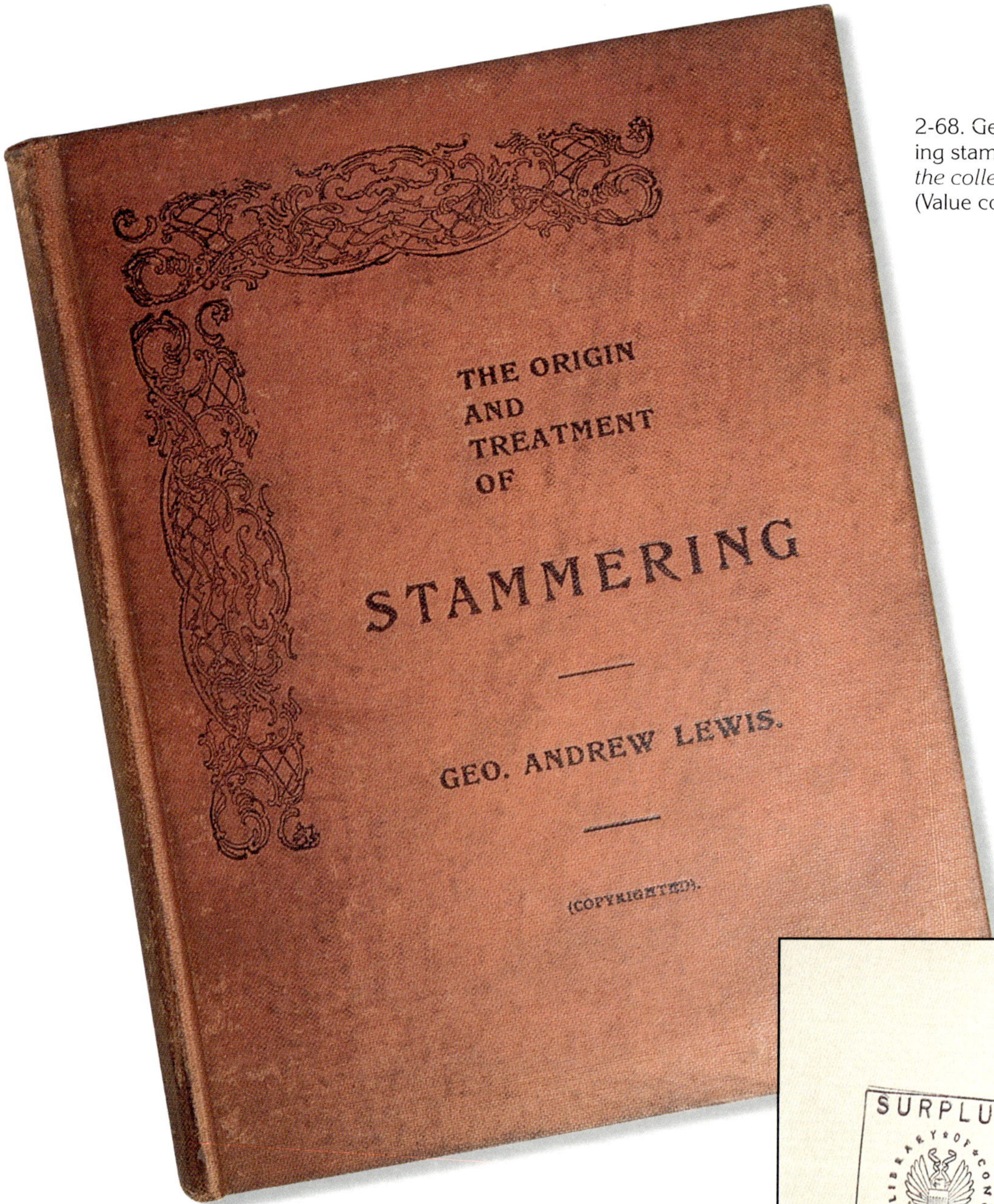

2-68. George Andrew Lewis' tract concerning stammering, 5 1/2" x 7". *Courtesy of the collection of Howard Hazelcorn.* (Value code: G)

2-69. Mr. Lewis' photo from his textbook. *Courtesy of the collection of Howard Hazelcorn.*

2-70. An Edison coin-operated Phonograph catalogue, 1906, measuring 4 1/2" x 8". The earliest exhibition talking machines were not fitted with a coin-activated mechanism, and required an operator to be present. From about 1890, various self-actuating devices were employed to allow talking machines to function automatically. Banks of these nickel-in-the-slot instruments appeared in arcades, train stations and other public places. Proliferation eventually brought the price of a recorded performance down, and Edison's 1906 line of coin-ops played a two-minute cylinder for the price of a penny. *Courtesy of the Tom and Sandi McCarthy collection.* (Value code: E)

2-71. The Talkophone Company of Toledo, Ohio survived for many years as an independent, despite relentless patent litigation initiated by both Victor and Columbia. This rare, wood-grained metal tip tray featured Talkophone's answer to Nipper: a parrot being entertained by the top-of-the-line "Sousa" model. Circa 1906, 4 1/4" diameter. *Courtesy of Robin and Joan Rolfs.* (Value code: VR)

2-72. A striking die-cut poster, 28 1/2" x 37 1/2" (without frame), depicting Victor record artists from the vaudeville stage, circa 1906. *Courtesy of the Tom and Sandi McCarthy collection.* (Value code: VR)

2-73. A very colorful die-cut poster, 28 1/2" x 37 1/2" (without frame), emphasizing Victor's exclusive Grand Opera talent, circa 1906. *Courtesy of the Tom and Sandi McCarthy collection.* (Value code: VR)

2-74. Curiously, chinaware bore a relation to talking machines. It was dinnerware that had helped inspire the concept of the phonograph as a retail sales incentive, when the East Liverpool China Company of Chicago began trading as the Standard Talking Machine Company, around 1905. Furthermore, "souvenir" plates were popular for interior decoration, and many early twentieth century homes had a "plate rail" placed high around the dining room. Shown here is a 10" diameter decorative plate, in faux oak design, advertising a Cleveland record brand. "Eagle" discs, circa 1906, were pressed from both Leeds & Catlin and International Record Company matrices. (Value code: F)

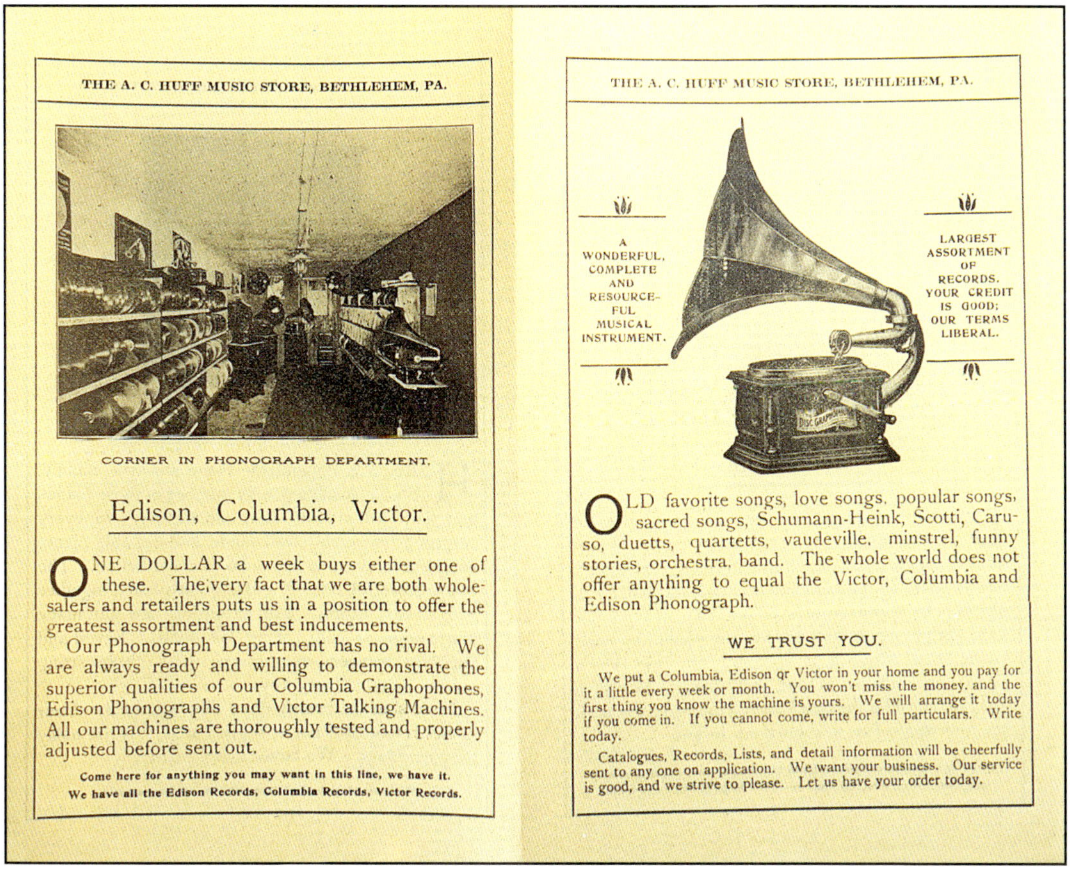

2-75. A Bethlehem, Pennsylvania dealer issued this 4 5/8" x 7" flyer showing the interior of its premises, and exhorting, "We put a Columbia, Edison or Victor in your home and you pay for it a little every week or month." (Value code: H)

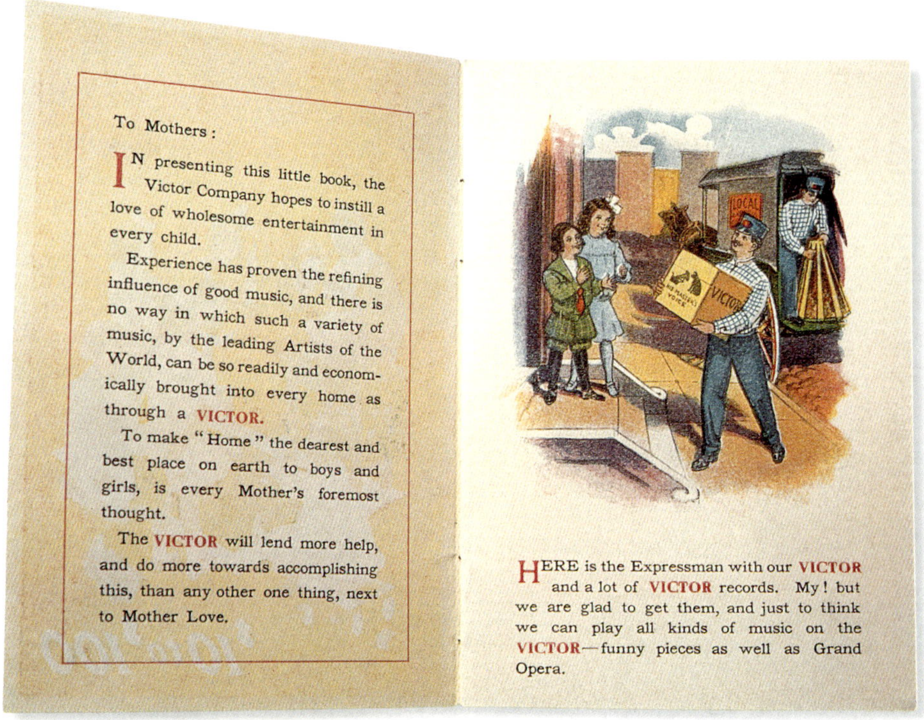

2-76. In January 1907, Victor first issued a charming 3 1/2" x 5" catalogue entitled "A Victor for Every Day of the Week." The cartoon-y color illustrations may have appealed to children, but, as the opening statement makes clear, the message was aimed directly at Mom and Dad's pocketbook. (Value code: F)

2-77. A clever Edison brochure shown unfolded. 4 1/2" high. (Value code: H)

2-78. The interior of the "circus" flyer.

2-79. Another articulated Edison item that received wide circulation, 3 1/4" x 5". (Value code: H)

2-80. Unfolded, the flyer showed what the boys discovered.

The EDISON PHONOGRAPH
TRADE MARK
Thomas A. Edison
Edison
VOICES FROM HOME
Form Nº 1189

Opposite page: 2-81. A 20" x 29 1/2" Edison advertising poster depicting cowboys listening to a disproportionately small Edison "Triumph" Phonograph. Public appreciation of the Westerner had not yet achieved the level of inaccuracy represented by the 1950s Hollywood gun-toter with clean-shaven face, vest, string tie and hat turned up at the sides. The rough and ready rounders shown here, though they expressed romantic imagery at the time, were much closer to the historical model. *Courtesy of Nina and Dave Heitz.* (Value code: VR)

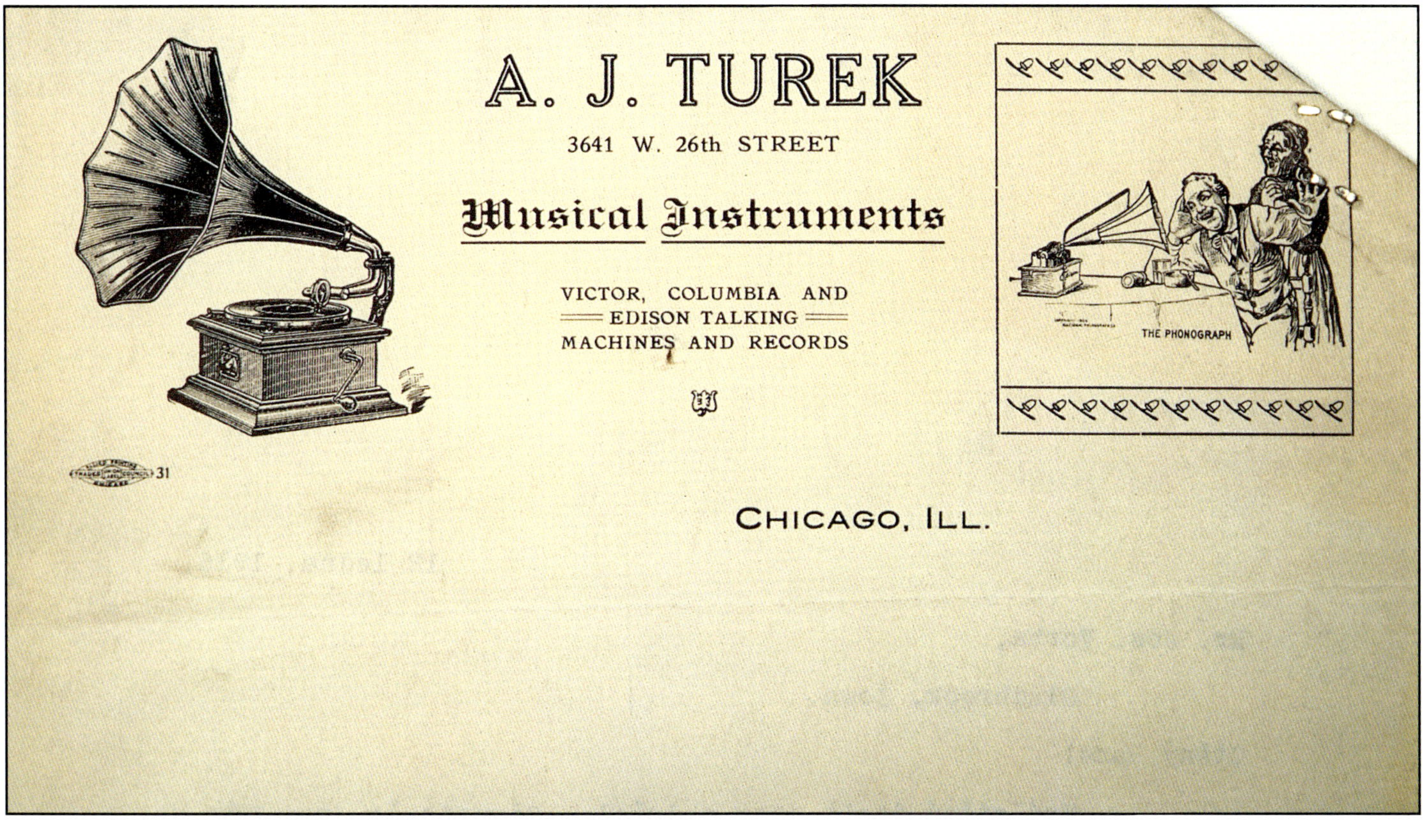

2-82. A dealer letterhead, featuring Edison's answer to the "His Master's Voice" trademark. Edison bought and adapted a painting by Italian artist Pompeo Massani, for use in its publicity during the period 1906 to 1910. Two delighted old-timers were depicted listening to an Edison Phonograph, the composition of which occasionally varied as new designs were introduced. In this instance, an artist's conception of a bizarrely tiny 1907 Edison flower horn is included. (Value code: H)

2-83. A charming Columbia record supplement. The "BK" or "Jewel" Graphophone was comparable to Edison's "Standard" Phonograph: a modest-sized, reasonably-priced model. *Courtesy of the Tom and Sandi McCarthy collection.* (Value code: H)

2-84. The colorful dealer decal of the Southern California Music Company can occasionally be found on Victor products which were sold in the Golden State. It is seen here on the side panel of a Victor "IV."

2-85. A very classy poster featuring Victor popular artists, circa 1907. Without frame, 25" x 34 1/2". *Courtesy of the Tom and Sandi McCarthy collection*. (Value code: (Value code: VR)

2-86. A poster, 25" x 34 1/2" (without frame), celebrating Victor's bevy of opera stars, already well-known in 1907. *Courtesy of the Tom and Sandi McCarthy collection.* (Value code: VR)

2-87. The celluloid cylinder record, technically feasible since the 1890s, developed with surprising slowness in the United States. After the Lambert Company of Chicago drifted into inactivity around 1905, the only American manufacturer of celluloid cylinders was gone. Then, in July 1906 the Indestructible Record Company of Albany, New York was formed, and began selling two-minute black celluloid cylinders in 1907. Shown here are three very early Indestructible record lists from late 1907 and 1908. At the center, a still from the stage production of Lehar's hit "The Merry Widow" announced a series of Indestructibles drawn from the score. The company remained active, producing cylinders and later discs, until destroyed by a disastrous fire in 1922. (Value code: H)

2-88. Two eye-catching Edison cylinder Phonograph flyers, circa 1907. The fingers represented the "Gem" ($10.00), "Standard" ($20.00), "Home" ($30.00) and "Triumph" ($50.00). (Value code: H)

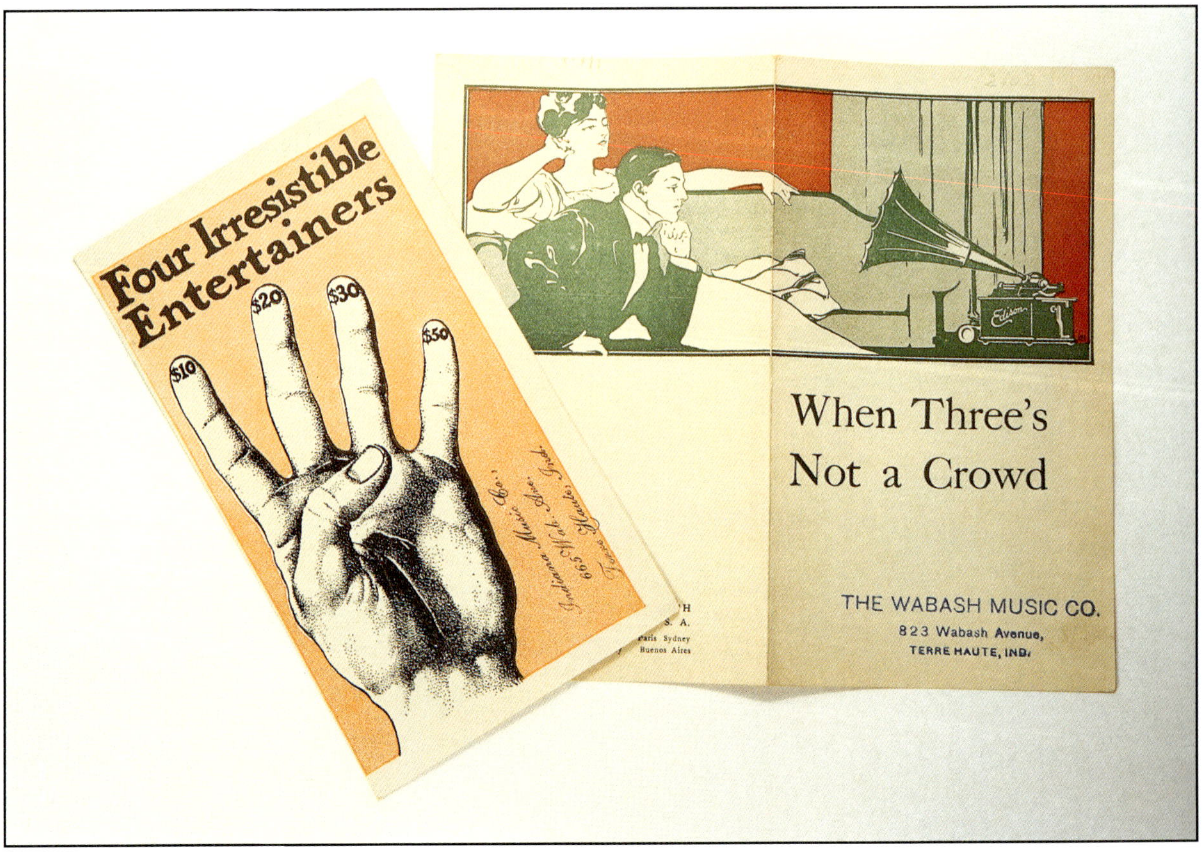

2-89. Automobiles, bicycles, talking machines – what will they think up next? An articulated dealer trade card, 4 1/2" long. *Courtesy of the Gfell family collection.* (Value code: F)

2-90. Nothing like a flash of petticoat to get the customer's attention. *Courtesy of the Gfell family collection.*

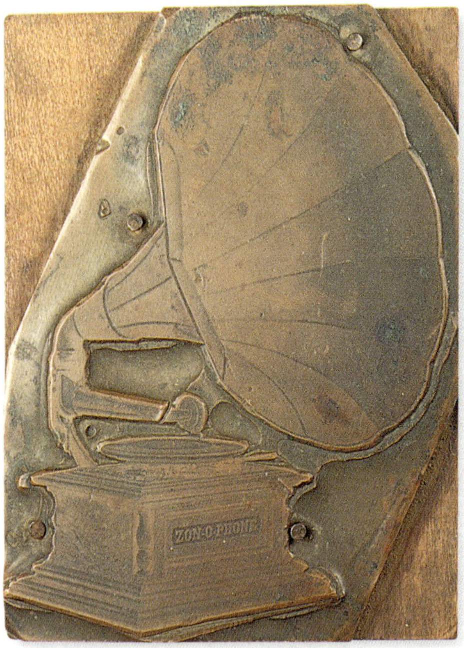

2-91. A 2 1/2" x 3" electrotype of a Zonophone "Grand Opera" talking machine, circa 1907. In 1899, the Zonophone had originated as the chief rival of Berliner's Gramophone. However, in 1903, Victor (effectively Berliner's successor) purchased the company that manufactured Zonophones. After that point, Zonophones became progressively more similar to Victor's own line of instruments. (Value code: G)

2-92. Preparing to deliver a treadle sewing machine, from a store that also sold Edison Phonographs, circa 1907. *Courtesy of Dennis Peterson.* (Value code: G)

2-93. A music store offering cylinder phonographs, circa 1907. As the modern collector appreciates, large horns can create quite a problem of space. Note the clever fashion in which the horns at the upper right have been mounted above the full display of cylinder records. *Courtesy of Dennis Peterson.* (Value code: G)

2-94. What appears to be a proof for Edison advertising, measuring 16" x 25 1/2", circa 1907. The eighteenth century-inspired finery of the female figure was unusual in Edison publicity of the period. *Courtesy of the Charles Hummel collections.* (Value code: VR)

2-95. Victor talking machines on sale in Redding, California, circa 1907. (Value code: H)

2-96. Photographs celebrating large shipments of phonographs or records were commonly shared among the trade, and often published in trade magazines. One day shy of Valentine's Day, a proud businessman posed with his employees as they took delivery of 23,000 cylinder records. The manufacturers, who encouraged others to emulate the "wide awake" attitude of those who placed large orders, viewed such scenes as trade stimulators. *Courtesy of the Charles Hummel collections*. (Value code: F)

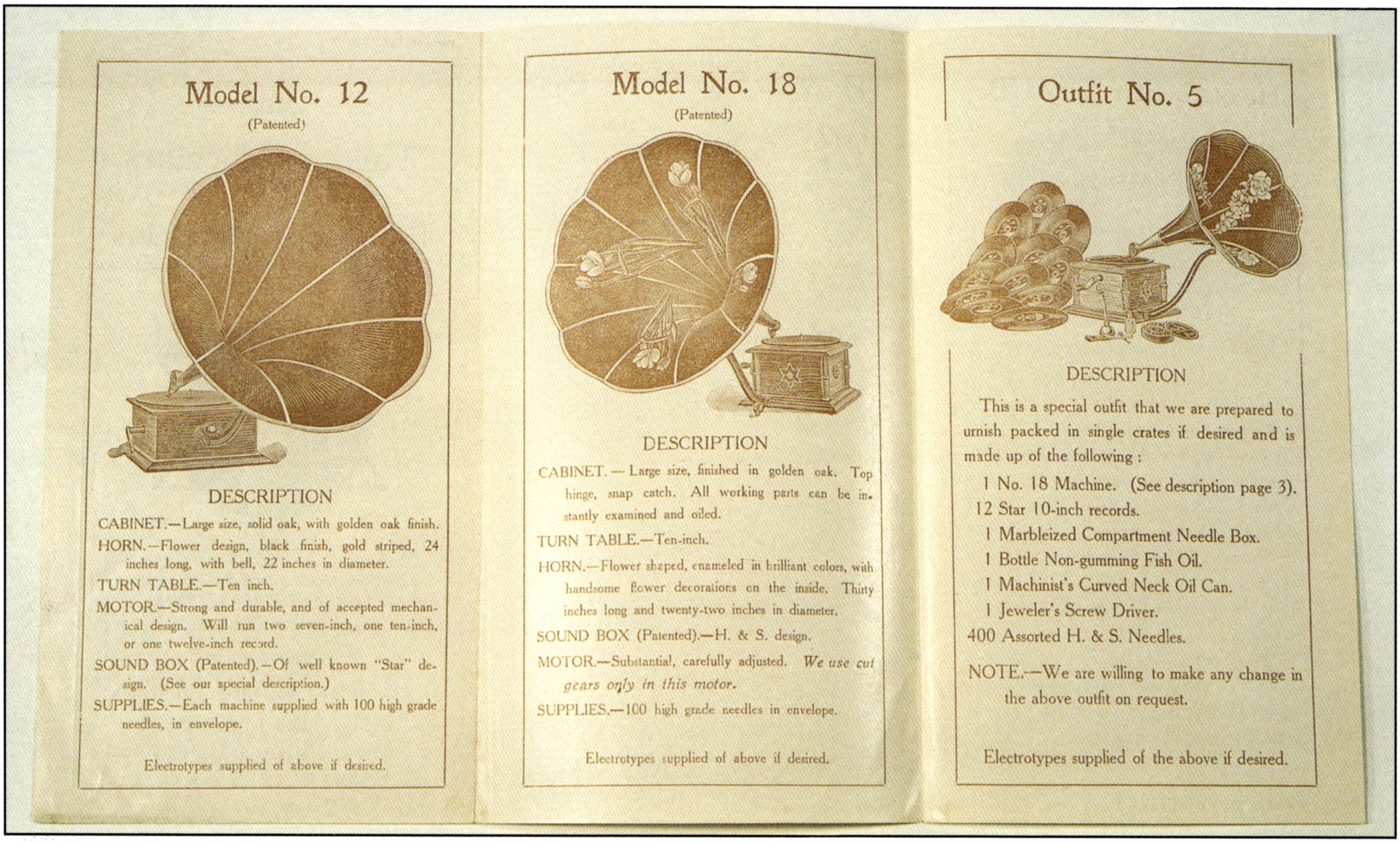

Model No. 12

(Patented)

DESCRIPTION

CABINET.—Large size, solid oak, with golden oak finish.

HORN.—Flower design, black finish, gold striped, 24 inches long, with bell, 22 inches in diameter.

TURN TABLE.—Ten inch.

MOTOR.—Strong and durable, and of accepted mechanical design. Will run two seven-inch, one ten-inch, or one twelve-inch record.

SOUND BOX (Patented).—Of well known "Star" design. (See our special description.)

SUPPLIES.—Each machine supplied with 100 high grade needles, in envelope.

Electrotypes supplied of above if desired.

Model No. 18

(Patented)

DESCRIPTION

CABINET.—Large size, finished in golden oak. Top hinge, snap catch. All working parts can be instantly examined and oiled.

TURN TABLE.—Ten-inch.

HORN.—Flower shaped, enameled in brilliant colors, with handsome flower decorations on the inside. Thirty inches long and twenty-two inches in diameter.

SOUND BOX (Patented).—H. & S. design.

MOTOR.—Substantial, carefully adjusted. *We use cut gears only in this motor.*

SUPPLIES.—100 high grade needles in envelope.

Electrotypes supplied of above if desired.

Outfit No. 5

DESCRIPTION

This is a special outfit that we are prepared to urnish packed in single crates if desired and is made up of the following :

1 No. 18 Machine. (See description page 3).
12 Star 10-inch records.
1 Marbleized Compartment Needle Box.
1 Bottle Non-gumming Fish Oil.
1 Machinist's Curved Neck Oil Can.
1 Jeweler's Screw Driver.
400 Assorted H. & S. Needles.

NOTE.—We are willing to make any change in the above outfit on request.

Electrotypes supplied of the above if desired.

2-97. A fold-out flyer for Hawthorne & Sheble "Star" talking machines. Model "12," at the left, was manufactured in great quantities for client firms, and sold under the "Busy Bee," "Harmony," "Aretino," and "True-Tone" brands (with minor variations). It is interesting to note that Model "18" employed a 31" long horn that was identical to the type H & S sold to fit cylinder talking machines. The distinctively-shaped H & S brass hanger (from which this type of horn was suspended when attached to a cylinder instrument) was left in place, however a small, identifying decal bearing the catalogue number of the horn was given the suffix "D" to indicate "disc." (Value code: F)

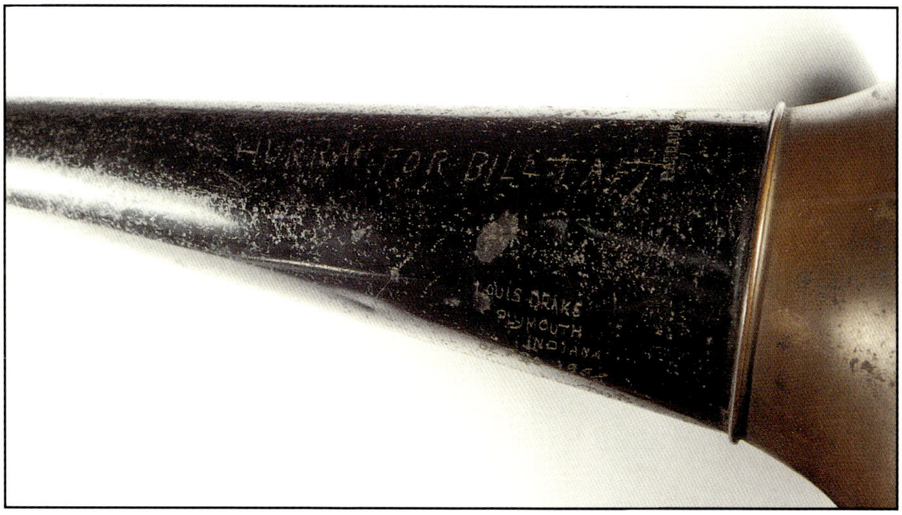

2-98. It's intriguing to imagine that this "politicized" phonograph horn was used by its owner to amplify the voice of William Howard Taft. As the Republican Presidential candidate in 1908, Taft made campaign speech cylinders for both Edison and Columbia (as did his opponent, Democrat William Jennings Bryan). Taft had been picked by Theodore Roosevelt as his anointed successor, but they would soon quarrel, prompting Roosevelt to return to Presidential politics in 1912. *Courtesy of Neal Hinchman.*

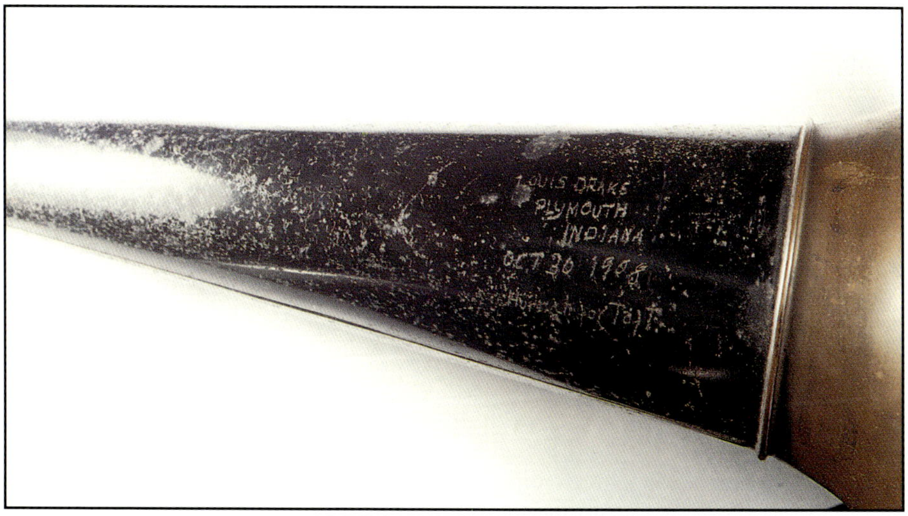

2-99. Mr. Drake's horn must have glowed red-hot with campaign verbiage on the eve of the election of his candidate, when he ebulliently inscribed it for posterity. *Courtesy of Neal Hinchman.*

2-100. This 7 3/4" square imitation delft tile (made of glossy paper of a composition core) promoted a French music store, and included a hanger on the reverse for displaying it. (Value code: G)

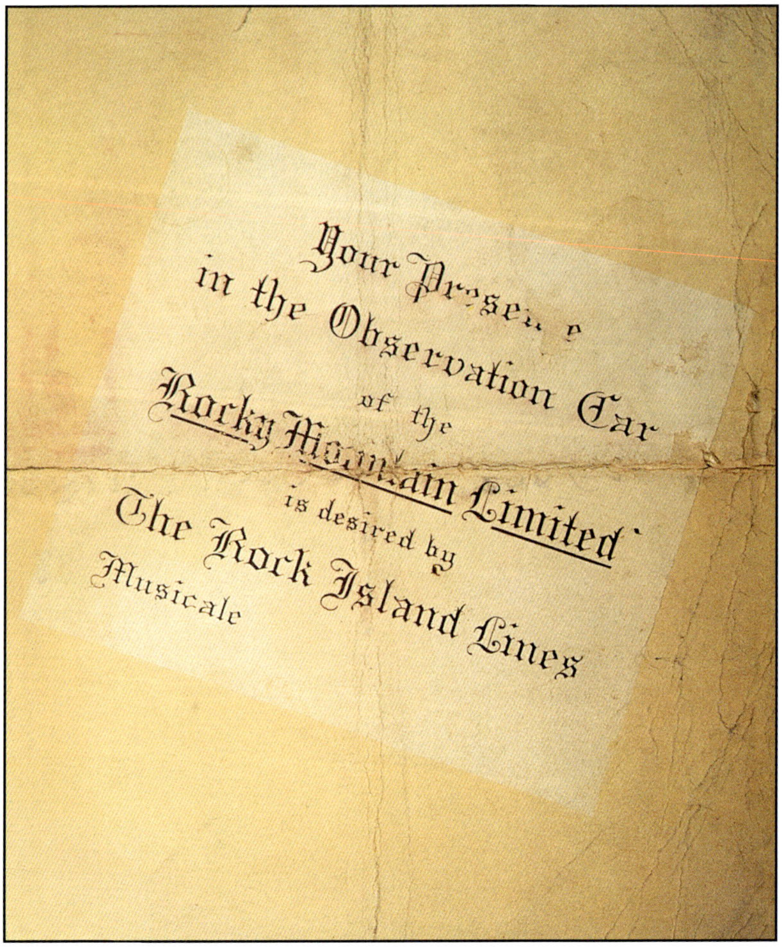

2-101. Why should a passenger train have any fewer amenities than were being offered by posh hotels or steamships of the period? In the instance of this "Musicale," the more confined space of a railroad coach might prove an advantage. An invitation, 5" x 6 1/4". *Courtesy of Ron Seavers.* (Value code: G)

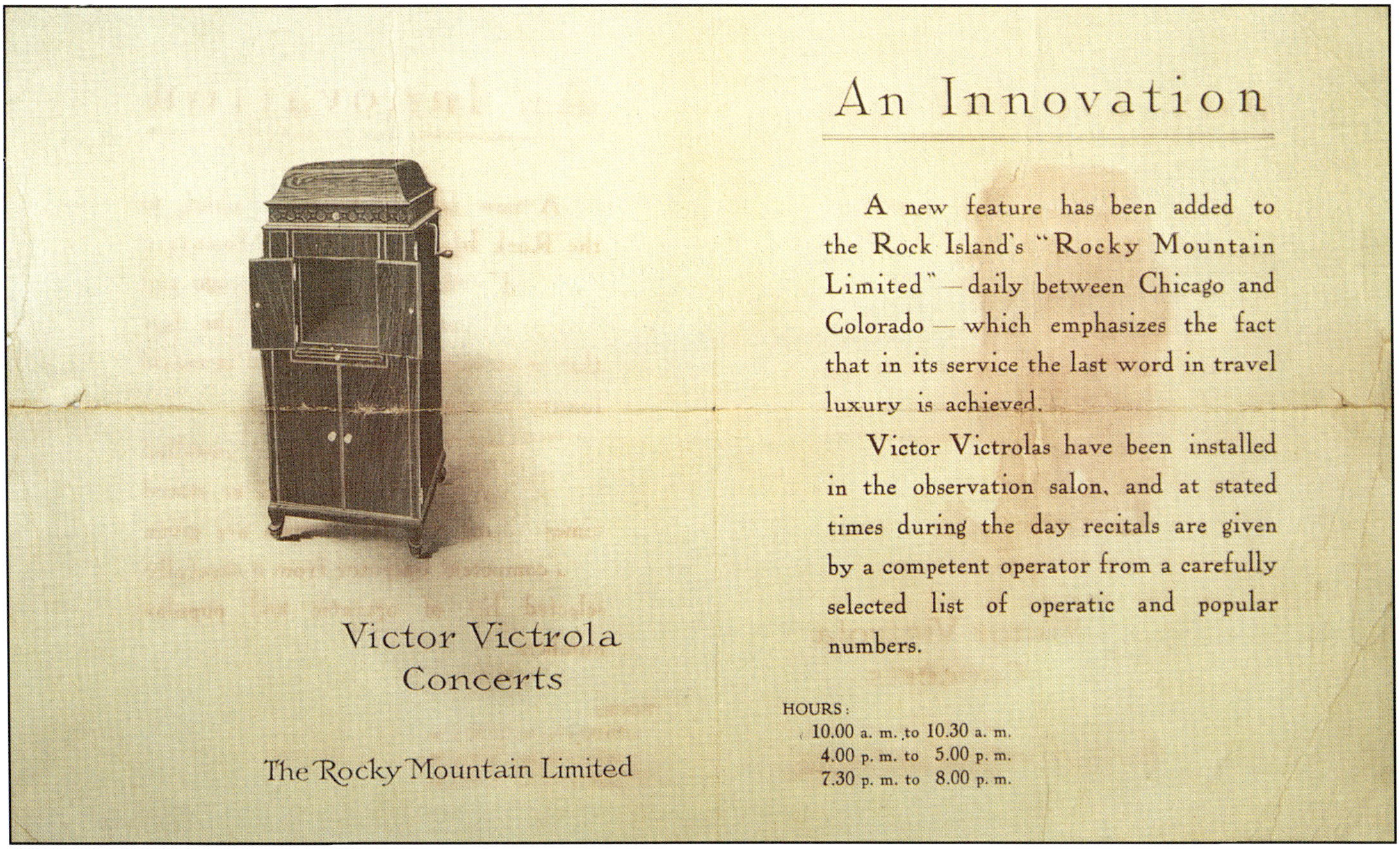

2-102. Luxury indeed, circa 1909, to have a "competent operator" playing Victor discs "from a carefully selected list of operatic and popular numbers." A "VTLA/Victrola XVI" was illustrated. *Courtesy of Ron Seavers.*

2-103. A Victor "Verdi" window display at the Thomas A. Purseglove store in 1909. The major talking machine brands supplied window designs and paraphernalia to their dealers. Note the meticulous care with which the modest space has been arranged. *Courtesy of the Tom and Sandi McCarthy collection.* (Value code: G)

2-104. There is only one effective method to show off a phonograph's capabilities: a live demonstration. When the "Auxeto Gramophone" (marketed in the United States by Victor as the Auxetophone) was introduced, written promotional material explained its stentorian principles. Compressed air was valved through the instrument's sound box, reinforcing and augmenting the mechanical components that produced sound from a record. Yet, phrases such as "Twice as Loud" or "Loudspeaking" lacked the impact of actually experiencing the Auxetophone's performance. The British Gramophone Company, Limited had one of its Auxeto Gramophones on display at Whitworth Park in Manchester, England, to demonstrate the machine's volume. Judging by the number of people seen here attentively listening to it, the crowd was impressed. This advertising postcard commemorating the event was postmarked August 9, 1909. (Value code: H)

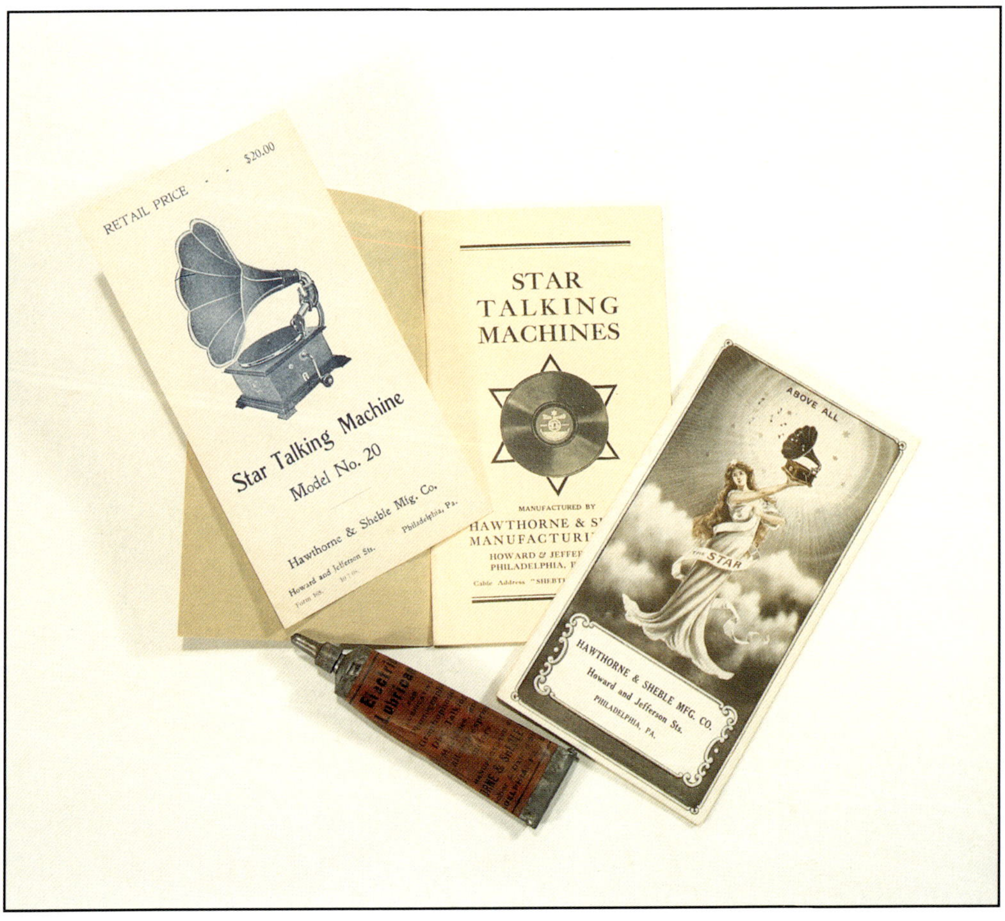

2-106. The success of the Standard disc talking machines as promotional goods was due to a gimmick employed by Standard and a number of other Chicago brands. The turntables of these instruments were designed to accept only their "house" brand of record. In the case of Standard, the turntable had a spindle of approximately 1/2" diameter, about twice the size of a conventional Victor or Columbia spindle. The retail promotions worked as follows. Standard sold a quantity of talking machines and the special records to fit them to a retail store. The shop gave coupons with cash purchases, in denominations such as 25 cents, 50 cents and a dollar. When the customer had collected enough coupons (say, $25.00 worth), he would receive a Standard instrument and a small quantity of records. Additional discs were sold by the store at the market price, which was about 65 cents. The participating shop made its money by selling the records – but also profited by enticing customers to spend more cash than they might ordinarily have done, or to pay off the balances on credit accounts. Shown here are rows of coupons as they would have been supplied to stores. (Value code: H)

2-107. Although the major record companies issued monthly lists of new records, the Standard Talking Machine Company required only quarterly updates. Standard's discs were supplied by Columbia, and were predominantly selections that were either out-of-date, or perennial favorites from the Columbia catalogue. It sometimes took two or three years for recorded trends to appear in Standard's catalogues. These examples, each with a splash of red, illustrate seasonal enjoyment of the Standard Model "X2." *Courtesy of the Gfell family collection.*

Opposite page, bottom: 2-105. The Hawthorne and Sheble Manufacturing Company of Philadelphia was an innovative and resourceful independent that reached its stride just as the major companies (Victor, Edison and Columbia) were evolving from the entrepreneurial toward the autocratic. Having begun in the 1890s as a retail outlet for Edison and Columbia, H & S soon ran afoul of Edison's suffocating dealer regulations, and was blackballed. H & S and Columbia, however, maintained their relationship, and Columbia would in the future acquire much of the legally enjoined and financially ruined Hawthorne and Sheble's inventory. Shown here are flyers and a catalogue illustrating H & S disc talking machines that were produced between 1906 and 1909, after which the firm collapsed under the weight of litigation by Victor. Left, the "Star" "No.20" featured the patented "Yielding Pressure Feed" arm, an attempt to circumvent the fundamental "Berliner patent" which Victor controlled. Center, a full catalogue of H & S disc machines. Right, the back cover of a flyer promoting the "Starola," a floor-standing internal horn cabinet model. Below, a tube of H & S talking machine lubricant. (Value code: G)

2-108. Pages from the 1910 John M. Smyth catalogue of cameras and talking machines. At the left, the "Geneva" talking machine was Columbia's own "BWT" which incorporated an oak cabinet originally manufactured by the (then defunct) Talkophone Company of Toledo, Ohio. Although Victor discs were illustrated in the background, Smyth at one point sold its own "Faultless Concert" brand. On the right-hand page, are two inexpensive machines, including the "Thomas" which was also produced by Columbia. *Courtesy of the Gfell family collection.* (Value code: VR)

JOHN M. SMYTH COMPANY'S Dictionary (44) of Economy No. 64—Chicago, U. S. A.

Our 1910 Geneva Home Entertainment Outfit $24.40

THE IDEAL HOME ENTERTAINER

OUR 1910 GENEVA HOME ENTERTAINMENT OUTFIT

THE CABINET

THE FLOWER HORN

THE MOTOR

OUTFIT NO. 45 CONSISTS OF OUR 1910 GENEVA ALUMINUM TONE-ARM TALKING MACHINE

OUTFIT NO. 46 CONSISTS OF OUR 1910 GENEVA ALUMINUM TONE-ARM TALKING MACHINE

JOHN M. SMYTH COMPANY'S Dictionary (45) of Economy No. 64—Chicago, U. S. A.

1910 Columbia "Peerless" Disc Talking Machine $7.25

7 DAYS FREE TRIAL

This Talking Machine Runs Perfectly Any Make of 7, 8, 10 or 12-inch Flat Disc Records. Select Your Records From the pages devoted to Flat Disc Records in This Catalog.

1910 Model "Thomas" Disc Talking Machine $14.50

7 DAYS FREE TRIAL

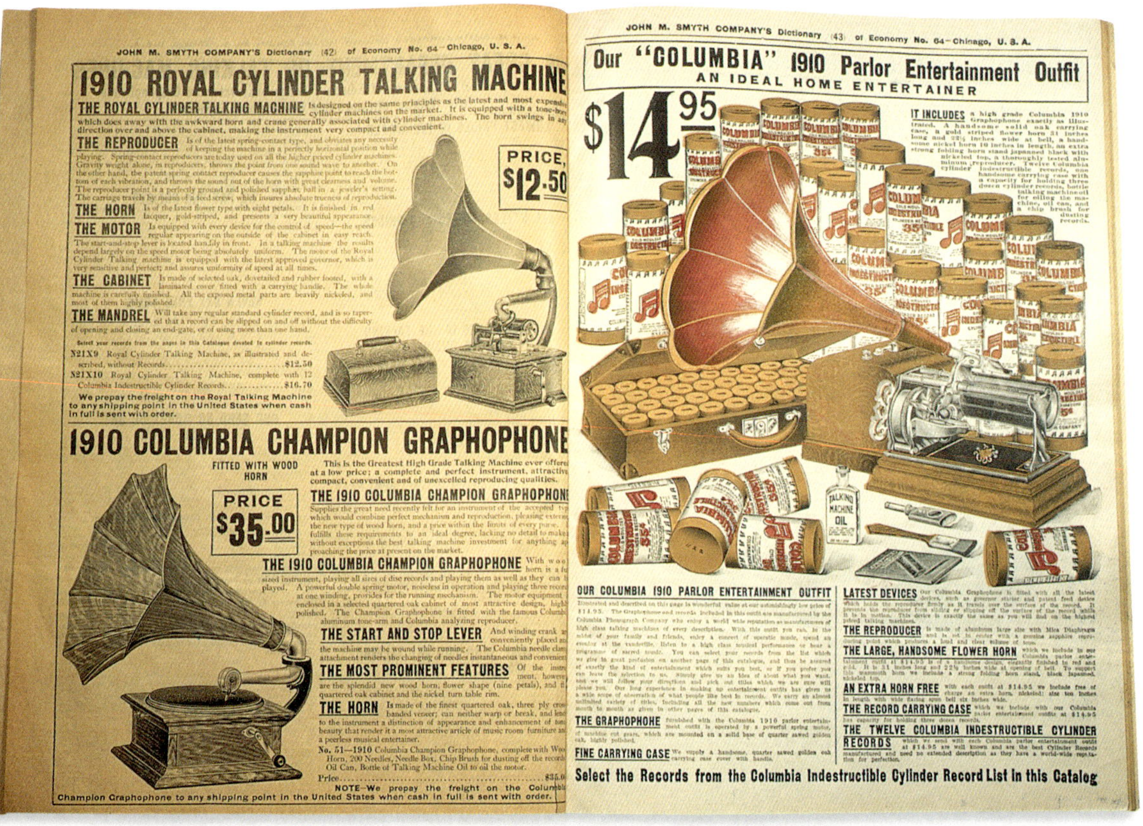
JOHN M. SMYTH COMPANY'S Dictionary (42) of Economy No. 64—Chicago, U. S. A.

1910 ROYAL CYLINDER TALKING MACHINE

THE ROYAL CYLINDER TALKING MACHINE

THE REPRODUCER

THE HORN

THE MOTOR

THE CABINET

THE MANDREL

PRICE, $12.50

We prepay the freight on the Royal Talking Machine to any shipping point in the United States when cash in full is sent with order.

1910 COLUMBIA CHAMPION GRAPHOPHONE

FITTED WITH WOOD HORN

PRICE $35.00

THE 1910 COLUMBIA CHAMPION GRAPHOPHONE

THE START AND STOP LEVER

THE MOST PROMINENT FEATURES

THE HORN

JOHN M. SMYTH COMPANY'S Dictionary (43) of Economy No. 64—Chicago, U. S. A.

Our "COLUMBIA" 1910 Parlor Entertainment Outfit

AN IDEAL HOME ENTERTAINER

$14.95

IT INCLUDES

OUR COLUMBIA 1910 PARLOR ENTERTAINMENT OUTFIT

THE GRAPHOPHONE

FINE CARRYING CASE

LATEST DEVICES

THE REPRODUCER

THE LARGE, HANDSOME FLOWER HORN

AN EXTRA HORN FREE

THE RECORD CARRYING CASE

THE TWELVE COLUMBIA INDESTRUCTIBLE CYLINDER RECORDS

Select the Records from the Columbia Indestructible Cylinder Record List in this Catalog

Opposite page: 2-110. Columbia attempted to compete with Victor in the operatic market, as this 24" x 37 1/2" (without frame) poster attests. Although Columbia recorded some noteworthy artists, it failed to crack Victor's popular hold as the great purveyor of high-class culture. *Courtesy of the Tom and Sandi McCarthy collection.* (Value code: D)

2-109. Further pages from the 1910 Smyth catalogue. At the left, a Columbia Graphophone "BVT," here called the "Royal," and a more up-to-date style of disc machine, with paneled wooden horn. At the right, the venerable Columbia "Q," twelve years after its introduction, was still being flogged. The "Q" played only two-minute cylinder records that were nearly obsolete – the four-minute cylinder, with double the playing time, had been introduced about two years earlier. However, the "Q" proved hard to kill, since it combined a low price with acceptable sound reproduction. Examples from 1911 are known with serial numbers over a million – though this is a bit misleading since the machines were numbered in blocks. Certainly, hundreds of thousands were produced. The flower horn was disproportionately represented by the artist. *Courtesy of the Gfell family collection.*

Columbia Records
CAMPANARI
THE FAMOUS ITALIAN BARITONE
SINGS EXCLUSIVELY
FOR THE
COLUMBIA
COLUMBIA
DOUBLE-DISC RECORDS
BY CAMPANARI

2-111. Independent talking machine brands of Chicago. Both "Busy Bee" (cylinder and disc machines) and "Aretino" (disc machines) were the brainchildren of master promoter Arthur J.O'Neill. O'Neill had grown up in Wisconsin, where a local newspaper referred to him (though misspelling his name) on January 19, 1902: "Arthur J. O'Neil of Prairie du Chien, is well known in the state not only as a most successful traveling salesman, but as the brother of the gifted elocutionist, Jennie O'Neil Potter… Mr. O'Neil has been on the road nine years, the last seven of which have been spent in the employ of the wholesale jewelry and novelty house of Robert Johns, Chicago…" Robert Johns was associated with the Standard Talking Machine Company, and no doubt introduced O'Neill to the concept of talking machines as "scheme goods." The Chicago firms that Arthur J. founded, the O'Neill-James Company (which sold "Busy Bee" machines) and the Aretino Company (which he ran with his brother Charles W.) would enjoy a considerable run of business between 1904 and 1914, despite being sued for patent infringement. O'Neill had a multi-faceted personality, as this excerpt from his poem *Passion* attests, "Oh Passion, oh Passion, I quite understand, why the devil and angels obey your command, for God in his wisdom made infinite man, and now you are a prisoner for him to command." (Value code: G)

2-112. This 3 3/4" x 5 1/4" paper label from the inside of a phonograph lid illustrates how frequently the Massani image of the "delighted old couple" was reconceived by the Edison company. This version, circa 1910, included the newest Edison innovation: the cygnet ("swan's neck") horn. *Courtesy of Pat and Jamie Jones.*

2-113. Two flyers issued by Thomas A. Edison, Incorporated promoting dealer window displays. It might seem strange to use an Edison "cygnet" horn as a sign holder, but the practice clearly was endorsed by the front office. *Courtesy of Tom and Joanna Broome.* (Value code: H)

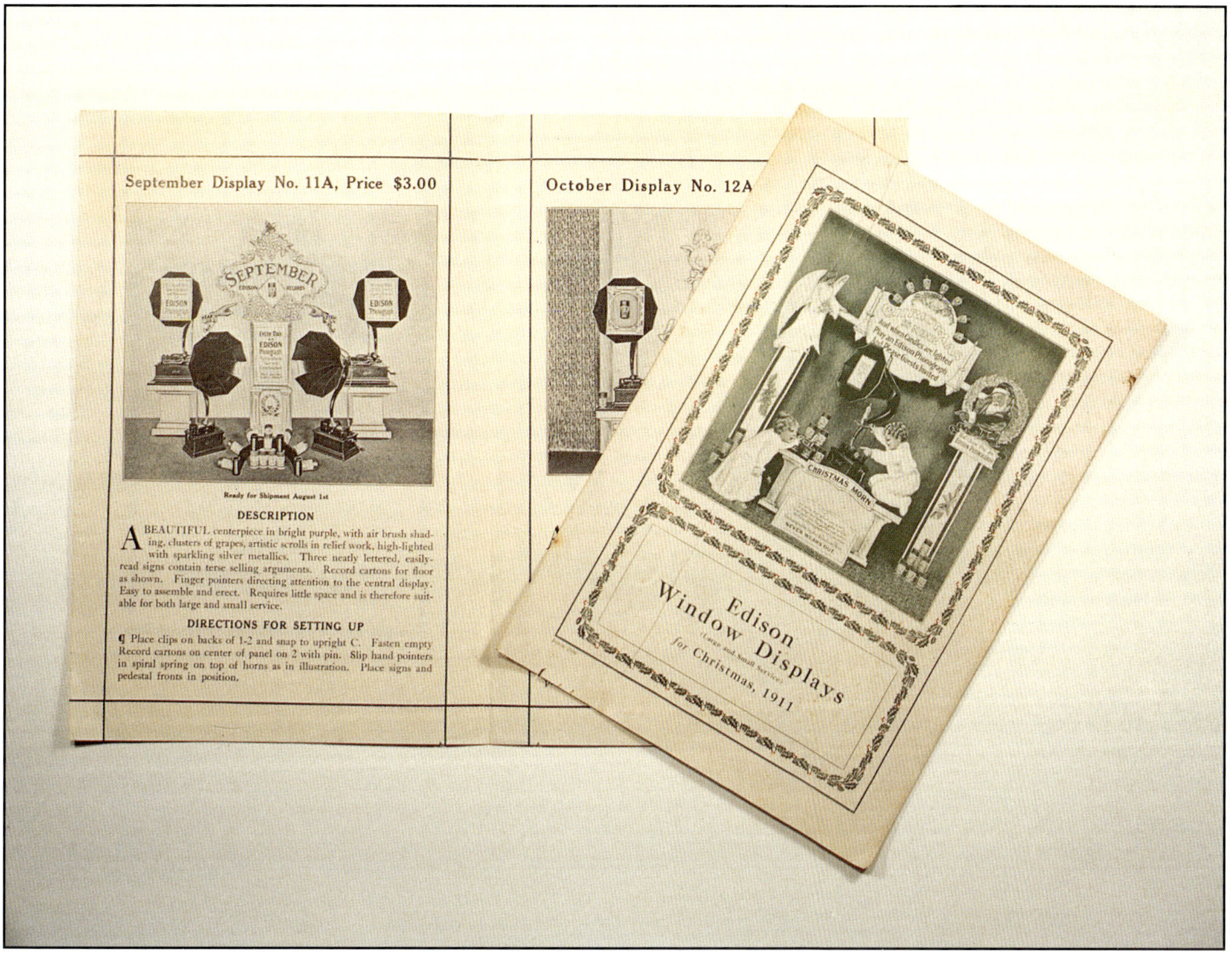

2-114. An enterprising dealer created this clever promotional postcard, circa 1910. The youngster in the Santa Claus costume holds an Edison cygnet horn, and a "Fireside" Phonograph sits on the floor. *Courtesy of Dennis Peterson.* (Value code: F)

2-115. The best material from which to manufacture talking machine horns was the subject of considerable debate. A wide variety of materials were tried, and were often touted as superior, including steel, brass, zinc, aluminum, cast iron, glass, paper, fiber, leather, celluloid and wood. Wood could be very eye-pleasing for an external horn, especially when finished to match the body of the talking machine. This factor was lost when horns moved inside the cabinet, however, many internal horns were constructed of (less beautifully finished) wood out of convenience. In 1907, Sheip & Vandegrift of Philadelphia introduced its solid wood (as opposed to laminated or veneered) horns, which were manufactured to fit both cylinder and disc phonographs. The black band encircling the horn a quarter of the way down from the edge of the bell was a reinforcing ring, to resist the tendency of the individual staves or panels to warp. A trade card, 3 5/8" x 5 5/8", circa 1909. *Courtesy of the Tom and Sandi McCarthy collection.* (Value code: H)

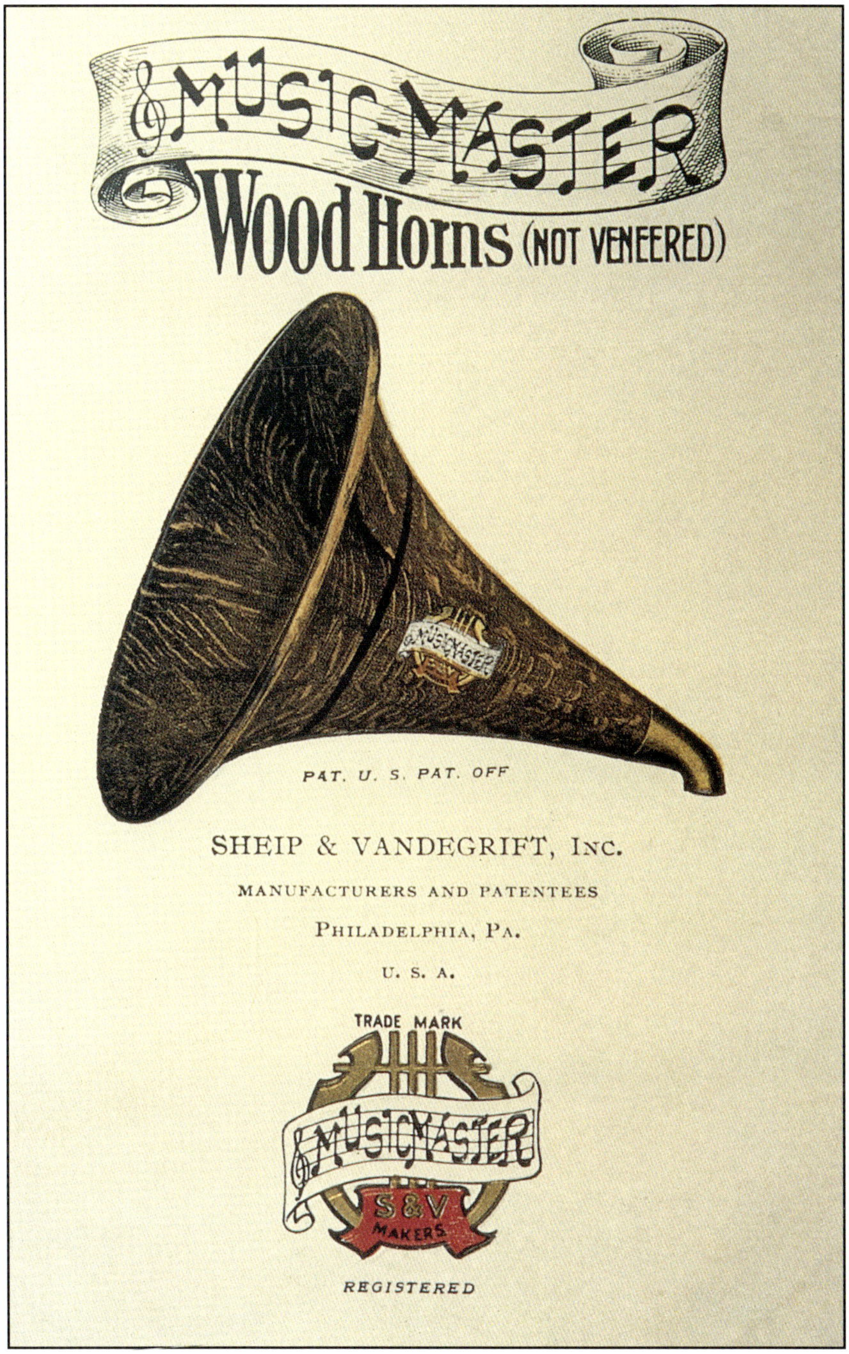

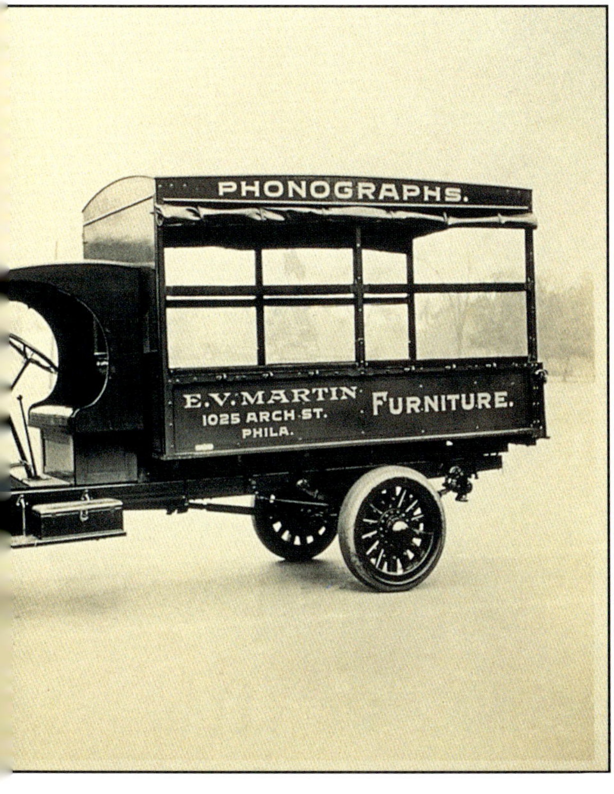

2-116. Commercial vehicles were as important an avenue of advertising in 1910 as they are today. *Courtesy of the Tom and Sandi McCarthy collection.* (Value code: G)

2-117. This electric delivery truck, barely evolved from a horse-drawn wagon, carried among its contents Victor and Edison instruments. July 30, 1910. *Courtesy of the Tom and Sandi McCarthy collection.* (Value code: G)

2-118. What is most charming about this photograph – the vintage automobile, pretty Nell M., or the roadside advertisement for phonographs? *Courtesy of Dennis Peterson.* (Value code: G)

2-119. A well-stocked Mabel, Minnesota Edison dealer in 1911. The sidewalk was paved, but the smartly decorated delivery wagon navigated the simple earthen streets of small town America. *Courtesy of Dennis Peterson.* (Value code: H)

2-120. In addition to its 24 electric lights, the Star Theatre in Ashland, Oregon employed a Victor Auxetophone (right) to promote its featured attractions. The Auxetophone utilized compressed air to increase the volume of its reproduction. Its placement outdoors along a busy street would have amply demonstrated the instrument's power as an attention-getter. Dated May 4, 1911. *Courtesy of Bob Carver.* (Value code: G)

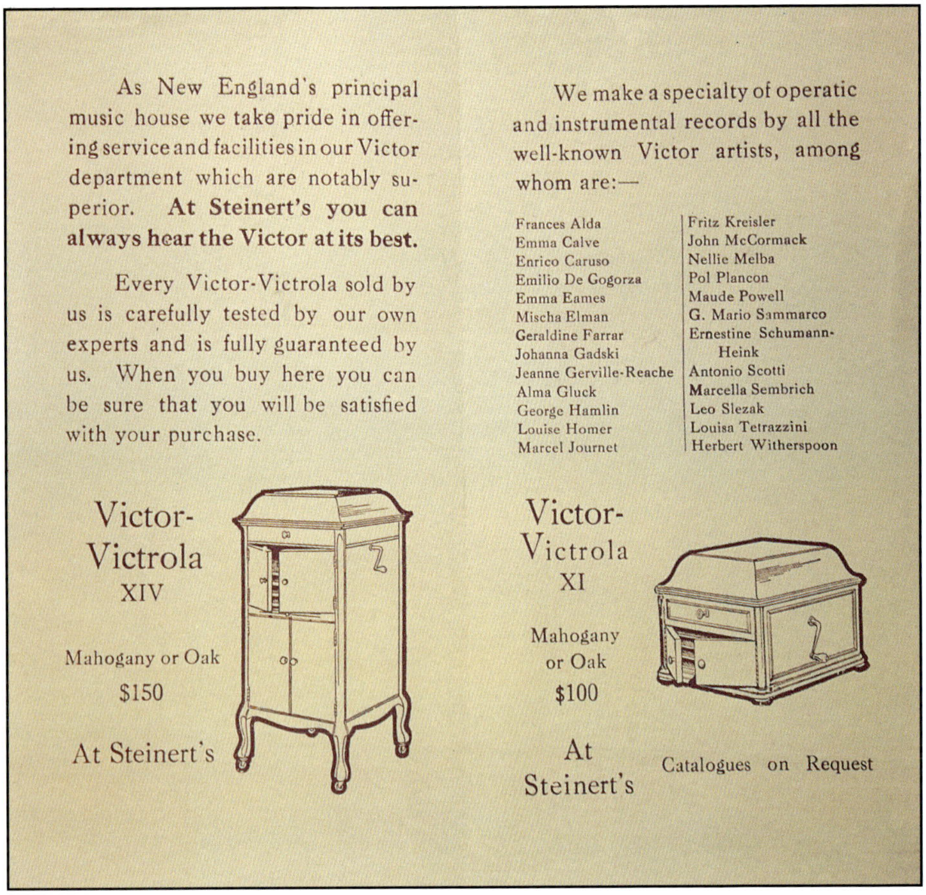

As New England's principal music house we take pride in offering service and facilities in our Victor department which are notably superior. **At Steinert's you can always hear the Victor at its best.**

Every Victor-Victrola sold by us is carefully tested by our own experts and is fully guaranteed by us. When you buy here you can be sure that you will be satisfied with your purchase.

We make a specialty of operatic and instrumental records by all the well-known Victor artists, among whom are:—

Frances Alda	Fritz Kreisler
Emma Calve	John McCormack
Enrico Caruso	Nellie Melba
Emilio De Gogorza	Pol Plancon
Emma Eames	Maude Powell
Mischa Elman	G. Mario Sammarco
Geraldine Farrar	Ernestine Schumann-Heink
Johanna Gadski	Antonio Scotti
Jeanne Gerville-Reache	Marcella Sembrich
Alma Gluck	Leo Slezak
George Hamlin	Louisa Tetrazzini
Louise Homer	Herbert Witherspoon
Marcel Journet	

Victor-Victrola
XIV
Mahogany or Oak
$150
At Steinert's

Victor-Victrola
XI
Mahogany or Oak
$100
At Steinert's

Catalogues on Request

2-121. Steinert's music store issued this 3 1/2" x 6 1/8" (folded) flyer, circa 1911, promoting the early line-up of Victrolas. The "XI" (right) would be redesigned as a floor-standing model in 1912. (Value code: H)

2-122. The Standard Talking Machine Company was closely related to two other Chicago phonograph companies. The three firms operated as subsidiaries of the same parent. Standard and Harmony disc talking machines were sold only with external horns (Type "X2" is pictured on the catalogue to the right) until 1911, after which internal horn models were concurrently offered. Also in 1911, the third subsidiary, the United Talking Machine Company, appeared. United sold internal horn "Symphony" disc instruments (inexpensively manufactured by Columbia). United's method of distribution was familiar. At the left are rows of uncut coupons used in store promotions. (Value code: H)

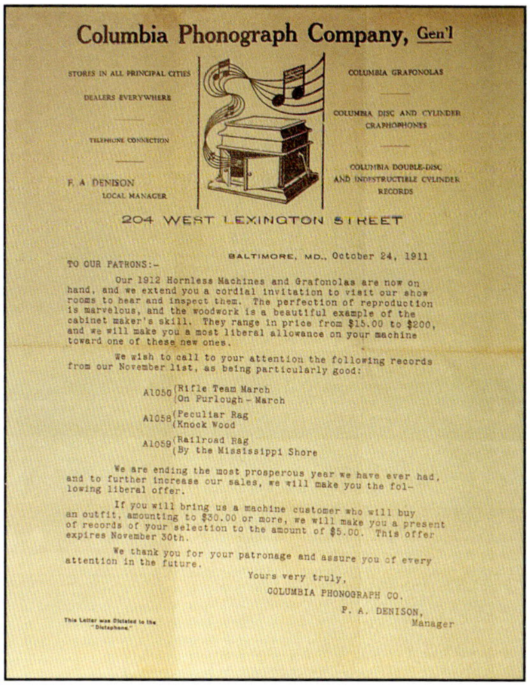

Columbia Phonograph Company, Gen'l

STORES IN ALL PRINCIPAL CITIES

DEALERS EVERYWHERE

TELEPHONE CONNECTION

F. A. DENISON
LOCAL MANAGER

COLUMBIA GRAFONOLAS

COLUMBIA DISC AND CYLINDER GRAPHOPHONES

COLUMBIA DOUBLE-DISC AND INDESTRUCTIBLE CYLINDER RECORDS

204 WEST LEXINGTON STREET

BALTIMORE, MD., October 24, 1911

TO OUR PATRONS:-

Our 1912 Hornless Machines and Grafonolas are now on hand, and we extend you a cordial invitation to visit our show rooms to hear and inspect them. The perfection of reproduction is marvelous, and the woodwork is a beautiful example of the cabinet maker's skill. They range in price from $15.00 to $200, and we will make you a most liberal allowance on your machine toward one of these new ones.

We wish to call to your attention the following records from our November list, as being particularly good:

A1050 (Rifle Team March
(On Furlough - March

A1058 (Peculiar Rag
(Knock Wood

A1059 (Railroad Rag
(By the Mississippi Shore

We are ending the most prosperous year we have ever had, and to further increase our sales, we will make you the following liberal offer.

If you will bring us a machine customer who will buy an outfit, amounting to $30.00 or more, we will make you a present of records of your selection to the amount of $5.00. This offer expires November 30th.

We thank you for your patronage and assure you of every attention in the future.

Yours very truly,
COLUMBIA PHONOGRAPH CO.
F. A. DENISON,
Manager

This Letter was Dictated to the "Dictaphone."

2-123. A letter mailed to prospective Grafonola buyers in 1911. Note reference to the practice of "bird-dogging" – anyone recommending a client who spent $30.00 or more would receive $5.00 worth of records. This promotional technique is still popular with automobile dealers. *Courtesy of Richard and Christine Mazur.* (Value code: H)

The Tragedy of a Young Girl

THROUGH the motley, out-at-elbows crowd in the Police Court in Montreal, a tearful girl was led before the magistrate. The air of the courtroom reeked with the fumes of the "hang-overs" of frowsy prisoners, and she shrank away from the outcasts as she passed them in the dock. The shrewd-eyed magistrate, hardened to tales of misery, true and false, quickly appraised the girl before him. Though but 22, her beauty had faded. Sobbingly she told the listening judge of the weary days of walking in search of employment as her funds grew low. Always the easy road was before her—the temptation of bright lights, pretty clothes and gaiety. When she had finished her story, the judge asked: "Why did you leave home? Why did you leave the free, pure life of the country for this place of tears?" And she answered: "Because there was no entertainment—it was so *lonesome!*" What a tragedy in this simple statement—a tragedy of a ruined life! A life that might have been saved for so little.

Could *YOUR* Girl Do Wrong?

Let us hope emphatically "no." **Your** girl, let us hope, is not only good, but strong in will, too—and temptations will not mean danger to her. Let us hope too—that she will never think of leaving home for the opportunities of the big city.

But—this girl in the picture above went away from her home because her home was "too lonesome." "Not a good excuse" you say—but remember that young folks are young folks, boys will be boys and girls will be girls.

Even if your daughter is the best, the finest girl in the world, when she is once away from her mother's watchful eye, other influences begin to work slowly but persistently. And even at twenty-five no woman is old enough or wise enough to withstand the influences of daily companionship.

She may not leave home, but if she shows a liking for "evenings out," perhaps for shows for circuses and late evening rides, she will have difficulty to keep from hearing and seeing things she had better not hear and see, and of meeting people she herself feels she had better not meet. And if after that she leaves home for the city, it is all the worse.

Keep Your Girl *at Home*

I gave a warning before about keeping the young men away from the cities and I say it is more important for the girls to be kept away from the cities.

When I see what becomes of the thousands and thousands of good, pure girls, where parents could not hold them in the village, when I see them pouring out of shops and factories and offices, tired and worn at half past five o'clock all to look for unhealthy entertainment for the night, when I see all this and picture the peaceful, happy homes from which they came, I ask myself **"why."**

"Why all this wandering about—this breaking of home ties—this awful inroad on pure girlhood?"

Well, perhaps it is because their happy peaceful village and farm homes were *too* peaceful—the kind of peace in which no bright young girl's heart can find entertainment. And I have said it myself. Perhaps the answer is here—as we show in the second picture—"that girl will not leave home—she will spend her evenings at home."

Anyway let's try it. You try it for **her** sake—and that is one of the reasons I offer you the free loan.

H..ppy at Her Mother's Side

Thomas A. Edison.

—*Page Twenty-Three*

2-124. For many years, the Babson name was associated with Edison Phonograph distribution in the Midwest. To induce its mail-order customers to buy, Babson marketing was frequently hyperbolic – and, in this instance, histrionic! A wealth of space has been devoted to assuring the largely rural audience of this catalogue, circa 1910, that the virtue of its daughters would not be sacrificed (the dire consequences of which were represented by the rumpled waif, above) if the pater familias administered salubrious doses of "healthy entertainment" from an Edison Phonograph. *Courtesy of Martin F. Bryan.* (Value code: G)

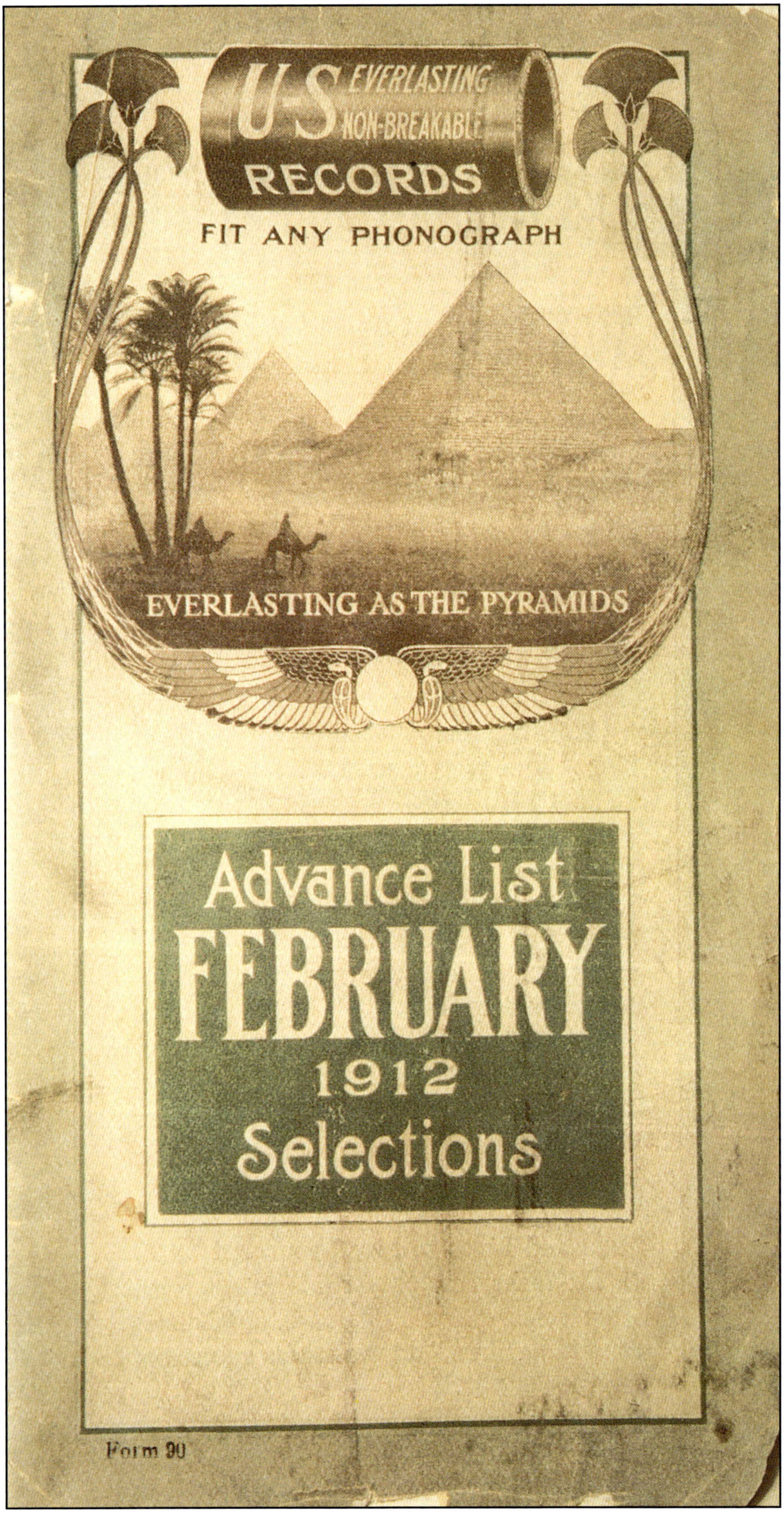

2-125. The U.S. Phonograph Company of Cleveland was the bête noir that drove Thomas A. Edison, Incorporated to paroxysms of litigation during the Ohio firm's brief life, 1910-1913. The "Everlasting" cylinders, produced by U.S. in both two and four minute formats, were well recorded and manufactured. These high-quality records must have been especially irksome to Edison, which did not introduce its own "Blue Amberol" celluloid cylinders until 1912. Thomas Edison had patented a celluloid record process in 1902 (No.713,209), and had employed the patent as heavy ammunition against the Lambert Company, which began manufacturing celluloid cylinders in 1900. Edison's attempt to stop Lambert backfired, however, when a court ruled the Edison patent invalid due to a technicality. Thereafter, Thomas Edison tenaciously sought to produce a super-hard version of the metallic soap compound (called "wax") that he was already using to mold cylinders. The task was impossible; harder wax proved brittle, and the result was that Edison records were breakable long after the rest of the industry switched to celluloid. As noted, Edison eventually (1912) introduced a superb quality celluloid four minute cylinder, yet was all the more determined to bring the U.S. Phonograph Company to ruin. A series of court battles gnawed at the resources of the little Ohio operation, and, coupled with the difficulties of independent enterprise, spelled its doom. *Courtesy of Ray Phillips.* (Value code: F)

2-126. Copper newspaper electrotypes. At the center, a Columbia BN, circa 1912. To the right, the Victor trademark as depicted in the 1920s. To the left, Edison storage battery advertising. (Value code: H)

2-127. A 15" diameter display clock, with spring movement, in the image of a Victor "Red Seal" record. Appropriately, the label is "I Hear You Calling Me" by John McCormack, No.64120, a record issued in 1910. *Courtesy of the Tom and Sandi McCarthy collection.* (Value code: VR)

REINCKE-ELLIS COMPANY,
CHICAGO. NEW YORK.

DIRECTIONS FOR SETTING THE CLOCK RUNNING AND KEEPING IT IN ORDER.

The Long Hand is the Minute Hand. The Short Hand is the Hour Hand

Remove the packing wire holding the pendulum rod, and hang the ball on the rod. The beat should be equal and regular and will be so if clock is hung in a correct position.

TO SET THE CLOCK.—Always use the minute hand (which can be turned in either direction without injury); never turn the hour hand.

The clock is regulated by means of a nut at the bottom of the pendulum. If the clock should go too fast, lower the ball; if too slow, raise it. One complete turn of the nut will make a difference of about 2½ minutes in 24 hours.

2-128. The manufacturer affixed these instructions to the reverse of the Victor clock. *Courtesy of the Tom and Sandi McCarthy collection.*

2-129. A 8" x 15 1/8" lithographed cardboard counter stand representing the Victor trademark. Note the care with which the shiny surface of the horn bell has been rendered to reflect an imaginary room. *Courtesy of Jim Kintzel.* (Value code: E)

2-130. This 14" x 22" poster promoted Edison's early synchronized sound-with-film system employing the Kinetophone. Despite the assertion that "millions are applauding," the Kinetophone system proved unreliable and its life was short. These July exhibitions occurred in 1913. *Courtesy of the Charles Hummel collections.* (Value code: VR)

2-131. The Standard Talking Machine Company of Chicago enjoyed ten years of vigorous activity as a client brand of Columbia. Standard had its origin in the East Liverpool China Company of Chicago, which in 1901 began distributing chinaware (manufactured in East Liverpool, Ohio) to be used as premiums in retail store promotions. Around 1905, the East Liverpool China Company began operating as the Standard Talking Machine Company, adding Columbia-made disc instruments to its line of pottery. Despite changes in ownership, Standard would disseminate huge numbers of its various talking machine models until subsumed by the Consolidated Talking Machine Company (also of Chicago) at the end of 1915. Among the items shown here is certainly one of the last record supplements to be issued by Standard. *Courtesy of Tom and Joanna Broome.* (Value code: H)

2-132. Victor's thoroughbred artists made the "Red Seal" discs a huge force in the record industry. Promotional postcards, circa 1913 – Ruffo, Kreisler, Homer, Farrar. (Value code: H)

2-133. This 22" x 27 7/8" dealer poster made its simple, perennial pitch by devoting more space to the text than to the illustration. From December 1913. *Courtesy of the Gfell family collection.* (Value code: F)

Chapter Three

THE PHONOGRAPH AND THE GREAT WAR, 1914~1918

History has a distressing way of repeating itself, particularly when a complacent people are confronted with war. In July 1861, before the American Civil War had fully ignited, breezy Washingtonians had packed picnic lunches and driven their buggies out to a creek known as Bull Run so that they might be entertained by the spectacle of splendidly uniformed men engaged in battle. Within a few hours, the Union troops were in disarray, and the pleasure-seekers were desperately galloping back to suddenly endangered homes, leaving their innocence behind on the gently rolling hills northeast of Manassas. Two generations later, in August 1914, the world learned of the outbreak of war in Europe. No longer regarding armed conflict as a circus, Americans nevertheless trusted that the chimera of isolationism would protect them. Meanwhile, they were determined that life would go on as usual. American manufacturers of phonographs and records were similarly determined. The Columbia Graphophone Company issued a circular on August 21, 1914, pertaining to the sale of dance records, that confidently stated,

> *Gentlemen:*
> *It is going to take more than* [a] *European war to interrupt the dancing vogue in* <u>*this country.*</u> *Folks have danced their way through Summer and they are going to dance their way through Fall and Winter...*

A fortnight's reflection may have suggested to Columbia's publicity staff that perhaps the war could, amid all the dancing, help stimulate certain other record purchases as well. In a circular dated September 4, 1914, the company made a different pitch:

> *Now that a great deal of interest is centered in anything and everything pertaining to the European war, it only needs slight effort to focus a large part of this interest on the patriotic music of these nations.*
> *Attached is a strikingly handsome hanger which, displayed in your window, will supply the attention-compelling and interest-arousing stimulus needed.*
> *Opposite the flag (in full color) of each nation at war is the national anthem or principal patriotic selection of that nation. You will notice that the poster is perforated so that the music which most appeals to your customers can be detached and displayed separately.*
> *Work your window!*

Columbia was not alone in its determination to maintain the status quo, particularly through the continued promotion of the "modern" dancing craze, which was in full flower. Victor trotted out Vernon and Irene Castle to make the point that its dance records were the only ones made under the Castles' expert supervision. Even Edison featured dancing in its advertising of the period, including a dealer poster depicting a couple in evening attire gliding across the floor to the sound of "Edison Blue Amberol Records for Dancing." The poster suggested that Edison records were noteworthy, "For Tone, For Time, and For Timeliness." There was, as yet, no mention of Tanks, Trenches, or Tourniquets.

3-1. This poster promoted Edison Blue Amberol cylinder records for dancing. Measures 23 1/8" x 27 1/4" framed. *Courtesy of the Tom and Sandi McCarthy collection.* (Value code: B)

Americans Awake

The illusion of normalcy gradually crumbled during the 32 months between the outbreak of the Great War and America's entry into the conflict. The United States was, after all, a nation of immigrants, and the appalling loss of life across the Atlantic was inevitably felt in America as well. After April 1917, phonographic advertising reflected the resolve of a nation intent on restoring peace to the world. The nobility of the cause might have been slightly overdone on the part of phonograph manufacturers. Their self-proclaimed mission was to bring a bit of home to our soldiers in the trenches, to remind them of what they were fighting for, and to help instill civility and reason in a world seemingly gone mad. These aspirations were pursued with the same energy as had been the attainment of "perfect tone and perfect time" a few years earlier.

Depictions of sanitized doughboys, cleaning their rifles in a dugout while listening to Caruso, were commonly seen in popular magazines. According to the advertisements, visions of home could be readily conjured by the lucky soldier or sailor whose family, church, or civic group cared enough to supply him with a talking machine. Quasi-patriotic appeals were made to demonstrate fidelity to the cause by purchasing the latest recorded martial music to entertain returning servicemen (probably the *last* thing they wanted to hear!). All of this was suggested at a time when the major talking machine factories were largely engaged in the manufacture of wartime supplies. Certain materials were restricted for the duration, and the usual range of talking machines was scaled back. These exigencies,

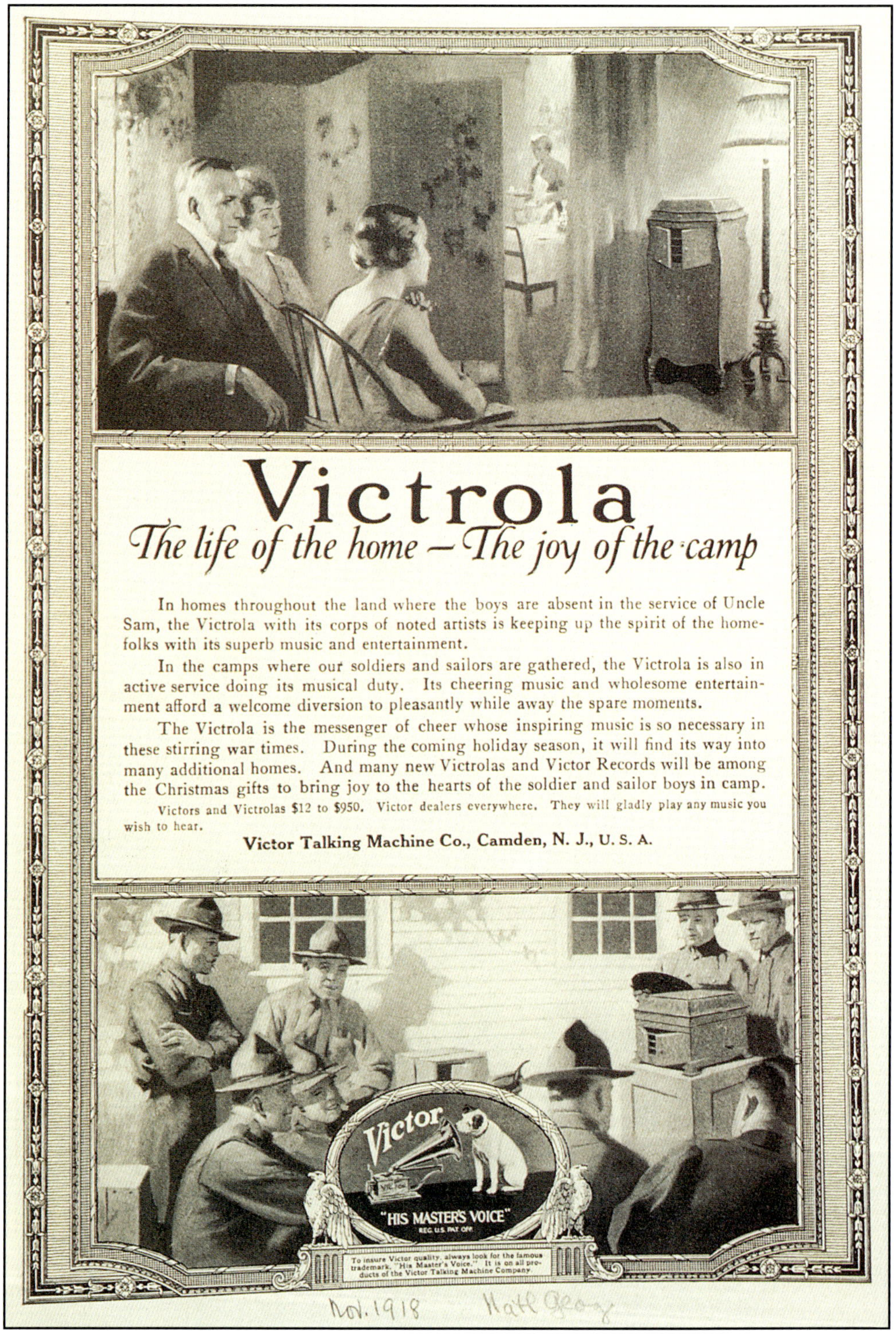

3-2. Reflecting common themes of the day, this November 1918 advertisement from *National Geographic* magazine united the folks at home with the boys at war through the music of the Victrola. (Value code: H)

rather than casting a pall over the phonograph trade, seemed to stimulate it. Voluntary and involuntary cutbacks were worn as badges of honor by the various companies, who exhorted the public to likewise do its duty by purchasing talking machines and records.

Perhaps the most striking phonographic advertisements of the war years were those that depicted home and family. Edison never wandered far from its perennial theme of young and old gathered by the fire to enjoy each other's company while being entertained by recorded music. Victor, strangely, put even more emphasis than usual on depicting bejeweled hostesses welcoming the vicarious talents of the Metropolitan Opera into their cavernous ballrooms. Such opulent scenes were colorful, and no doubt served to elevate the status of the Victrola, but lacked any universal empathy beyond simply keeping-up-with-the-Joneses.

For spirituality, nothing else equaled the wartime advertisements for Columbia. Other-worldly images of loved ones and dreams of "home" could be seen among towering cumulus over the vast seas. Heavenly choruses and orchestras shared the firmament with monolithic Grafonolas, from which flowed their healing art. These depictions better represented the yearnings of a war-torn world than did a bevy of opera stars arrayed on acres of polished parquet floors.

The one constant message throughout the numerous talking machine ads that appeared during the war years was that "normalcy" could be reestablished in the home through the purchase of a phonograph and records. Despite the slightly self-righteous tone of some wartime phonograph advertisements, there is no doubt that talking machines indeed brought a great deal of comfort to a great many on both sides of the Atlantic during and immediately after the First World War.

3-3. The April 25, 1914 issue of *The Saturday Evening Post* carried this Victor advertisement featuring the endorsement of prominent dance instructors, Vernon and Irene Castle. This 12 1/2" x 20 1/2" proof was sent to Victor dealers for display. *Courtesy of the Tom and Sandi McCarthy collection.* (Value code: VR)

3-4. Another proof for dealer use. This panoramic constellation of operatic legends measures 11 1/4" x 26 1/2" (without mat). *Courtesy of the Tom and Sandi McCarthy collection.* (Value code: VR)

3-5. The commercial product is shown here in original frame. In this form (11" x 23 1/2" framed), a key to the artists' names was included on the back. *Courtesy of Rae Ann Rieping.* (Value code: F)

3-6. A glass advertising slide for use in theatres. All major talking machine companies made such slides available to their dealers for promotional purposes.3 1/8" x 4". *Courtesy of Steve and Ellie Saccente.* (Value code: F)

3-7. During the early war years, prior to America's involvement, Victor's advertising was often focused on "snob appeal." Victrolas were depicted as the indispensable entertainers of the wealthy, whether at home, on the porch of the beach "cottage," or wherever the pursuit of recreation should lead. In this 1914 card, the average American housewife was advised that, after a seven-course dinner in the gilded dining room aglow with candlelight, her guests should be entertained... (Value code: G)

3-8. Previous item, opened. No barn dance, this, but the Metropolitan Opera House brought into a muraled ballroom (or is it merely a salon?). If the Victrola could transform the polished parquet caverns of the Vanderbilts into the Met, it could easily elevate the parlor of hometown America into an oasis of culture. Couldn't it? Such "lifestyle merchandising" proved to be enormously successful.

3-9. The onetime hardware store of Mr. C.J. Tierney, located in the sleepy hamlet of Wallace, New York. In 1914, Mr. Tierney decided to put in a line of Columbia Grafonolas and records. Evidently, his flirtation with Columbia was brief (June–October 1914), but fortunately, Mr. Tierney kept the advertising materials and correspondence that Columbia sent to him – even after the hardware store closed in the late 1930s. Time often passes slowly in rural New York State. Miraculously undisturbed, the materials pictured on the following pages remained together in this building from the summer of 1914 until November 1995.

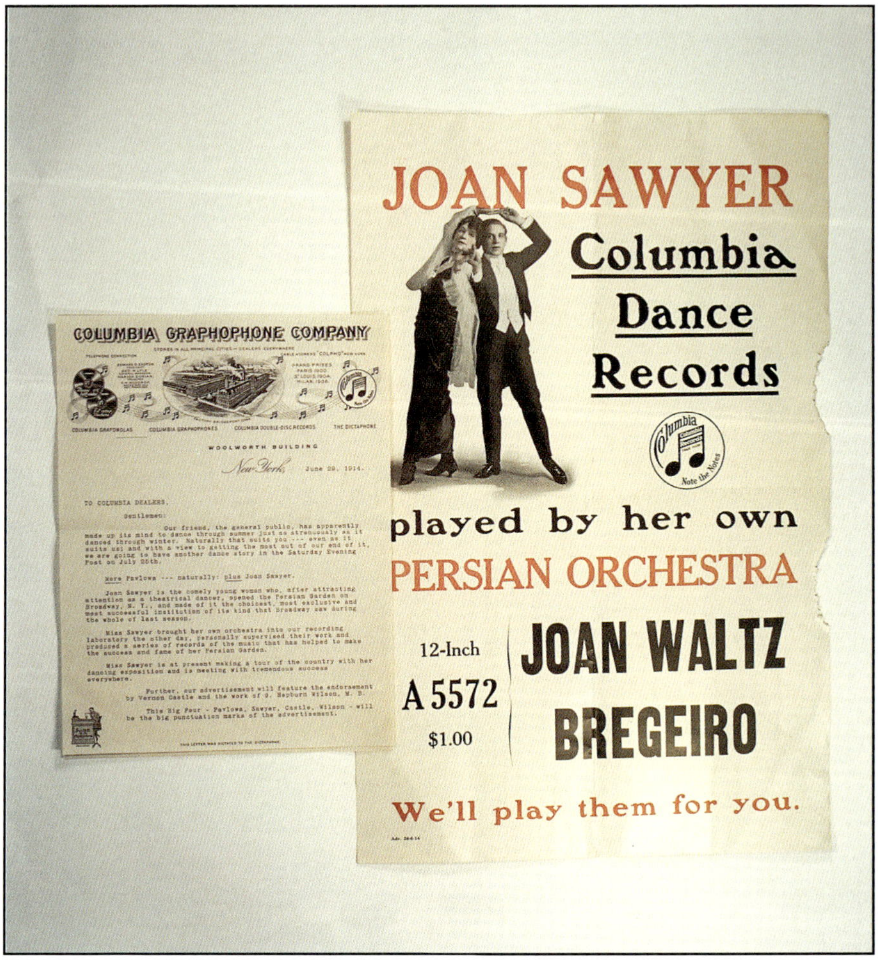

COLUMBIA GRAPHOPHONE COMPANY

COLUMBIA GRAFONOLAS — COLUMBIA GRAPHOPHONES — COLUMBIA DOUBLE-DISC RECORDS — THE DICTAPHONE

WOOLWORTH BUILDING

New York, June 29, 1914.

TO COLUMBIA DEALERS,

Gentlemen:

Our friend, the general public, has apparently made up its mind to dance through summer just as strenuously as it danced through winter. Naturally that suits you --- even as it suits us; and with a view to getting the most out of our end of it, we are going to have another dance story in the Saturday Evening Post on July 25th.

More Pavlowa --- naturally; plus Joan Sawyer.

Joan Sawyer is the comely young woman who, after attracting attention as a theatrical dancer, opened the Persian Garden on Broadway, N. Y., and made of it the choicest, most exclusive and most successful institution of its kind that Broadway saw during the whole of last season.

Miss Sawyer brought her own orchestra into our recording laboratory the other day, personally supervised their work and produced a series of records of the music that has helped to make the success and fame of her Persian Garden.

Miss Sawyer is at present making a tour of the country with her dancing exposition and is meeting with tremendous success everywhere.

Further, our advertisement will feature the endorsement by Vernon Castle and the work of G. Hepburn Wilson, M. B.

This Big Four - Pavlowa, Sawyer, Castle, Wilson - will be the big punctuation marks of the advertisement.

3-10. The day after the assassination of the Austrian Archduke Ferdinand, Columbia sent hardware dealer C.J. Tierney this announcement of new Joan Sawyer records, plus this 12 1/2" x 19" poster for his store. It was the death of Austrian Archduke Francis Ferdinand, gunned down by a Serb nationalist, which precipitated Austria-Hungary's declaration of war against Serbia in July 1914. By early August, Germany, Russia, France, and Great Britain had been drawn into the war by treaty obligations. (Value code: H)

COLUMBIA GRAPHOPHONE COMPANY

STORES IN ALL PRINCIPAL CITIES — DEALERS EVERYWHERE

TELEPHONE CONNECTION

CABLE ADDRESS "COLPHO" NEW YORK.

EDWARD D. EASTON, PRESIDENT
GEO. W. LYLE, GENERAL MANAGER
MARION DORIAN, TREASURER
C. W. WOODROP, SECRETARY AND ASST. TREASURER

GRAND PRIZES
PARIS 1900.
ST LOUIS, 1904.
MILAN, 1906.

FACTORY: BRIDGEPORT, CONN.

COLUMBIA GRAFONOLAS   COLUMBIA GRAPHOPHONES   COLUMBIA DOUBLE-DISC RECORDS   THE DICTAPHONE

WOOLWORTH BUILDING

New York, July 20, 1914.

TO COLUMBIA DEALERS,

Gentlemen:

Mr. John Hofman, a Columbia dealer of 1346 South 13th Street, Omaha, Neb., sent us a sketch and a brief description the other day of a window display that he has been using with excellent results.

It looks just so good that we made one up ourselves in this Department and photographed it, so that you can all have the benefit of the idea.

To begin with, like most good ideas, it is so beautifully simple that it is a wonder that nobody ever thought of it before.

The display does not cost much: about a dollar for the dolls and maybe another half a dollar for some ribbon to dress them with.

Then place them in pairs on the turn-table of an "Eclipse". If they are too uncertain on their feet to stand by themselves, a dab of mucilage will steady them sufficiently. Then start the machine. It is a simple matter, by pulling the starting lever only part of the way over, to bring down the speed of the turn-table to less than 12 revolutions a minute. And at that rate the machine will run an hour or two without re-winding. You will find that the circular motion of the miniature dancing floor will give the dolls a really excellent suggestion of actual dancing.

Mr. Hofman found that playing dance records on a nearby instrument served a double purpose: it helped along the display and at the same time of course demonstrated the records and generally helped a good deal toward the excellent results he got from the display.

Mr. Hofman, by the way, went a little bit further than we did, because he fixed up a card-board roof and a railing around the machine so as to convey the idea of a piazza.

This is an idea which has already proved of value and which is obviously simple and not at all costly. It is distinctly worth your while to duplicate it in your own window or store.

Yours very truly,

COLUMBIA GRAPHOPHONE COMPANY.

THIS LETTER WAS DICTATED TO THE DICTAPHONE

3-11. This illustration of an eye-catching window display was sent to dealers in July. Summer was traditionally a slow time for phonograph and record sales, and novelty displays such as this one attempted to maintain the public's interest. (Value code: H)

COLUMBIA GRAPHOPHONE COMPANY

STORES IN ALL PRINCIPAL CITIES — DEALERS EVERYWHERE

TELEPHONE CONNECTION

CABLE ADDRESS "COLPHO" NEW YORK.

EDWARD D. EASTON, PRESIDENT
GEO. W. LYLE, GENERAL MANAGER
MARION DORIAN, TREASURER
C. W. WOODROP, SECRETARY AND ASST. TREASURER

GRAND PRIZES
PARIS 1900,
ST LOUIS, 1904.
MILAN, 1906.

FACTORY: BRIDGEPORT, CONN.

COLUMBIA GRAFONOLAS   COLUMBIA GRAPHOPHONES   COLUMBIA DOUBLE-DISC RECORDS   THE DICTAPHONE

WOOLWORTH BUILDING

New York, August 21, 1914.

TO COLUMBIA DEALERS,

Gentlemen:

It is going to take more than an European war to interrupt the dancing vogue in this country. Folks have danced their way through Summer and they are going to dance their way through Fall and Winter.

Just by way of keeping Columbia dance product well to the front and prominently before the public eye, we have prepared a large and striking window poster showing the opinions that eighteen of the foremost dancing authorities in the country entertain regarding Columbia modern dance records. At the head of the list are the big four - Pavlowa, Hepburn Wilson, the Castles and Joan Sawyer.

The others are not only from New York but from mighty distant parts of the country.

This poster presents a pretty powerful battery of endorsements and enthusiastic praise.

We enclose one sample copy. Display it prominently in your window or inside your store. If you can use any additional copies, notify your distributor and he will supply you for the asking.

Yours very truly,

COLUMBIA GRAPHOPHONE COMPANY.

THIS LETTER WAS DICTATED TO THE DICTAPHONE

3-12. By the end of August 1914, the war had erupted in Europe. This letter from Columbia gamely predicted business as usual, while describing, "…a large and striking window poster…" which was enclosed. (Value code: H)

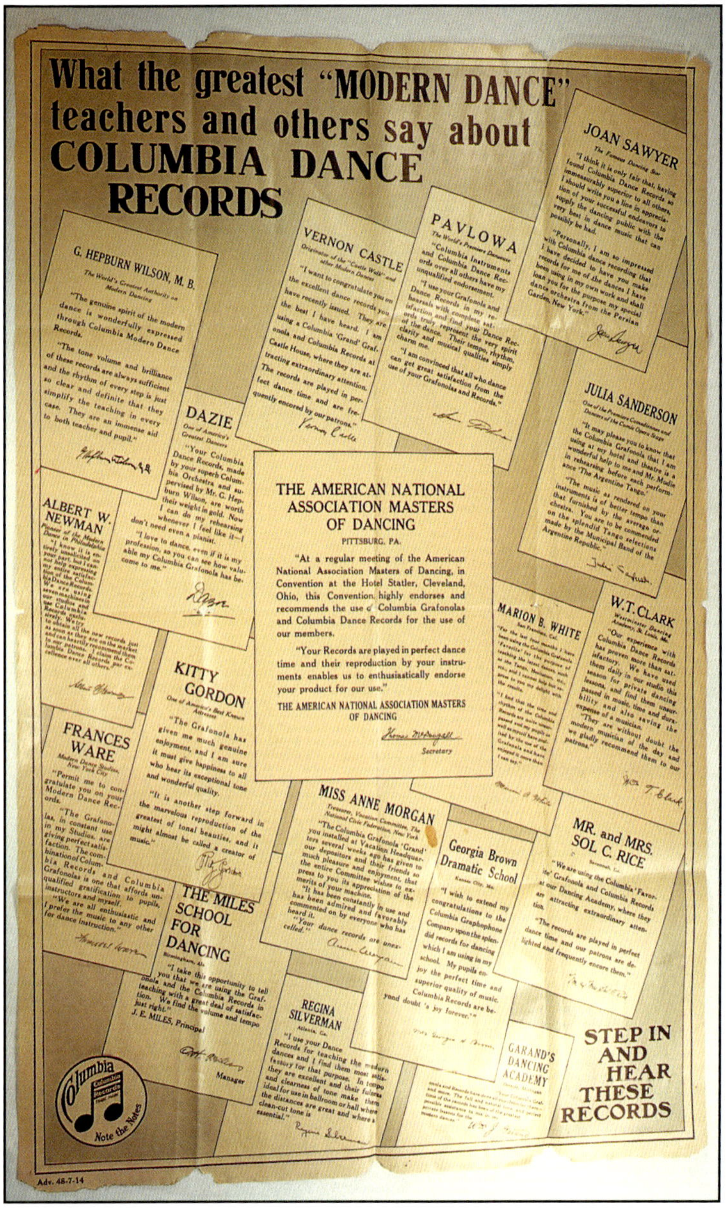

3-13. The window poster that accompanied the previous letter measured 24 1/2" x 38 1/4". The endorsement by Vernon Castle is interesting in light of his previous support of Victor products. (Value code: G)

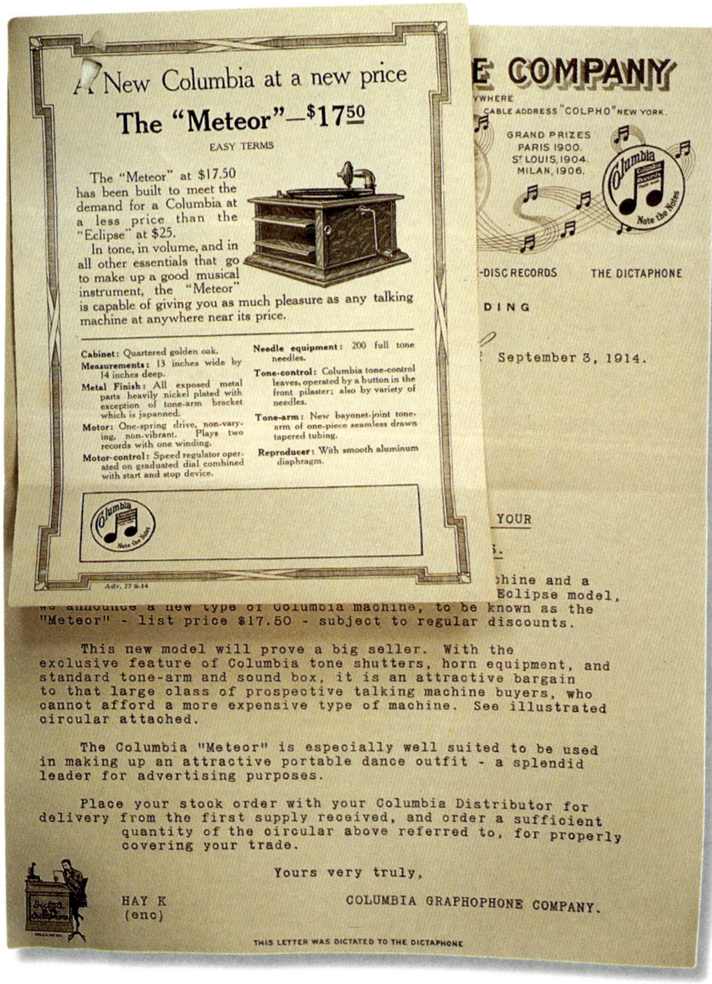

3-14. Early September 1914 brought the announcement of the "Meteor" and a promotional circular to advertise it. (Value code: H)

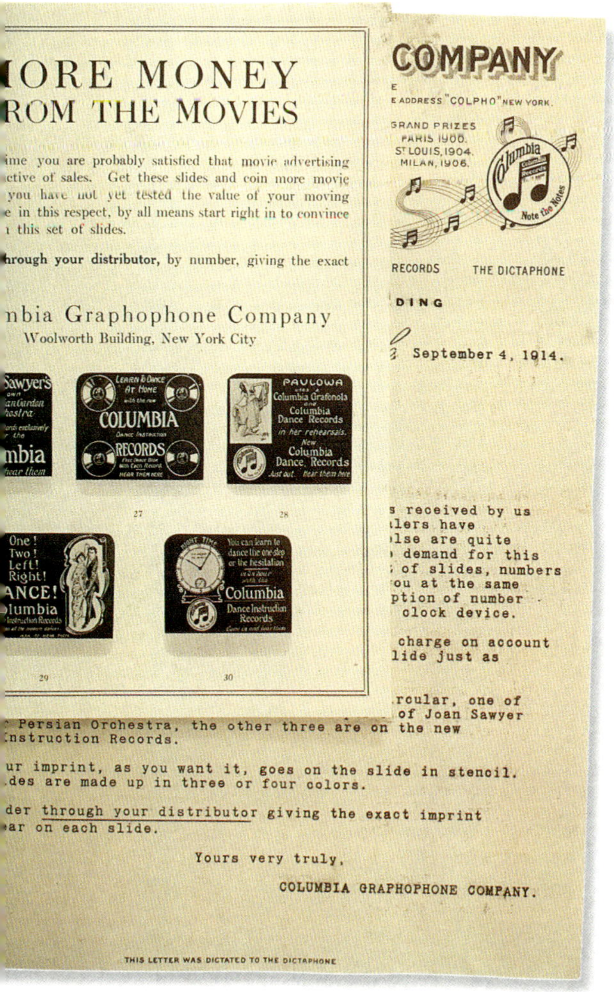

3-15. Like other talking machine companies, Columbia offered its dealers glass advertising slides for use in theatres. Note the clock device on the slide to the lower right, to be set by the projectionist. (Value code: H)

3-16. Columbia (much like the rest of America) grudgingly acknowledged the war's presence, but suggested ways to capitalize on it. "Display a map of Europe… Put small flags of the warring countries in their proper places on the map. From these, run ribbons to the patriotic Columbia record…" (Value code: H)

COLUMBIA GRAPHOPHONE COMPANY

TELEPHONE CONNECTION

STORES IN ALL PRINCIPAL CITIES — DEALERS EVERYWHERE

CABLE ADDRESS "COLPHO" NEW YORK

GRAND PRIZES PARIS 1900. ST LOUIS, 1904. MILAN, 1906.

COLUMBIA GRAFONOLAS

COLUMBIA GRAPHOPHONES

FACTORY: BRIDGEPORT, CONN.

COLUMBIA DOUBLE-DISC RECORDS

THE DICTAPHONE

WOOLWORTH BUILDING

New York, October 1, 1914.

COLUMBIA DEALERS,

Gentlemen:

An entirely new note in color work has been struck in our Saturday Evening Post back cover for October 24th. That it is at the same time artistic and striking, you can judge from the advance proof attached.

The advertisement is built around the "Mignonette" - "The greatest $100 worth ever offered".

The proof pasted in your window and the enclosed advertising run in your local papers will link up your store to your share of the Post's two million readers.

Yours very truly,

COLUMBIA GRAPHOPHONE COMPANY.

THIS LETTER WAS DICTATED TO THE DICTAPHONE

3-17. This ad proof for an upcoming issue of *The Saturday Evening Post* was the last item found in C.J. Tierney's files. Despite the appeal of the "Mignonette" ("the greatest $100 worth ever offered"), Mr. Tierney evidently closed out his Columbia sideline at this point. Ironically, he had attempted his new venture during the slowest 90 days of the talking machine business year, dropping his franchise just as the Christmas business was gaining momentum. Despite his poor timing, Mr. Tierney preserved these and many other documents in voluminous files, allowing later generations a glimpse, however brief, of Columbia's marketing during a momentous, long-ago summer. (Value code: H)

3-18. In December 1914, Victor issued this flyer urging the presence of music in every home on Christmas morning. (Value code: F)

3-19. Opened, the flyer depicted the now-customary palatial surroundings, adorned by the Victrola "XVI." The flyer opened a third time to show the usual Victrola line, with prices.

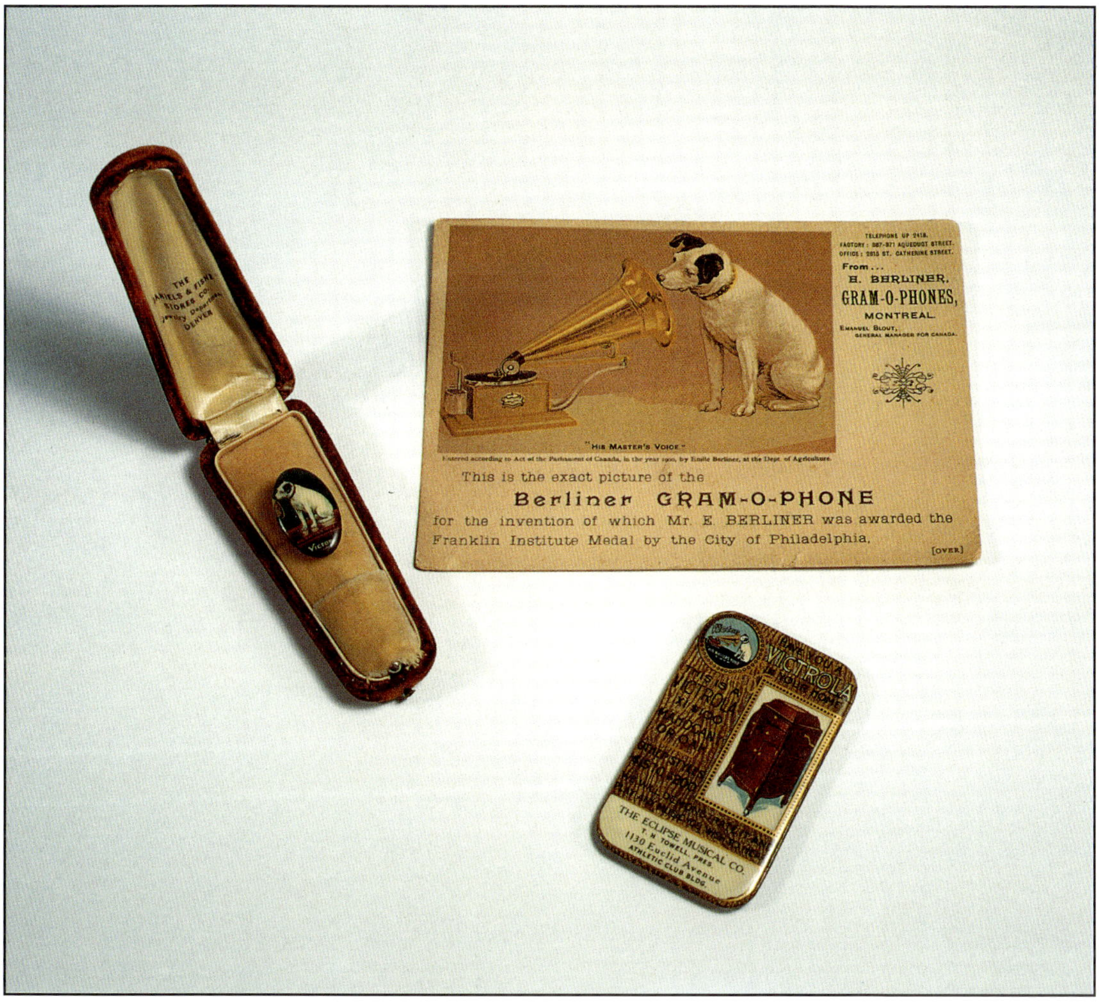

3-20. Three varied objects bearing the universally-recognized image of "Nipper." A celluloid stick-pin in its original padded box, a trade card from the Berliner Gramophone Company of Canada (which, during the first two decades of the twentieth century, functioned as a close cousin of, and was ultimately acquired by, Victor); and a celluloid advertising mirror prominently featuring a Victrola. (Value code: F)

3-21.An 11" x 21" trolley card extolling the realism of Victor records. *Courtesy of Alan H. Mueller.* (Value code: E)

3-22. Another trolley card measuring 11" x 21", emphasizing the variety of entertainment available from the Victrola. *Courtesy of Alan H. Mueller.* (Value code: E)

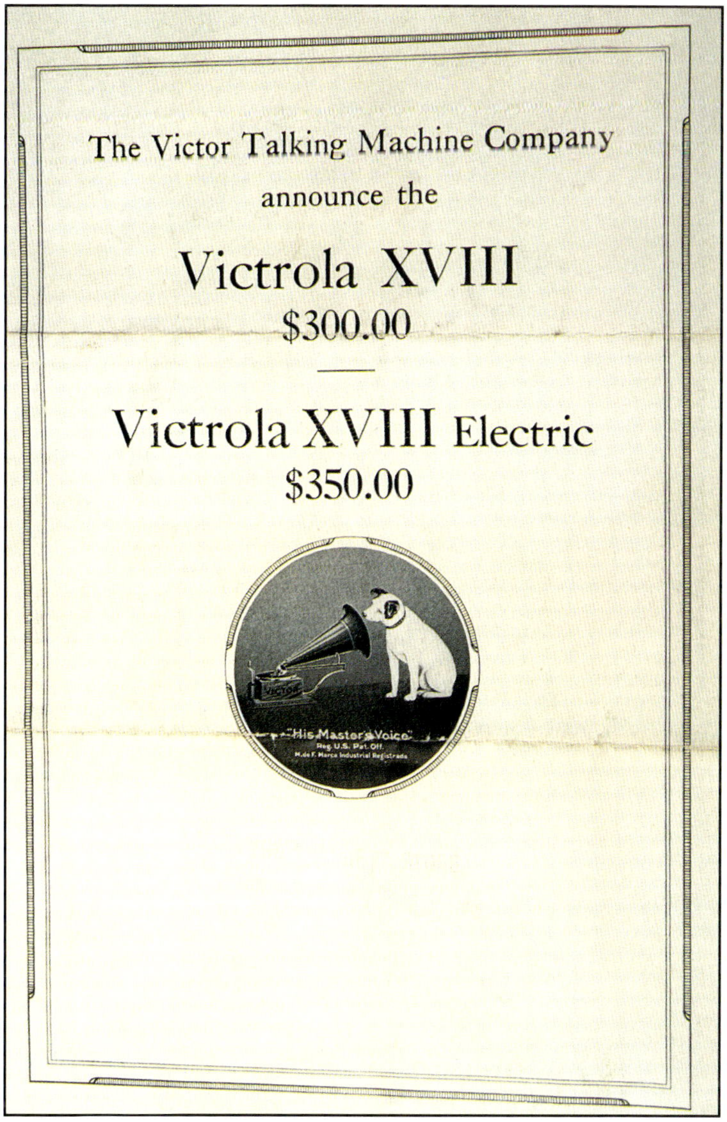

The Victor Talking Machine Company
announce the

Victrola XVIII
$300.00

Victrola XVIII Electric
$350.00

3-23. From June 1915 until December 1916, The Victrola "XVIII" was the top of the catalogued line at $300.00. This elegant model warranted a special brochure (printed in July 1915) to announce its introduction. *Courtesy of Bruce and Linda Peterson*. (Value code: F)

Victrola XVIII
Mahogany, $300
Circassian or American Walnut, $350

Victrola XVIII Electric
Mahogany, $350
Circassian or American Walnut. $400

This beautiful and artistic cabinet is exclusively our own design and manufacture. No expense has been spared in making this instrument representative of the very highest type of construction known to the art of cabinet making, and we make this announcement to the public with a degree of pride that is unanswerable from a quality standpoint from any other source.

Only the finest figured mahogany veneers (matched V-shaped) are used on its front and two sides, and the completed doors, sides and back are of 7-ply veneers, properly cross-banded, which is the strongest and most costly construction known in the art and manufacture of the finest furniture.

Like all other Victrolas the Victrola XVIII will bring to you the world's best music, sung and played by the world's greatest artists.

Victrola XVIII—$300.00

Matched Mahogany Cabinet with paneled moulding, swell front and sides. Contains sixteen (eleven 10-inch and five 12-inch) Victor Record Albums for 160 records. 48⅛ inches high, 23¼ inches wide, 25¼ inches deep.

12-inch gold-plated turntable, gold-plated exhibition sound box, Victor tapering tone arm and goose-neck sound-box tube, brake, speed regulator and indicator. Nickel-plated, extra heavy, triple spring, spiral drive motor (can be wound while playing); all metal parts 24 karat gold plated.

Victrola XVIII Electric—$350.00. Equipped with Universal Motor applicable to all currents and voltages. Fitted with safety device to automatically shut off current if forgotten by operator. Incandescent lamp on motor board which lights with opening of lid and is shut off when lid is closed.

Specifications for Circassian or American Walnut same as Mahogany. (See opposite page for prices).

3-24. Mechanical specifications were those of the $200.00 Victrola "XVI," but the elaborate cabinet was a departure from Victor tradition. *Courtesy of Bruce and Linda Peterson*.

3-25. The back cover of the brochure was devoted to the seven-ply lamination process featured in the construction of this model. *Courtesy of Bruce and Linda Peterson*.

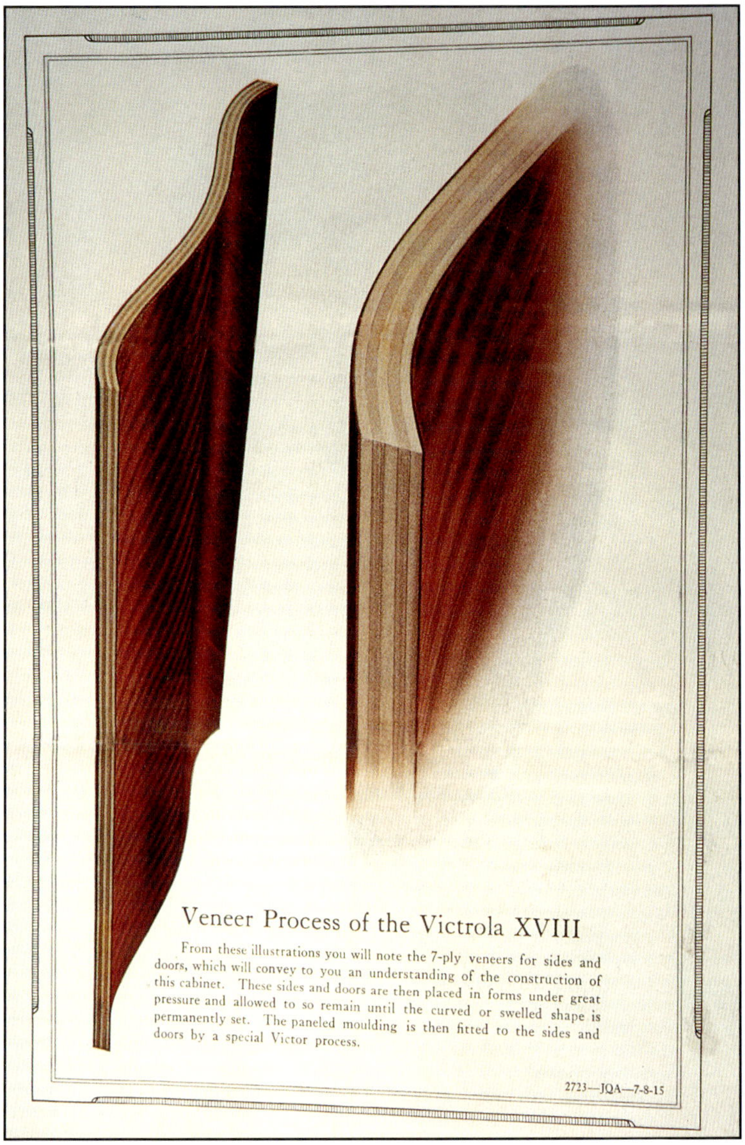

3-26. Victor had no monopoly on expensive instruments. Shown on this advertising card is Edison artist Marie Kaiser listening to an Edison Diamond Disc Phonograph, Model "375." This model first retailed at a heady $375.00. (Value code: H)

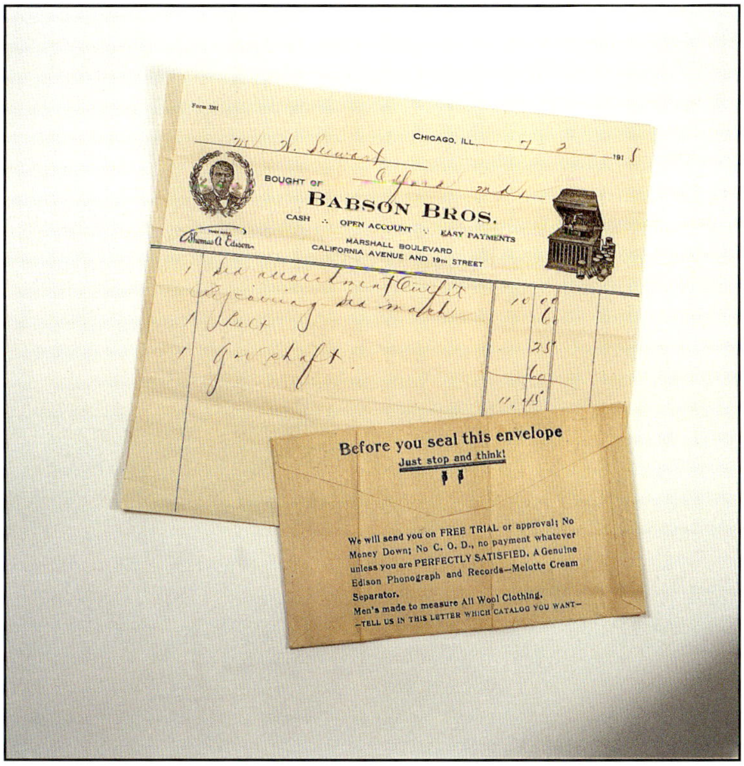

3-27. In 1915, the Edison Amberola "30" illustrated on this Babson Brothers invoice was a brand new product. A confusing gaggle of earlier Amberolas was reduced to three models ("30," "50" and "75") by the Edison company. Babson did a great deal to market the improved Edison Amberolas by mail-order. Below, a customer reply envelope delineated the practically irresistible terms under which Babson did business. However, if a Genuine Edison Phonograph was not to your liking, perhaps you'd prefer a cream separator or some men's all wool clothing? (Value code: H)

3-28. One of a series of Victor mailing cards from the 1915 Panama-Pacific International Exposition in San Francisco. Note the three-dimensional effect of the vertical portion. World's Fairs and expositions were prime venues for phonograph advertising over the years. *Courtesy of Robin and Joan Rolfs*. (Value code: VR)

3-29. Not all advertising of the period was provided by the talking machine companies. This 12" x 36" metal sign was clearly executed by the local sign painter of Mount Airy, Maryland. The charming depiction of a Victrola appears to be either a Model "XVIII" or "XVII." *Courtesy of William G. Meyer.* (Value code: E)

3-31. This 3 1/2" x 6 1/4" Victor advertising card depicted Caruso knocking at the front door, eager to perform. *Courtesy of the Tom and Sandi McCarthy collection.* (Value code: G)

3-30. The E.A. Schweiger store in Brooklyn, New York, returned its customers' processed snapshots in sleeves such as this one, advertising its line of Victrolas. *Courtesy of Fred Guenther.* (Value code: G)

3-32. The Edison "Amberola Store" was sold to dealers for $15.00 as a place to store, display, and demonstrate the Amberola "30" and Amberola "50." Four receptacles above held catalogues and supplements. Space was provided for a stock of Edison Blue Amberol records as well. Traces of the unfaded bright blue paint suggest the visual impact that this simple cupboard must have had when new. In the October 1916 issue of the *Edison Phonograph Monthly*, the company announced the availability of this display: "'The New Amberola Store' is not only designed to contain New Diamond Amberolas and Blue Amberol records, but to advertise them as well." Measures 38 1/4" wide x 24" deep x 34" tall (excluding sign). *Courtesy of Jen and Ken Flaherty*. (Value code: VR)

3-33. Open view of the Edison "Amberola Store." "While the 'New Amberola Store' has been designed primarily for new dealers, it can be secured by merchants who are now handling the Amberola line and who feel that the new method is an improvement over their present way of displaying the instruments and records." The five trays to the right could hold 185 cylinder records. An Amberola "30" could be stored in the lower left cubicle, and an Amberola "50" in the upper left. *Courtesy of Jen and Ken Flaherty*.

3-34. Victor dealerships were often adorned with framed photogravures of famous recording artists, frequently listening to – what else – a Victrola. Shown is a page from an advertising catalogue offering these items to Victor dealers. *Courtesy of Martin F. Bryan*. (Value code: G)

3-35. John McCormack was an enormously popular Victor artist, and his youthful smile was suitably displayed in this 25" x 31 1/2" photogravure with original frame. *Courtesy of the Tom and Sandi McCarthy collection*. (Value code: E)

3-36. Violinist Mischa Elman was likewise showcased in a 25" x 31 1/2" Victor photogravure. *Courtesy of the Tom and Sandi McCarthy collection*. (Value code: E)

3-37. ...And no Victor dealership would be complete without the likeness of Enrico Caruso. Measures 39 1/4" x 51" in original frame. *Courtesy of the Tom and Sandi McCarthy collection*. (Value code: E)

3-38. Caruso, shown here in identical regalia, merited his own Victor catalogue. (Catalogue issued February 1922.) (Value code: H)

3-39. Victor drew Caruso out of its advertising arsenal like a gunfighter flashing a six-gun. Undeniably, Enrico Caruso was a formidable weapon. The operatic tenor first had made an impact at La Scala in Milano, and recorded both cylinders and discs, before leaving Italy to enter a long residence at the Metropolitan Opera in New York City. Victor signed him to an exclusive contract, and released a protracted series of his recordings, beginning in 1904. Caruso's popular fame became enormous, aided of course by Victor's successful distribution of his records. In this publicity photo, Victor's prize property is arrayed in the costume of his most widely recognized role from Leoncavallo's "Pagliacci." *Courtesy of Tom and Sandi McCarthy collection.* (Value code: F)

3-40. Edison dealers may not have had many glamorous operatic recording artists to flaunt on their walls, but the famed inventor and leader of the company that bore his name was frequently displayed. This framed portrait measures 15 1/2" x 21 3/4". *Courtesy of Martin F. Bryan.* (Value code: E)

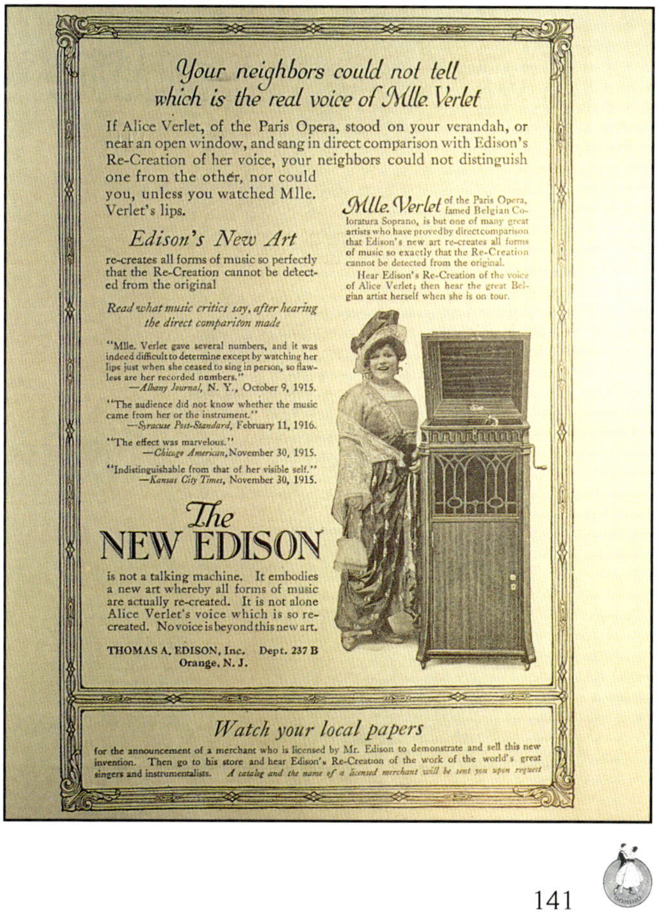

3-41. One of the most notable phonograph advertising campaigns was the Edison "Tone Tests" which occurred across the country for several years. The "Tone Tests" hearkened back to the "Tinfoil" Phonograph exhibitions of the late 1870s, which had been underwritten by the old Edison Speaking Phonograph Company. The "Tone-Tests," sponsored by Thomas A. Edison, Incorporated, were given free of charge, usually in a large municipal auditorium or opera house. The usual performance called for a well-known Edison recording artist such as violinist Albert Spaulding, comic duet Collins and Harlan, or (as here) singer Alice Verlet to perform a selection for the audience. Standing onstage was an Edison Diamond Disc Phonograph – usually the Model "C-250" as pictured in this ad. Sometime during the performance, the house lights would be gradually diminished to total darkness while the performance continued. A few moments later, the lights would return, to reveal the Edison Phonograph, alone on the stage, carrying on the performance without the recording artist present. The artists would sing duets with their recorded voices, add harmony, and demonstrate other effects to point out the realism of the recorded reproduction. Independent critics and newspaper reporters were almost unanimous in their praise for the fidelity of the Edison, and the effectiveness of the demonstrations. The "Tone Tests" were a brilliant success for Edison during the teens and early 1920s. *Courtesy of Gilbert (Bert) Pasley.* (Value code: H)

Trade Mark Thomas A. Edison

A PRODUCT OF THE EDISON LABORATORIES

CERTIFICATE OF AUTHENTICITY

OFFICIAL LABORATORY MODEL

THE NEW EDISON

"THE PHONOGRAPH WITH A SOUL"

I hereby certify that the Official Laboratory Model New Edison No. ______ encased in a Chippendale period cabinet purchased on ______ 19__, by ______ of ______ from ______ of ______ is an exact duplicate in realism and tonal quality of the Official Laboratory Model New Edison with which I made the famous Tone Test comparison at School Auditorium on May 13th, and that it will sustain the test of direct comparison with living artists in the same successful manner. Given under my hand and seal this 13th day of May 1920

Attest: Victor Young Alice Verlet

AMERICAN BANK NOTE CO. LITHO.

3-42. Alice Verlet and her accompanist, Victor Young, signed this "Certificate of Authenticity" for a local Edison dealer after giving a "Tone Test." The dealer could then supply the artists' personal assurance that a customer's new Edison was, "…an exact duplicate in realism and tonal quality of the Official Laboratory Model New Edison with which I made the famous Tone Test comparison…" This particular certificate was supplied to the purchaser of an Edison "C-19" Diamond Disc Phonograph (formerly the "C-250," but often called the "Chippendale"). Dated May 13, 1920. *Courtesy of Gilbert (Bert) Pasley.*

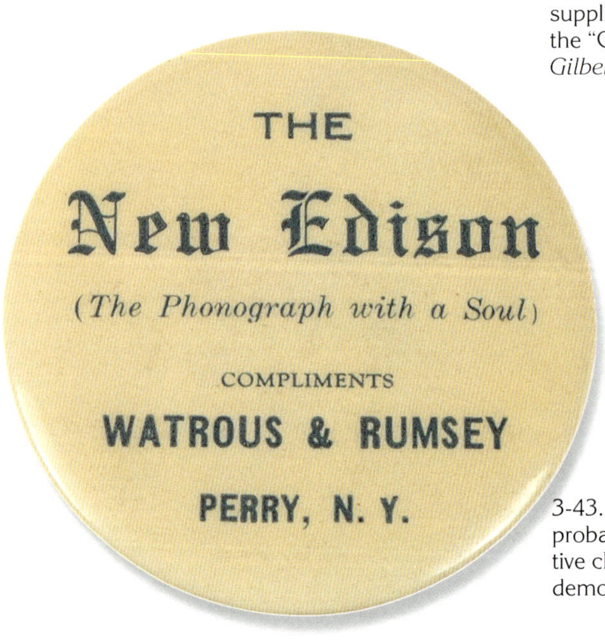

3-43. A celluloid advertising mirror, 2" diameter, probably given by the identified dealer to prospective clients who attended "Tone Tests" and other demonstrations. (Value code: F)

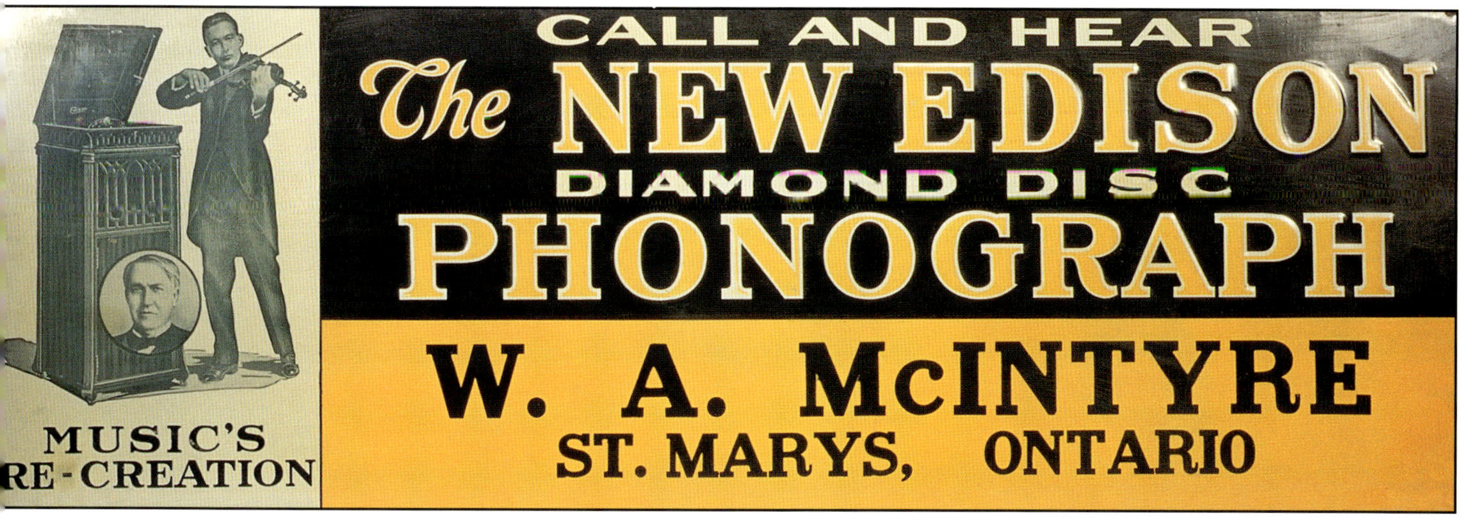

3-44. The Edison "Tone Tests" were even depicted on dealers' metal signs such as this one. In this instance, Albert Spaulding plays in unison with a Model "C-250." Measures 11 3/4" x 35 1/4". *Courtesy of the Tom and Sandi McCarthy collection*. (Value code: D)

3-45. A 7" x 10" souvenir photo of an Edison "Tone Test," signed by Edison artist Cecil Arden.

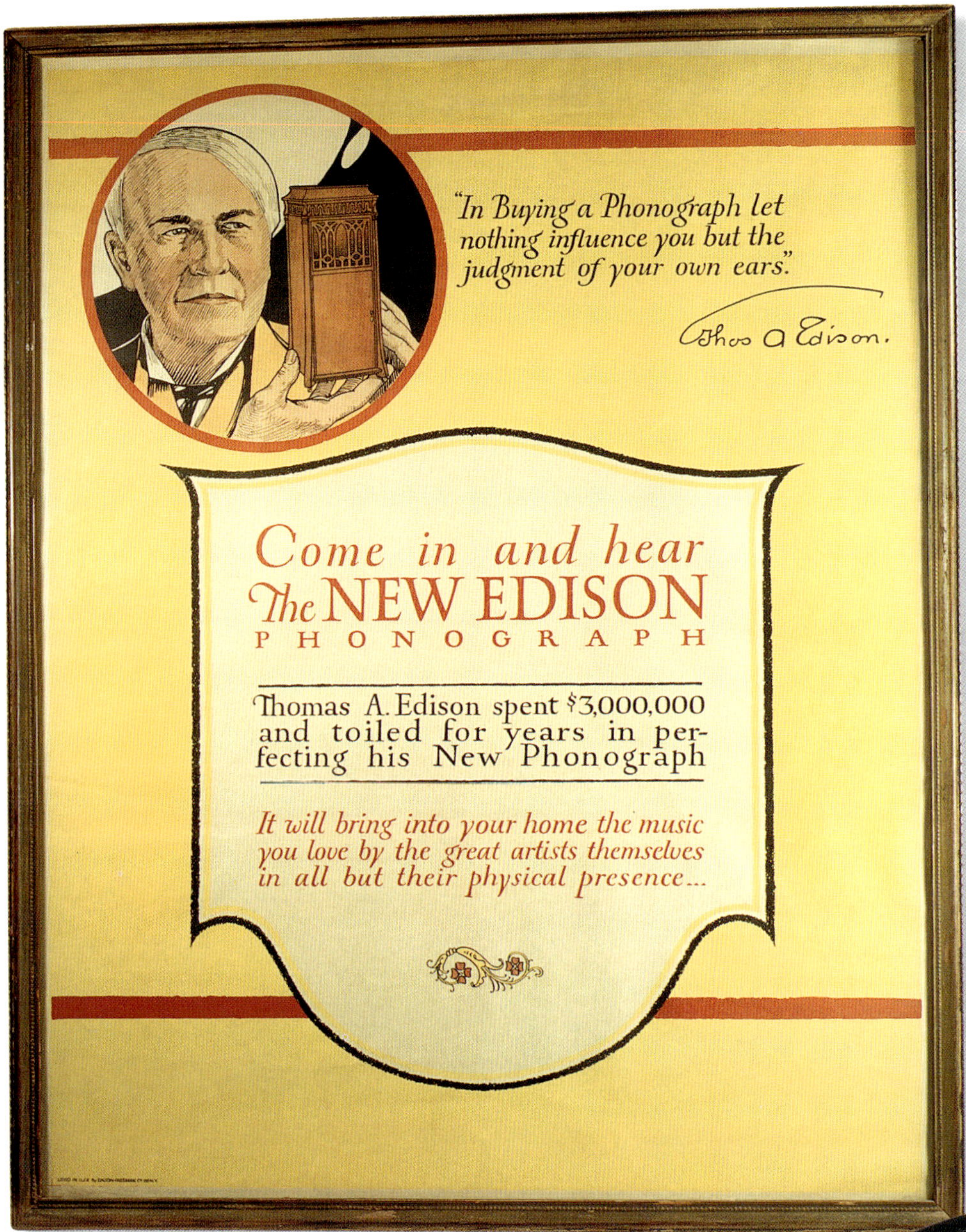

3-46. History has vindicated Mr. Edison's toil and expenditure of money by judging the Diamond Disc Phonograph the first disc talking machine system designed from the ground up. A poster, 23" x 29". *Courtesy of the Gfell family collection.* (Value code: F)

3-47. Several talking machine and record manufacturers offered imitation records to be placed on the turntables of display phonographs. Usually made of metal, these items would protect the turntable felt from fading in a shop window, where dust, sunlight, and handling could damage an actual record. This Pathé example, made of pressed cardboard, measures 10" in diameter. *Courtesy of the Charles Hummel collections.* (Value code: F)

3-48. A lithographed metal Vocalion imitation 10" record duplicated the brick-red color of the actual discs. *Courtesy of the Charles Hummel collections.* (Value code: F)

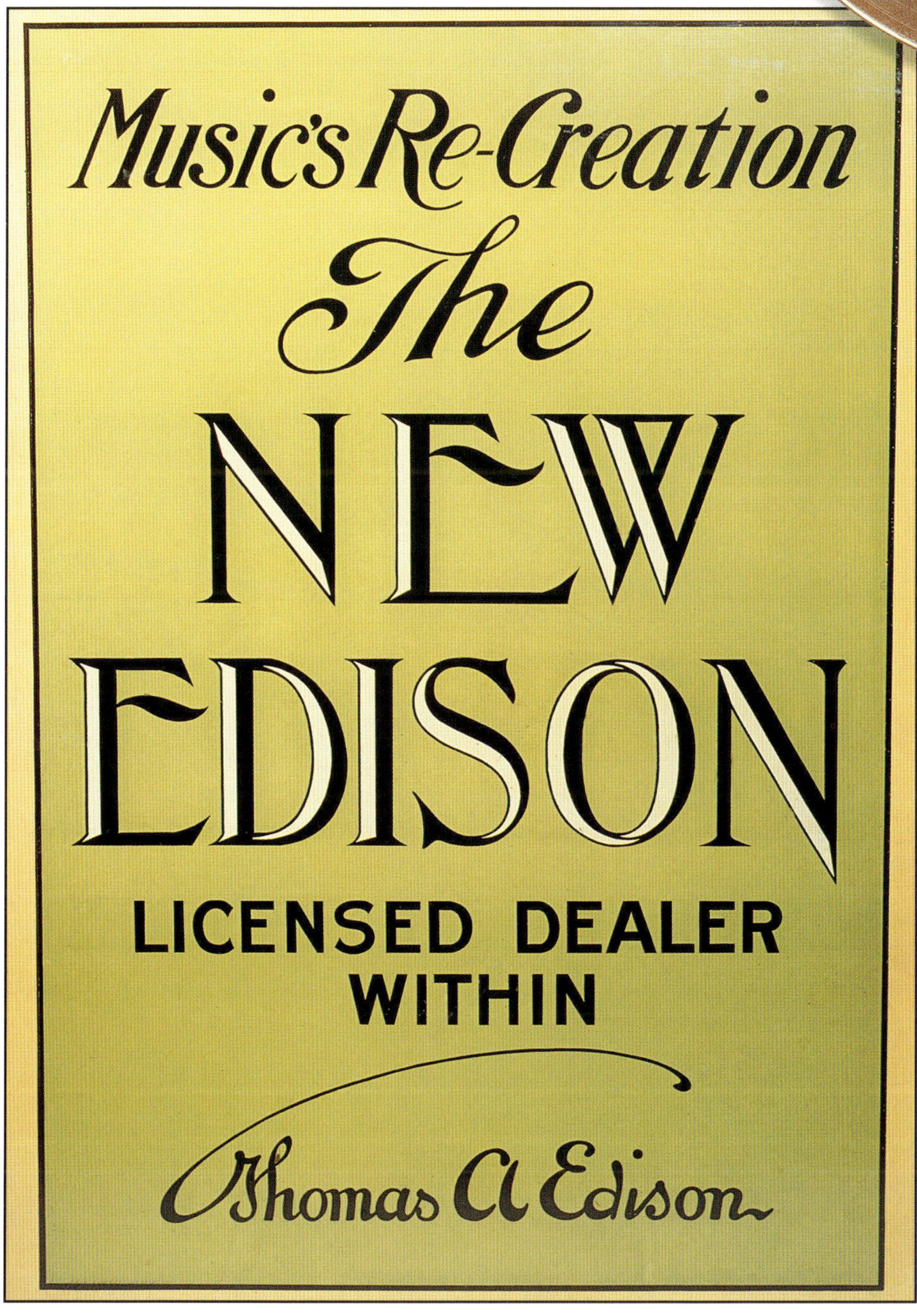

3-49. This Edison dealer's metal sign measures 19" x 27 1/2". The understated text and coloring are in stark contrast to some more decoratively designed signs of the period. *Courtesy of Jim Kintzel.* (Value code: D)

3-50. This Pathé metal advertising sign (10" x 27 1/2") illustrates the truth of the previous caption. *Courtesy of the Charles Hummel collections.* (Value code: D)

3-51. A magazine advertisement from June 1916 stressed the value of the Columbia Grafonola during increasingly turbulent times. "The music-hour has taken the place of the story-hour at dusk…" Dad may have been missing from the picture, but the serene mother and happy children were evidence of the Grafonola's ability to impart, "…the vivid, human quality of *life*…" (Value code: H)

3-52. The *Woman's Home Companion* of July 1916 was the perfect venue for this sentimental treatment. The young couple staring wistfully toward a celestial vision of "family" recalls Wordsworth, "The child is father of the man; And I could wish my days to be bound each to each by natural piety." (*My Heart Leaps Up When I Behold,* 1802.) (Value code: H)

3-53. This 12" tall plush "Nipper," manufactured by J. Henry Smythe, Jr., New York City, was offered to dealers as an advertising item. Dealer cost was $8.00 per dozen (for the 12" size; 15", 17", and 19" sizes were also available). The presentation of such a toy to the child of a prospective customer could have been a powerful inducement to "Look for the Dog" beneath the lid when buying a talking machine. When sold to the customer, the 12" size cost $1.00. *Courtesy of the Tom and Sandi McCarthy collection.* (Value code: E)

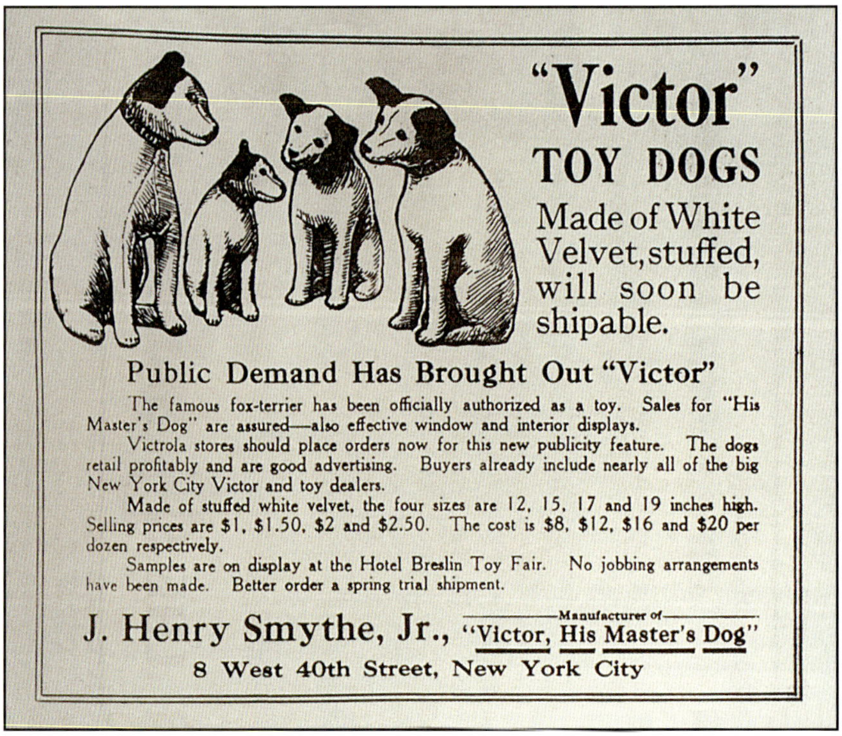

"Victor" TOY DOGS

Made of White Velvet, stuffed, will soon be shipable.

Public Demand Has Brought Out "Victor"

The famous fox-terrier has been officially authorized as a toy. Sales for "His Master's Dog" are assured—also effective window and interior displays.

Victrola stores should place orders now for this new publicity feature. The dogs retail profitably and are good advertising. Buyers already include nearly all of the big New York City Victor and toy dealers.

Made of stuffed white velvet, the four sizes are 12, 15, 17 and 19 inches high. Selling prices are $1, $1.50, $2 and $2.50. The cost is $8, $12, $16 and $20 per dozen respectively.

Samples are on display at the Hotel Breslin Toy Fair. No jobbing arrangements have been made. Better order a spring trial shipment.

J. Henry Smythe, Jr., Manufacturer of "Victor, His Master's Dog"

8 West 40th Street, New York City

3-54. A February 1916 advertisement from *Talking Machine World*. Interestingly, this toy was marketed as "Victor, His Master's Dog," contributing to confusion that still exists regarding the animal's name.

3-55. These Victor signs were used in tandem. The 10" x 28" dealer identification was suspended below the 28" diameter "Red Seal" record. Introduced in 1916, the set was offered to dealers for $6.00. *Courtesy of the Tom and Sandi McCarthy collection.* (Value code: A)

3-56. In 1916, the Paroquette Record Manufacturing Company was formed. One of the brands designed to capitalize on the vertical cut craze, "Par-O-Ket" records had a relatively short life, although the number of surviving examples suggests that they sold well. Shown is "List No. 1," with an 8" Par-O-Ket record (the only size manufactured). *Courtesy of Alan H. Mueller.* (Value code: H)

3-57. This dealer sign was proud to proclaim the Edison Diamond Disc Phonograph to be "A Vital Factor In The Nation's Life." Made of pasteboard on a wooden frame, measures 16 3/4x 23 3/4". *Courtesy of the Gfell family collection.* (Value code: E)

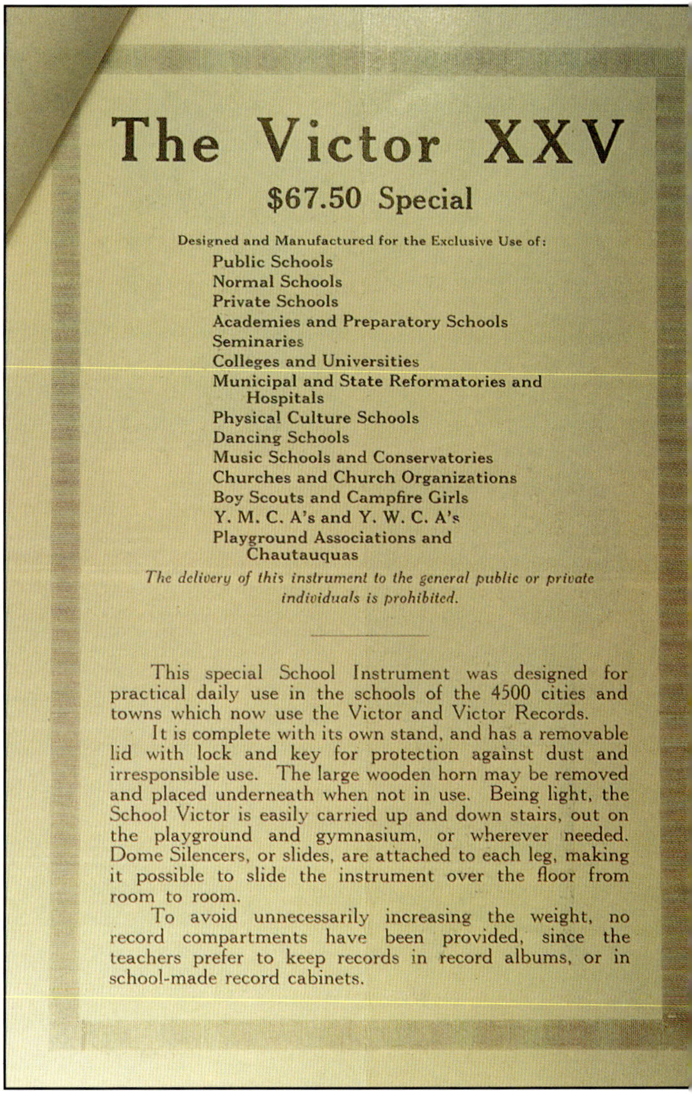

The Victor XXV

$67.50 Special

Designed and Manufactured for the Exclusive Use of:

- Public Schools
- Normal Schools
- Private Schools
- Academies and Preparatory Schools
- Seminaries
- Colleges and Universities
- Municipal and State Reformatories and Hospitals
- Physical Culture Schools
- Dancing Schools
- Music Schools and Conservatories
- Churches and Church Organizations
- Boy Scouts and Campfire Girls
- Y. M. C. A's and Y. W. C. A's
- Playground Associations and Chautauquas

The delivery of this instrument to the general public or private individuals is prohibited.

This special School Instrument was designed for practical daily use in the schools of the 4500 cities and towns which now use the Victor and Victor Records.

It is complete with its own stand, and has a removable lid with lock and key for protection against dust and irresponsible use. The large wooden horn may be removed and placed underneath when not in use. Being light, the School Victor is easily carried up and down stairs, out on the playground and gymnasium, or wherever needed. Dome Silencers, or slides, are attached to each leg, making it possible to slide the instrument over the floor from room to room.

To avoid unnecessarily increasing the weight, no record compartments have been provided, since the teachers prefer to keep records in record albums, or in school-made record cabinets.

3-58. This flyer, dated January 22, 1917, advertised the Victor "XXV." Note the admonition, "The delivery of this instrument to the general public or private individuals is prohibited." Victor placed great emphasis on the use of its products for teaching, devoting far more advertising to these machines than did Edison or Columbia with respectively similar instruments. *Courtesy of Ron Seavers.* (Value code: F)

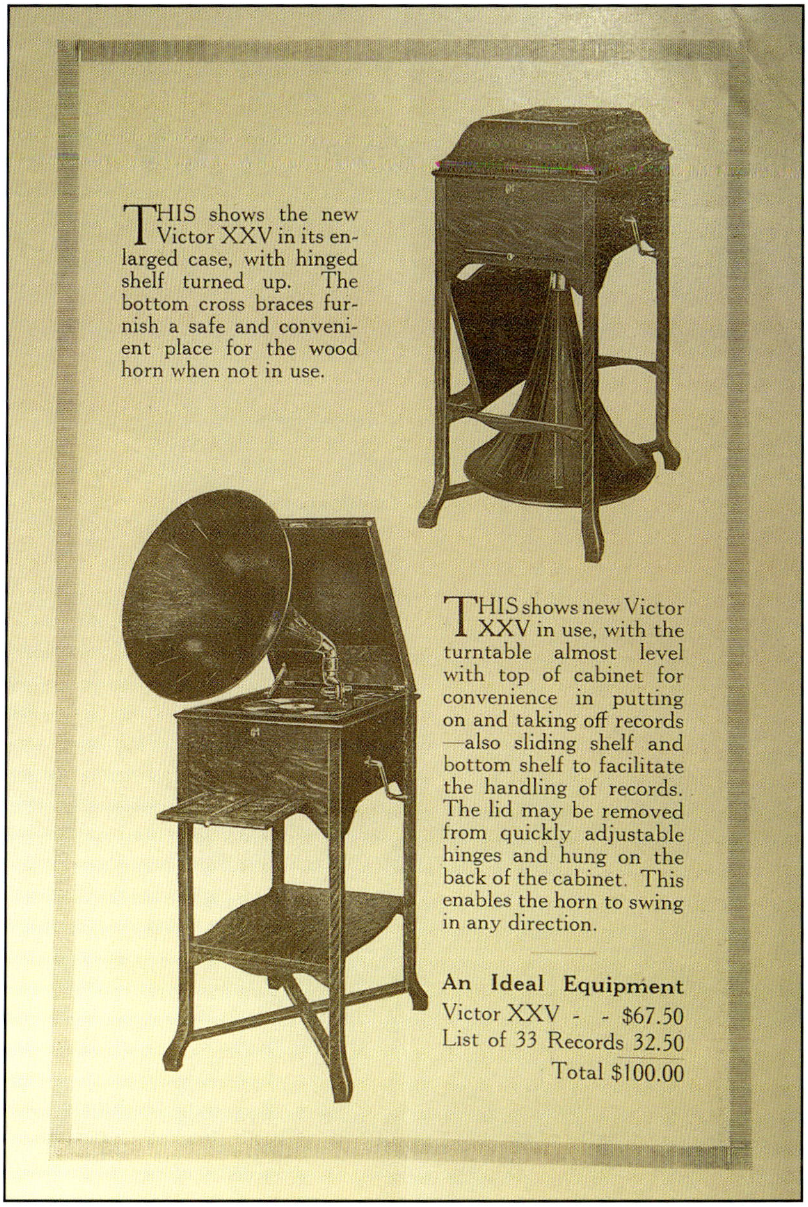

3-59. Another page of the flyer for the Victor "XXV." This was the only instrument marketed by the company that began life as a "Victor," and was later marketed as a "Victrola." In both instances, the "XXV" designation was used. *Courtesy of Ron Seavers.*

3-60. This British postcard included song lyrics, and prominently depicted a reflex-horn talking machine. It is obvious that the smiling Tommies are transported back home to sweethearts and mothers simply by playing their phonograph. *Courtesy of Dennis Peterson.* (Value code: G)

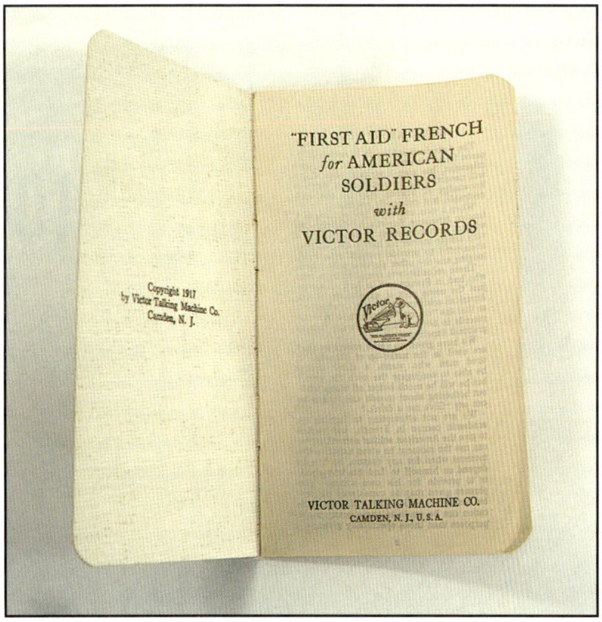

3-61. One of the undeniable contributions the Victor Talking Machine Company made to the war effort. Shown is a 3" x 5" booklet meant to teach "First Aid French" to Allied soldiers fighting in a foreign land. *Courtesy of Alan H. Mueller*. (Value code: H)

3-62. This 27 1/2" x 38 3/4" poster depicted a lanky American conversing with a pretty French peasant, while her languid countryman looked on. This promotion was clearly aimed at United States soldiers bound for Europe. *Courtesy of Nina and Dave Heitz*. (Value code: B)

3-63. A bizarre composition for a photograph: a Victrola "IX" topped with a naval cap from the "Kronprinz Wilhelm," flanked by two cats. This German postcard was mailed in August 1917. The sailor and tents in the background suggest that the photograph was taken at a military establishment. *Courtesy of Dennis Peterson.* (Value code: G)

3-64. "Imagine, if you can, a nation going off into war without the thrill of music!" This December 1917 magazine advertisement embodies virtually all the emotional selling points employed by talking machine companies during the Great War. Perhaps lacking the spirituality offered in some Columbia ads, Victor was nevertheless the champion flag-waving phonograph firm of the war years. Implicit in these appeals was, of course, a self-serving message: "The Victrola performs no mean service to the nation." *Courtesy of Alan H. Mueller.* (Value code: H)

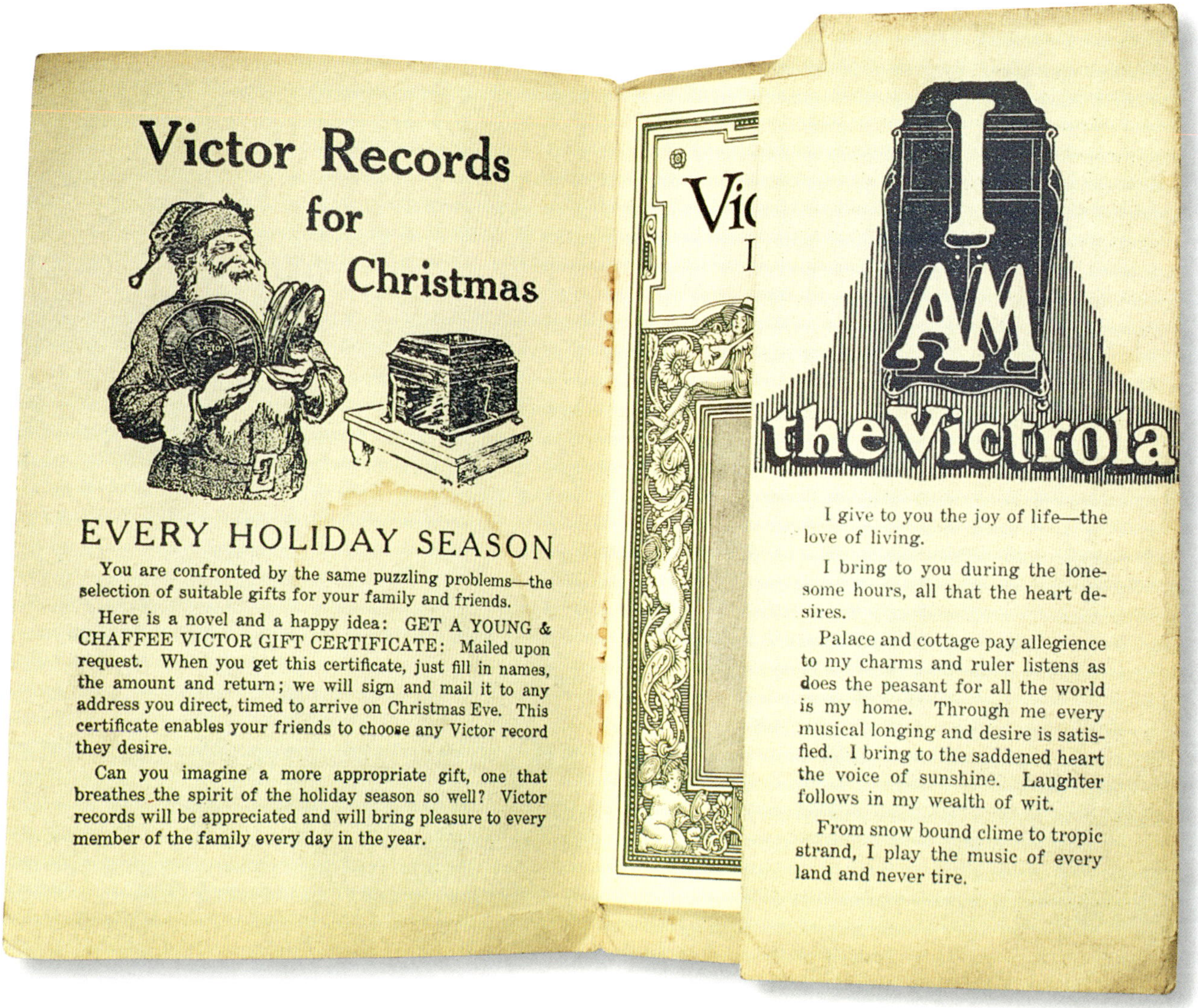

3-65. Over the years, monthly record supplements became enormously influential in stimulating sales. The major record manufacturers distributed supplements to their dealers in large numbers, to be handed out or mailed to customers. In this instance, the Young & Chaffee Furniture Company of Newago, Michigan employed this distinctive jacket to enclose direct-mail copies of Victor's December 1917 supplement. (Value code: H)

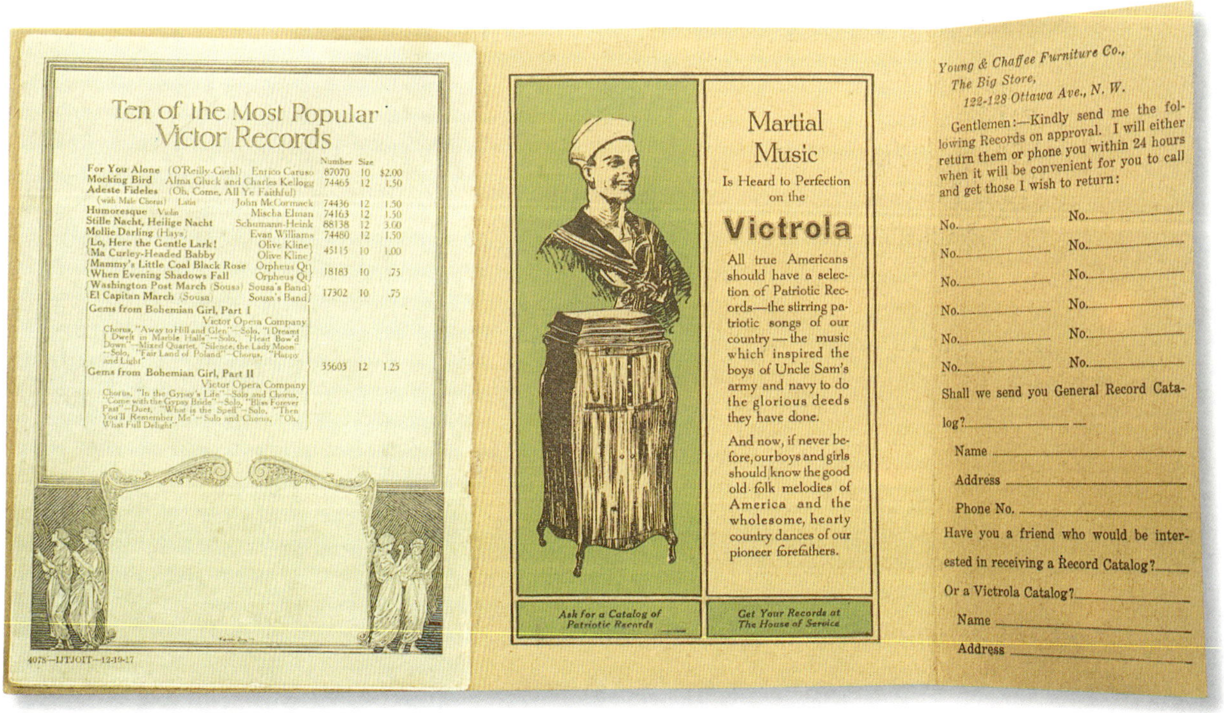

3-66. This February 1918 Victor supplement was mailed to a potential customer in an advertising jacket plugging martial music. The Young & Chaffee Furniture Company encouraged all "true Americans" to purchase "Patriotic Records." *Courtesy of Alan H. Mueller.* (Value code: H)

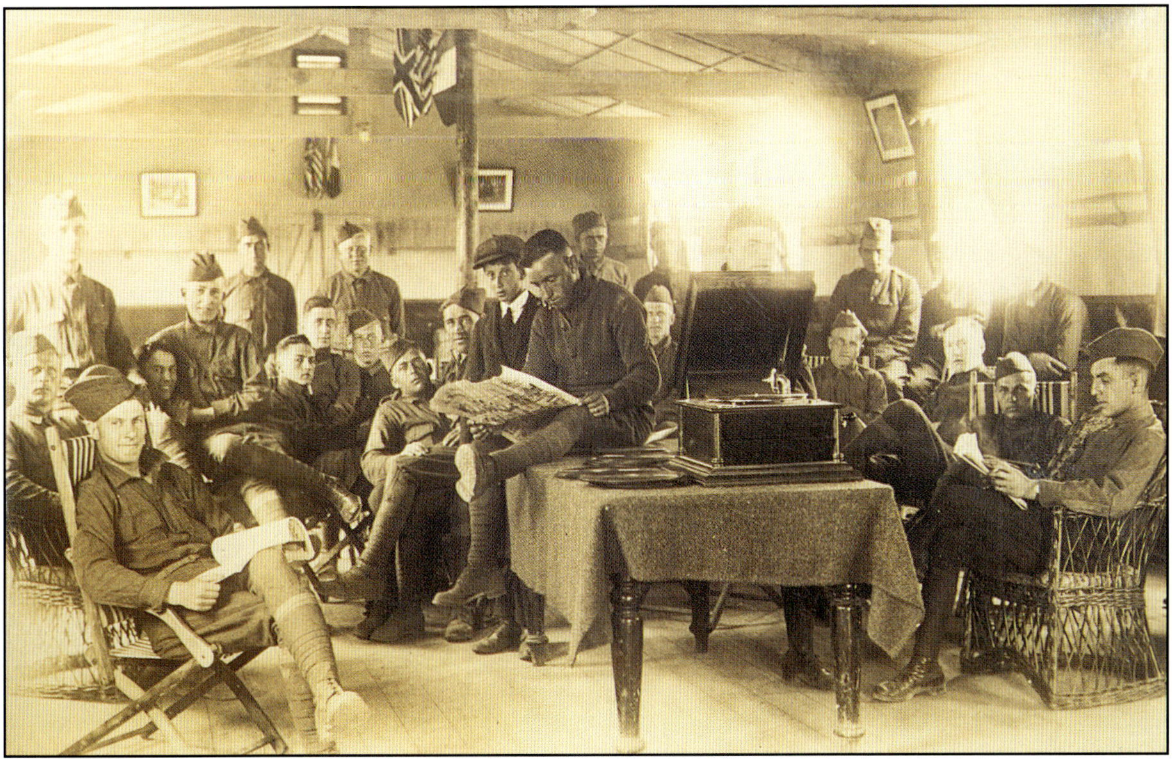

3-67. Soldiers relax away from the front beneath British, French, and United States flags, while listening to a Columbia Grafonola. *Courtesy of Dennis Peterson*. (Value code: G)

52 The Literary Digest for May 18, 1918

The Literary Digest for May 18, 1918 53

By these men we shall conquer!

Spread before you is a panorama of patriotism.

The world must be made safe for democracy. Here are the men who will make it so.

The moral and spiritual forces that will carry us on to victory no man can measure. The books you send, the letters you write, the music the men have to enjoy—do not for one moment underestimate the weight they will throw into the final balance of success.

The pictures shown here are typical of the spirit of Uncle Sam. He has a song in his heart, a tune on his Yankee lips, and an iron resolve deep in his liberty-loving soul.

This company is proud that its products are a mighty Armament of Hope, cheering and strengthening the spirit of our fighting men.

Wherever the soldiers and sailors of Uncle Sam and his Allies are gathered, there the Victrola is singing its song of courage. The Victrola is literally following the flag. Through the unseen power of music, it supplies and renews that vast human dynamo that is driving our war machine to its goal of glory.

Across the shadows of No Man's Land stand the embattled foes. But there are more foes than these to be vanquished. In the stern work of war, fatigue, discouragement, hesitation are inevitably encountered. Bullets will not suffice in these battles of the soul. In these sore trials, music is the great physician. It satisfies the hunger of the mind, the thirst of the spirit, the deep and hidden yearning of the wearied soul for words of comfort that cannot be spoken and that only music can whisper.

In camp and trench, on transport and battleship, in hospital, church and cantonment, in the welfare houses of the Y. M. C. A., the K. of C., and the Y. M. H. A., the Victrola is the unflagging, and often the *only*, source of music and entertainment. It is so portable that it can be taken anywhere and *unaided* it gives forth the music and laughter of the world's greatest artists. The Victrola is teaching wireless and French to our Army and Navy. Victrolas and Victor Records are day and night advancing the cause of freedom on the battlefields of the entire world.

Every Victrola in the service of Uncle Sam is a source of actual war strength. Every Victor Record at the front is a winged messenger of victory, doing its humble but by no means unimportant bit to vanquish the powers of darkness and make the world safe for democracy.

Victor Talking Machine Co., Camden, N. J., U. S. A.

The Victrola enlisted in the War for Democracy

Victor

"HIS MASTER'S VOICE"

3-68. Victor presented this "panorama of patriotism" in magazines during May 1918. Shown are uniformed music-lovers in training camps, on board ship, on duty in the snowy Alps, in stateside community/civic halls such as the Knights of Columbus, YMCA, and Young Men's Hebrew Association, vigilant in the trenches at Gallipoli, relaxing behind the lines, and even in a hospital, trying to "forget" the horrors of war. In every photograph is the stalwart Victrola, "…a source of actual war strength," and Victor records, "…winged messenger[s] of victory…" *Courtesy of Alan H. Mueller*. (Value code: H)

3-69. Men, not nations, fought wars. These German officers, like their American, British, and French counterparts, enjoyed recorded music beside a trench in a quiet sector of the front. *Courtesy of Dennis Peterson.* (Value code: G)

3-70. Three advertising electrotypes for use in newspapers. Edison's sales organization provided stock electrotypes such as these at little or no cost to dealers for many years. Usually, the dealer was required to submit a clipping to Thomas A. Edison Inc.: proof that the electrotype had been used. This image has been reversed so that the items can be more easily read. *Courtesy of the Gfell family collection.* (Value code: G)

3-71. Another cut, this one measuring 8 3/4" x 12 1/4", for the Edison Amberola. This image has been reversed so that the item can be more easily read. *Courtesy of Brady Jeffcoat.* (Value code: F)

3-72. This festive horse-drawn parade float, circa 1918, was sponsored by Steving and Streams, Undertaking and Furniture. *Courtesy of the Tom and Sandi McCarthy collection.* (Value code: G)

3-73. This articulated trade card from the late teens established the hoity-toity setting without presenting the product. (Value code: F)

3-74. The side leaves of the card open to reveal the luxurious scene into which the smartly-attired visitors enter. An appropriately puffed-up Sonora awaits them.

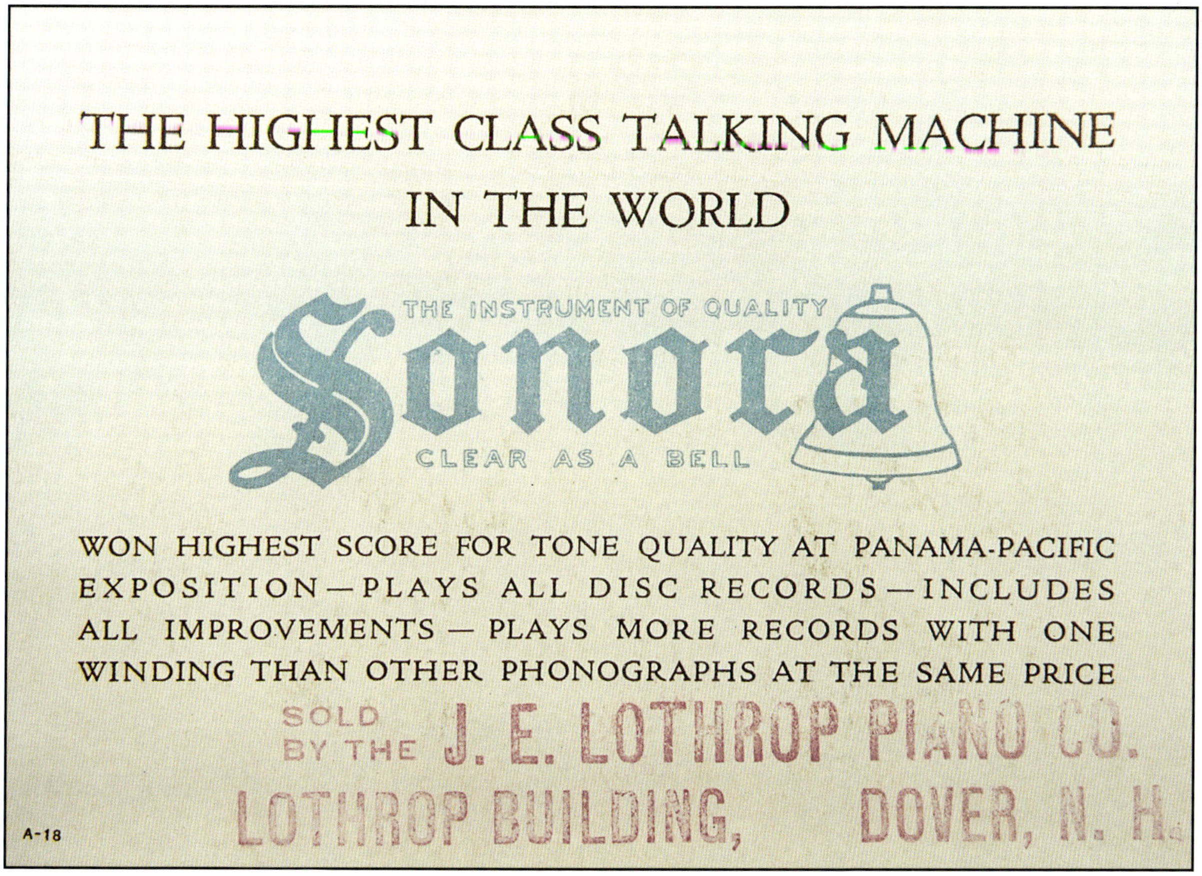

3-75. On its reverse side, the card lists some key selling points. Measures 3 1/2" x 5", folded.

3-76. The Sonora department of this store resembles a Mae West look-alike contest, with shoulder-to-shoulder voluptuaries. *Courtesy of Dennis Peterson.* (Value code: G)

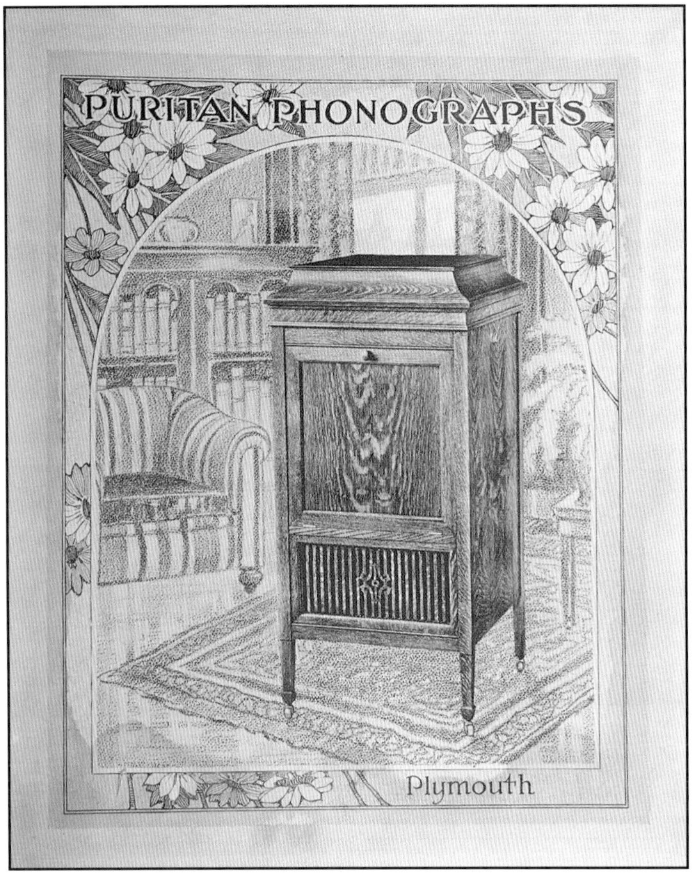

3-77. In the mid-teens, the Wisconsin Chair Company of Port Washington began manufacturing cabinets for phonograph companies. Rapid expansion in the talking machine market tempted the Chair Company to launch its own line of instruments. Late in 1916, a subsidiary of Wisconsin Chair was re-christened the United Phonographs Corporation, and set up a factory in Sheboygan. The trade name "Puritan" was chosen, although the firm also produced machines that were sold under various "client" brands. The gimmick of the "Puritan" was an elongated internal sound chamber which dispensed the sound from the lower portion of the cabinet. A dealer display card showing a rather basic model, the "Plymouth." *Courtesy of David P. Graber.* (Value code: F)

3-79. The most recognized of the "Puritan" models is the "Artline." Who could forget its Marie-Dressler-without-her-corset look? The merit of the instrument's "ground-level" horn opening is debatable – a deep shag carpet might render it mute. *Courtesy of David P. Graber.* (Value code: F)

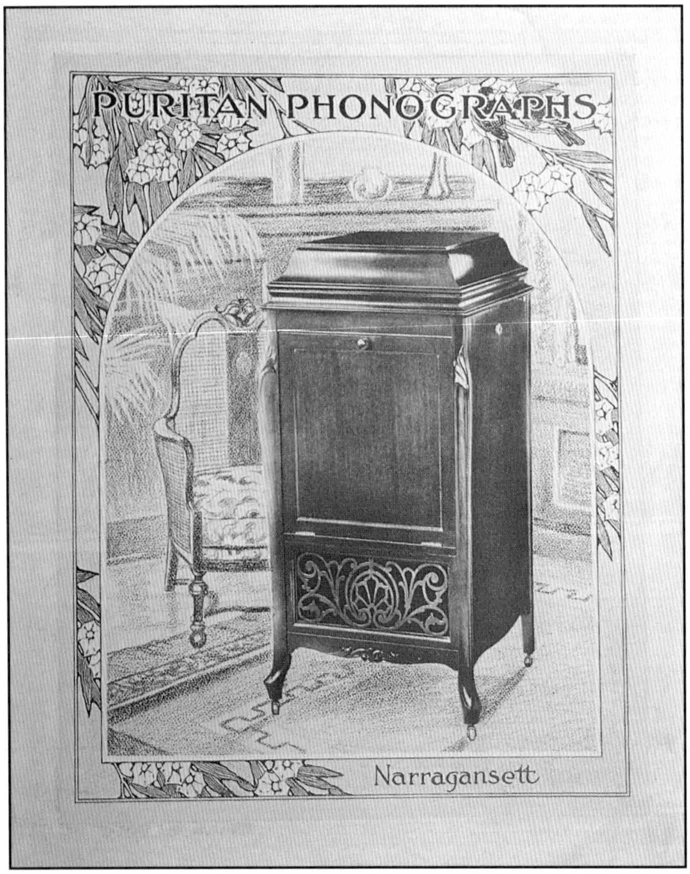

3-78. Somewhat up the ladder of importance was the "Narragansett." The cupboard above the horn grille contained record storage space. *Courtesy of David P. Graber.* (Value code: F)

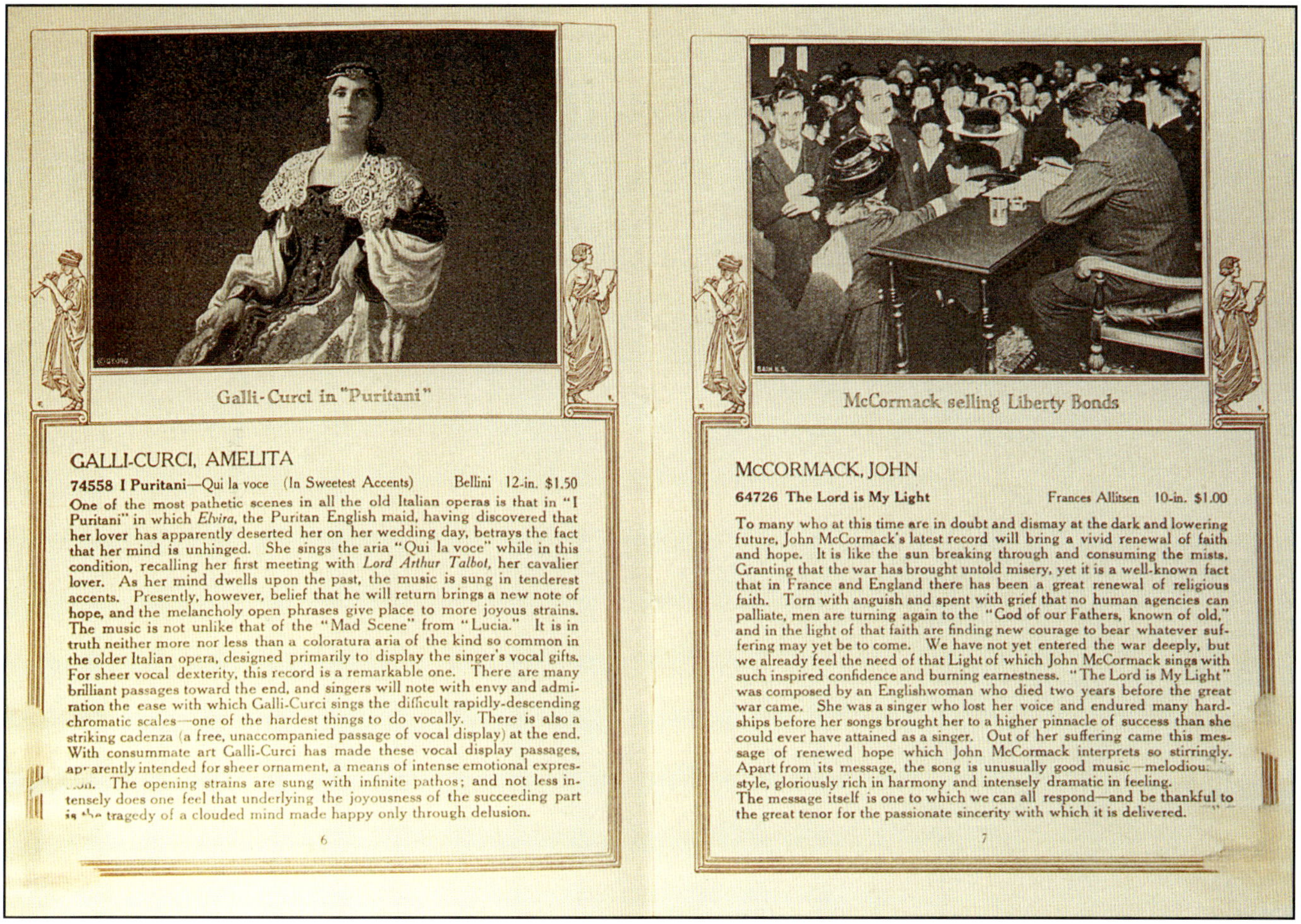

Galli-Curci in "Puritani"

GALLI-CURCI, AMELITA

74558 I Puritani—Qui la voce (In Sweetest Accents) Bellini 12-in. $1.50

One of the most pathetic scenes in all the old Italian operas is that in "I Puritani" in which *Elvira*, the Puritan English maid, having discovered that her lover has apparently deserted her on her wedding day, betrays the fact that her mind is unhinged. She sings the aria "Qui la voce" while in this condition, recalling her first meeting with *Lord Arthur Talbot*, her cavalier lover. As her mind dwells upon the past, the music is sung in tenderest accents. Presently, however, belief that he will return brings a new note of hope, and the melancholy open phrases give place to more joyous strains. The music is not unlike that of the "Mad Scene" from "Lucia." It is in truth neither more nor less than a coloratura aria of the kind so common in the older Italian opera, designed primarily to display the singer's vocal gifts. For sheer vocal dexterity, this record is a remarkable one. There are many brilliant passages toward the end, and singers will note with envy and admiration the ease with which Galli-Curci sings the difficult rapidly-descending chromatic scales—one of the hardest things to do vocally. There is also a striking cadenza (a free, unaccompanied passage of vocal display) at the end. With consummate art Galli-Curci has made these vocal display passages, apparently intended for sheer ornament, a means of intense emotional expres-[illegible]on. The opening strains are sung with infinite pathos; and not less intensely does one feel that underlying the joyousness of the succeeding part is the tragedy of a clouded mind made happy only through delusion.

6

McCormack selling Liberty Bonds

McCORMACK, JOHN

64726 The Lord is My Light Frances Allitsen 10-in. $1.00

To many who at this time are in doubt and dismay at the dark and lowering future, John McCormack's latest record will bring a vivid renewal of faith and hope. It is like the sun breaking through and consuming the mists. Granting that the war has brought untold misery, yet it is a well-known fact that in France and England there has been a great renewal of religious faith. Torn with anguish and spent with grief that no human agencies can palliate, men are turning again to the "God of our Fathers, known of old," and in the light of that faith are finding new courage to bear whatever suffering may yet be to come. We have not yet entered the war deeply, but we already feel the need of that Light of which John McCormack sings with such inspired confidence and burning earnestness. "The Lord is My Light" was composed by an Englishwoman who died two years before the great war came. She was a singer who lost her voice and endured many hardships before her songs brought her to a higher pinnacle of success than she could ever have attained as a singer. Out of her suffering came this message of renewed hope which John McCormack interprets so stirringly. Apart from its message, the song is unusually good music—melodiou[illegible] style, gloriously rich in harmony and intensely dramatic in feeling.
The message itself is one to which we can all respond—and be thankful to the great tenor for the passionate sincerity with which it is delivered. [illegible]"

7

3-80. In this April 1918 Victor supplement, Galli-Curci may have appeared radiant, but it was John McCormack selling Liberty Bonds that would magnify his popularity with the American public. *Courtesy of Alan H. Mueller*. (Value code: H)

3-81. The soldiers aboard *Transport Mercury* enjoyed books, cards, a banjolin, and of course, the Victrola. *Courtesy of Dennis Peterson*. (Value code: G)

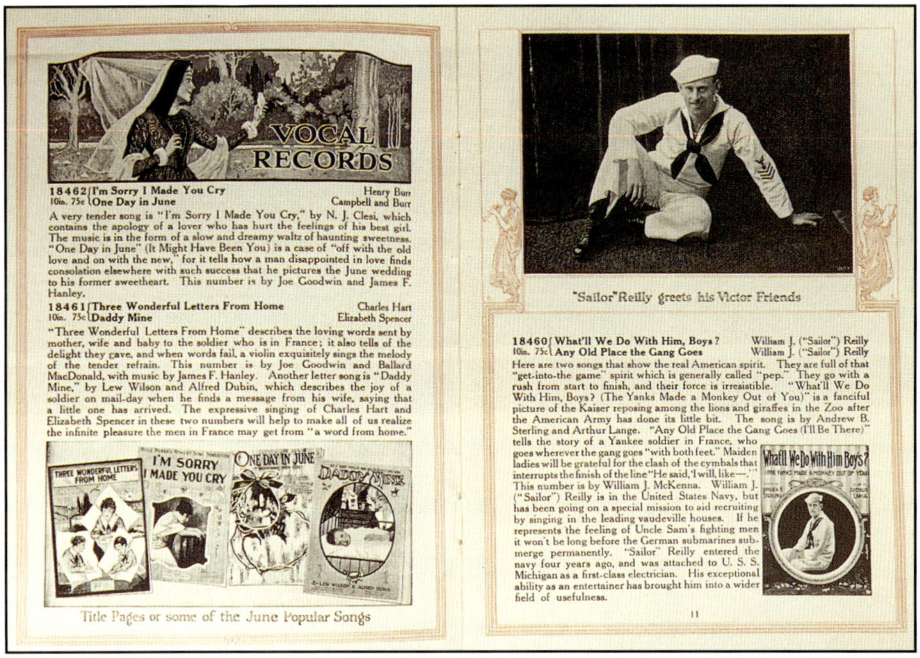

VOCAL RECORDS

18462 { **I'm Sorry I Made You Cry** — Henry Burr
10in. 75c { **One Day in June** — Campbell and Burr

A very tender song is "I'm Sorry I Made You Cry," by N. J. Clesi, which contains the apology of a lover who has hurt the feelings of his best girl. The music is in the form of a slow and dreamy waltz of haunting sweetness. "One Day in June" (It Might Have Been You) is a case of "off with the old love and on with the new," for it tells how a man disappointed in love finds consolation elsewhere with such success that he pictures the June wedding to his former sweetheart. This number is by Joe Goodwin and James F. Hanley.

18461 { **Three Wonderful Letters From Home** — Charles Hart
10in. 75c { **Daddy Mine** — Elizabeth Spencer

"Three Wonderful Letters From Home" describes the loving words sent by mother, wife and baby to the soldier who is in France; it also tells of the delight they gave, and when words fail, a violin exquisitely sings the melody of the tender refrain. This number is by Joe Goodwin and Ballard MacDonald, with music by James F. Hanley. Another letter song is "Daddy Mine," by Lew Wilson and Alfred Dubin, which describes the joy of a soldier on mail-day when he finds a message from his wife, saying that a little one has arrived. The expressive singing of Charles Hart and Elizabeth Spencer in these two numbers will help to make all of us realize the infinite pleasure the men in France may get from "a word from home."

THREE WONDERFUL LETTERS FROM HOME — I'M SORRY I MADE YOU CRY — ONE DAY IN JUNE — DADDY MINE

Title Pages or some of the June Popular Songs

"Sailor" Reilly greets his Victor Friends

18460 { **What'll We Do With Him, Boys?** — William J. ("Sailor") Reilly
10in. 75c { **Any Old Place the Gang Goes** — William J. ("Sailor") Reilly

Here are two songs that show the real American spirit. They are full of that "get-into-the game" spirit which is generally called "pep." They go with a rush from start to finish, and their force is irresistible. "What'll We Do With Him, Boys? (The Yanks Made a Monkey Out of You)" is a fanciful picture of the Kaiser reposing among the lions and giraffes in the Zoo after the American Army has done its little bit. The song is by Andrew B. Sterling and Arthur Lange. "Any Old Place the Gang Goes (I'll Be There)" tells the story of a Yankee soldier in France, who goes wherever the gang goes "with both feet." Maiden ladies will be grateful for the clash of the cymbals that interrupts the finish of the line "He said, 'I will, like—.'" This number is by William J. McKenna. William J. ("Sailor") Reilly is in the United States Navy, but has been going on a special mission to aid recruiting by singing in the leading vaudeville houses. If he represents the feeling of Uncle Sam's fighting men it won't be long before the German submarines submerge permanently. "Sailor" Reilly entered the navy four years ago, and was attached to U. S. S. Michigan as a first-class electrician. His exceptional ability as an entertainer has brought him into a wider field of usefulness.

What'll We Do With Him Boys?

11

3-82. This June 1918 Victor supplement featured a record by William J. ("Sailor") Reilly. The copy writer boasted, "If he represents the feeling of Uncle Sam's fighting men it won't be long before the German submarines submerge permanently." *Courtesy of Alan H. Mueller.* (Value code: H)

3-83. The transition of phonograph advertising in magazines from dancing to doughboys was sometimes gradual, depending on the audience. Even after more than a year of American involvement in the war, this Victor advertisement that appeared in the July 1918 issue of *Woman's Magazine* stressed that, "Any time is dancing time," with only one bit of khaki evident among the dancers (fifth from the right). (Value code: H)

3-84. The presence on deck of a posh Columbia "BY" Graphophone with its mahogany horn might seem odd to us today. It should, however, be remembered that the machine was a decade out-of-date; probably donated by its original owner. The no-nonsense tars listening to the music were no slaves to phonographic fashion. *Courtesy of Dennis Peterson.* (Value code: G)

3-85. The Army-Navy Club of Minneapolis, along with pool tables and a bar discreetly tucked into the background, featured an oak Victrola "X." *Courtesy of Dennis Peterson.* (Value code: G)

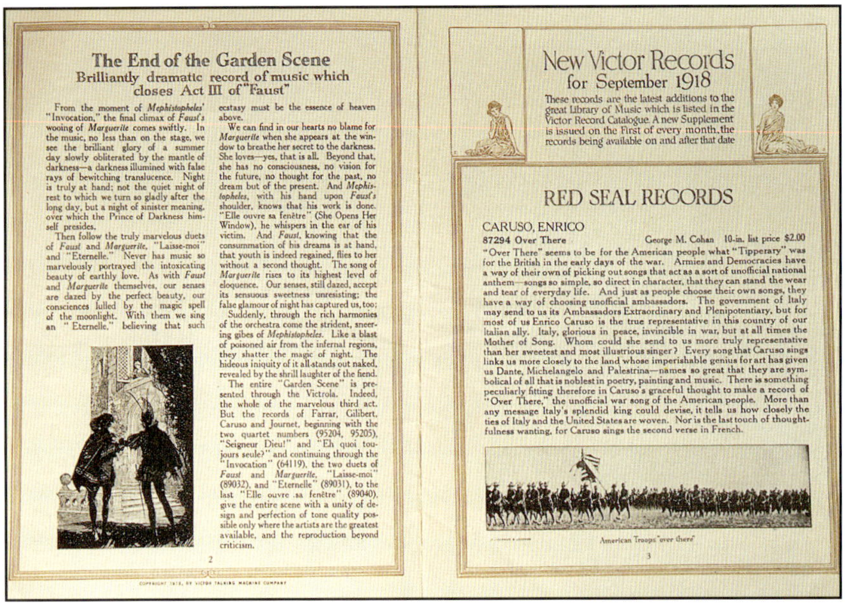

The End of the Garden Scene

Brilliantly dramatic record of music which closes Act III of "Faust"

From the moment of *Mephistopheles'* "Invocation," the final climax of *Faust's* wooing of *Marguerite* comes swiftly. In the music, no less than on the stage, we see the brilliant glory of a summer day slowly obliterated by the mantle of darkness—a darkness illumined with false rays of bewitching translucence. Night is truly at hand; not the quiet night of rest to which we turn so gladly after the long day, but a night of sinister meaning, over which the Prince of Darkness himself presides.

Then follow the truly marvelous duets of *Faust* and *Marguerite*, "Laisse-moi" and "Eternelle." Never has music so marvelously portrayed the intoxicating beauty of earthly love. As with *Faust* and *Marguerite* themselves, our senses are dazed by the perfect beauty, our consciences lulled by the magic spell of the moonlight. With them we sing an "Eternelle," believing that such ecstasy must be the essence of heaven above.

We can find in our hearts no blame for *Marguerite* when she appears at the window to breathe her secret to the darkness. She loves—yes, that is all. Beyond that, she has no consciousness, no vision for the future, no thought for the past, no dream but of the present. And *Mephistopheles*, with his hand upon *Faust's* shoulder, knows that his work is done. "Elle ouvre sa fenêtre" (She Opens Her Window), he whispers in the ear of his victim. And *Faust*, knowing that the consummation of his dreams is at hand, that youth is indeed regained, flies to her without a second thought. The song of *Marguerite* rises to its highest level of eloquence. Our senses, still dazed, accept its sensuous sweetness unresisting; the false glamour of night has captured us, too;

Suddenly, through the rich harmonies of the orchestra come the strident, sneering gibes of *Mephistopheles*. Like a blast of poisoned air from the infernal regions, they shatter the magic of night. The hideous iniquity of it all stands out naked, revealed by the shrill laughter of the fiend.

The entire "Garden Scene" is presented through the Victrola. Indeed, the whole of the marvelous third act. But the records of Farrar, Gilibert, Caruso and Journet, beginning with the two quartet numbers (95204, 95205), "Seigneur Dieu!" and "Eh quoi toujours seule?" and continuing through the "Invocation" (64119), the two duets of *Faust* and *Marguerite*, "Laisse-moi" (89032), and "Eternelle" (89031), to the last "Elle ouvre sa fenêtre" (89040), give the entire scene with a unity of design and perfection of tone quality possible only where the artists are the greatest available, and the reproduction beyond criticism.

2

New Victor Records for September 1918

These records are the latest additions to the great Library of Music which is listed in the Victor Record Catalogue. A new Supplement is issued on the First of every month, the records being available on and after that date

RED SEAL RECORDS

CARUSO, ENRICO

87294 Over There — George M. Cohan 10-in. list price $2.00

"Over There" seems to be for the American people what "Tipperary" was for the British in the early days of the war. Armies and Democracies have a way of their own of picking out songs that act as a sort of unofficial national anthem—songs so simple, so direct in character, that they can stand the wear and tear of everyday life. And just as people choose their own songs, they have a way of choosing unofficial ambassadors. The government of Italy may send to us its Ambassadors Extraordinary and Plenipotentiary, but for most of us Enrico Caruso is the true representative in this country of our Italian ally. Italy, glorious in peace, invincible in war, but at all times the Mother of Song. Whom could she send to us more truly representative than her sweetest and most illustrious singer? Every song that Caruso sings links us more closely to the land whose imperishable genius for art has given us Dante, Michelangelo and Palestrina—names so great that they are symbolical of all that is noblest in poetry, painting and music. There is something peculiarly fitting therefore in Caruso's graceful thought to make a record of "Over There," the unofficial war song of the American people. More than any message Italy's splendid king could devise, it tells us how closely the ties of Italy and the United States are woven. Nor is the last touch of thoughtfulness wanting, for Caruso sings the second verse in French.

American Troops "over there"

3

3-86. This Victor supplement announced the fact that the great Enrico Caruso had recorded the "...unofficial war song of the American people." George M. Cohan's "Over There" had indeed inspired the nation, and the addition of the legendary Caruso as one of the song's exponents was a coup for Victor. In a delirious burst of fervor for war-stricken France, the supplement assured the reader that, as a "...last touch of thoughtfulness," Caruso had sung the second verse in French. *Courtesy of Alan H. Mueller*. (Value code: H)

3-87. In what appears to be a hospital ward, soldiers in non-combat dress relax with a phonograph. *Courtesy of Dennis Peterson*. (Value code: G)

3-88. Marching soldiers, a pining sweetheart, and stalwart wireless operators all lent atmosphere to record advertising. The April 1918 Victor supplement to the right advertised the company's wireless telegraphy teaching discs. The Victor supplement in the center was issued four months after the war's end, but is a reminder that it took a long time for the last of the fighting men to return home. Inside, the text opined, "How little we know even of our own Navy – especially that section of it which existed before the war and will go on existing, silently, efficiently, now the war is over." (Value code: H)

3-89. In late 1918, the J.W. Rowlands Company of Lima, Ohio sent this 3 1/2" x 5 1/4" Christmas postcard, complete with a depiction of a Victor record featuring John McCormack singing "The Star Spangled Banner." *Courtesy of the Tom and Sandi McCarthy collection.* (Value code: H)

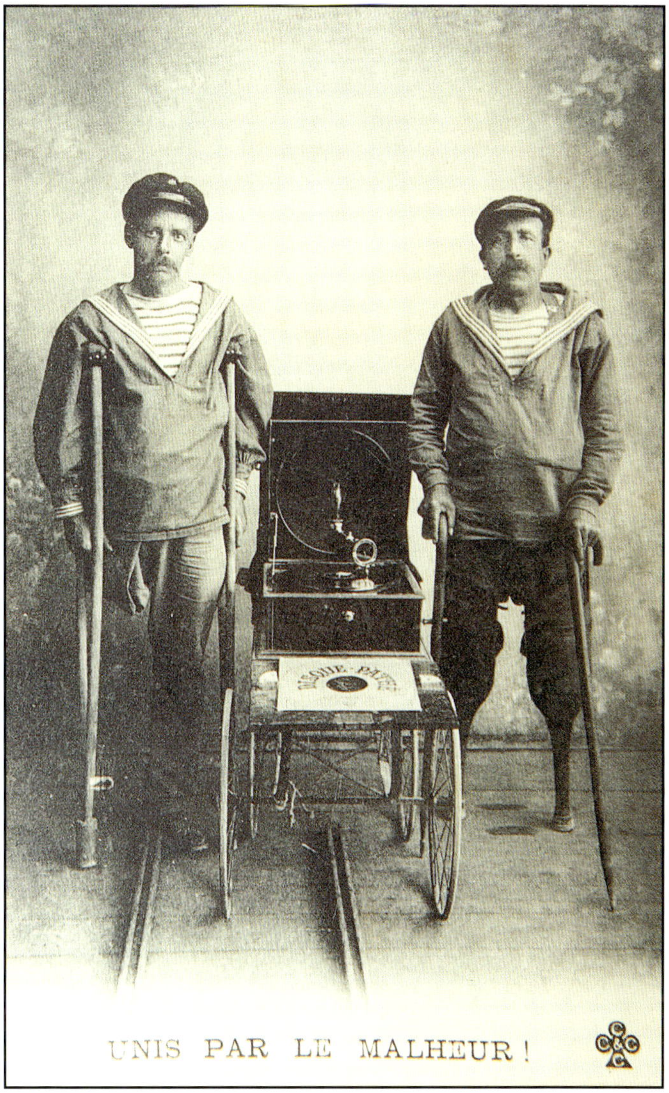

3-90. "Together in misfortune." The attention of passersby was drawn to the plight of maimed Great War veterans by the music of a phonograph. The captions explained that one man (Mr. Desjardins) was paralyzed and the other (Mr. Souque) was blind. A cup collected donations as the Pathé Modèle "D" played. The machine was about ten years out-of-date, probably the old family instrument. "Albert Desjardins, Ex-Representative of Commerce, victim of duty [to his country], family man. 42, Rue Clodion, Nancy." *Courtesy of Philippe Le Ray.* (Value code: H)

3-91. The aftermath of vicious conflict; "together in misfortune." A talking machine provided musical background to a heart-wrenching scene. Like their comrades in the previous illustration, these Frenchmen dressed in their navy uniforms were not really begging, but carrying on a little enterprise: open-air concerts, in this instance employing a Pathé "reflex" instrument mounted on a cart. *Courtesy of Philippe Le Ray.* (Value code: H)

Chapter Four

MODERN TIMES, 1919~1929

It has often been remarked that First World War was the end of the "old" world, and the beginning of an entirely new one. Buried in the mud of trenches, along with the sabers and plumes of nineteenth century military glory, were the rigid societal constraints of a western civilization that had all but blown itself up. Into the limitless void of this catastrophic explosion were sucked the brittle, desiccated Victorian manners and mores of the survivors.

The 1920s were like the 1960s, periods when many persons' life focus was suddenly immediate. The vicious Great War erased in many a desire to contemplate the past or to hope for the future. In the 1960s, the cumulative anxiety of twenty years living under the threat of The Bomb produced a similar reaction. Each of these decades was a *gestalt*, greater than the sum of its parts. However, specific circumstances ineluctably determined the trajectory of the 1920s.

There was considerable inflation and shortage of raw material during the war. Columbia 10" "popular" disc records cost 65 cents in 1915. In 1916, they rose to 75 cents, which might have been attributed to ordinary inflation. However, the war economy produced a further increase to 85 cents in 1918. Columbia popular records had risen nearly 25% in a handful of years. Talking machines were similarly affected, with the retail tickets of Edison's cylinder and disc Phonographs, originally conceived as "model-number-designates-price," rising steadily. The Diamond Disc "C-150," introduced in 1915 at $150.00, rose to $175.00 after September 1918. Edison's cylinder Amberola "75," inexpensively constructed and no particular bargain at $75.00 in 1915, cost the customer $100.00 by the end of 1918.

Although many prices came down after the Armistice, the overheated American economy continued to chug at full speed. A post-war boom resulted, but recession hit in 1921. The elation over the war finally ending was replaced by the realities of a world profoundly altered. American soil had not been rent by bombs, but Americans, bent by their first experiences in a world theatre, were no longer the same. Dozens of independent brands of talking machine that had sprung up like mushrooms after a rainstorm during the late teens and start of the 1920s, and which had poured thousands and thousands of advertising dollars into the economy, began to disappear. Even the major companies were in trouble, particularly Columbia. A vast and varied visual feast of advertising signs, posters, trade cards and promotional objects, which had been generated by the proliferation of the independents, evaporated.

Yet, this was prelude to the main event. The American economy rebounded, and began its dizzying rise to the fragile heights from which it would plunge in 1929. We see reflected in the advertising of the 1920s the abandonment of traditional expression. The plucky yet demure Gibson Girl became the irreverent Flapper. Traditional product lines, too, were deserted. The Victor company, after struggling to maintain the time-honored appearance of its Victrolas in the face of an ever less interested public, introduced dramatic departures of design in 1925. Its rivals followed suit. The latter half of the 1920s would bring fresh ideas, new imagery and another spending-spree to talking machine advertising.

4-1. A 10" diameter Columbia pressing made for the Olds Motor Works, circa 1919. Records such as this, distributed to employees for their amusement, were more commonly produced than advertising records. About ten years later, Victor would press a genuine advertising disc for Olds. (Value code: H)

4-2. Columbia had developed a significant sideline in "vanity recordings" which lasted for several years, so promotional records were not new when the National Biscuit Company wanted to have a recording made by its Shredded Wheat Band. The "Trumpet and Drum Corps and Pipers" tooted the "Shredded Wheat March" on this Columbia 12" disc. Also shown is a postcard of the Nabisco factory in Niagara Falls, New York.

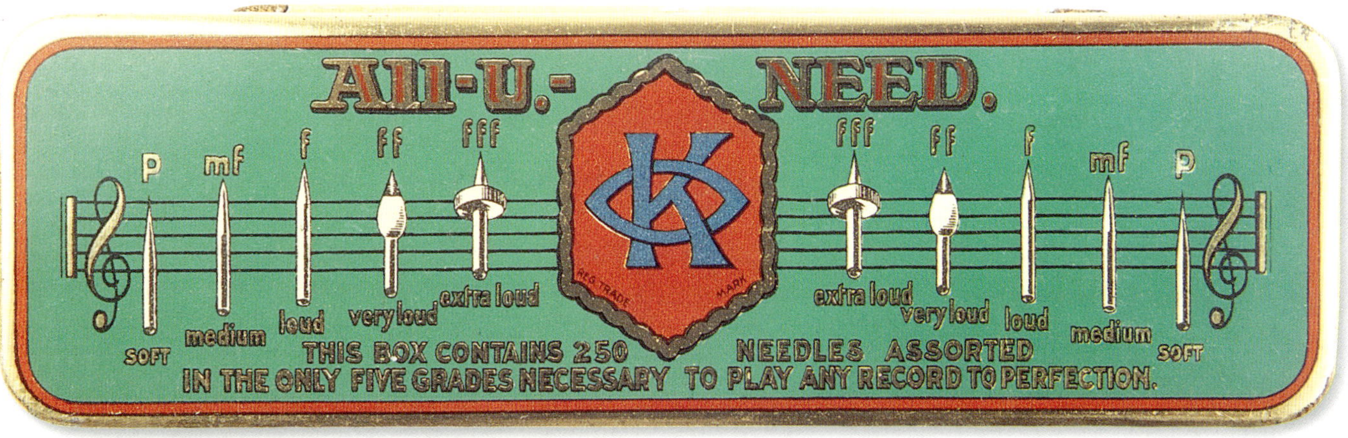

4-3. In 1899, the National Biscuit Company introduced its "Uneeda Biscuit" crackers. The coined name was an admonition to the customer, a not-so-subliminal seduction. The twentieth century would abound with such nomenclature, from Sav-mor to No-nox. Here, the practice has been extended to a 5 1/4" long tin of multi-grade steel talking machine needles. (Value code: G)

Advertising Records Evolve

The advertising disc, exploited by talking machine companies to promote themselves, began to attract the interest of outside firms. In 1918, Columbia pressed an "Advertising Talk On Mrs. Rorer's Own Blend – America's Finest Coffee," commissioned by the Climax Coffee and Baking Powder Company. Yet, it seems surprising that more firms did not employ pre-recorded advertising.

At the end of the 1920s, and during the early 1930s, Victor would record another pep talk to dealers, and produce advertising discs for the Olds Motor Works and Aunt Jemima pancake mix. Columbia culled pop records from its subsidiary brands catalogue to promote various MGM and Paramount movies. These film-related discs were sold in theatre lobbies.

4-4. Emerson record: "Brothers," recorded in January 1921.

Speaking Your Mind

One of the oddest recordings commissioned by an industrial firm was an Emerson 10" disc made in January 1921. One side is entitled "'Brothers' An Editorial From The Detroit News, December 13th, 1920." On the reverse is the "Dodge Brothers March" by the Dodge Brothers Industrial Band, composed by Victor Herbert. "Manufactured especially for Dodge Brothers."

A number of commercial enterprises recorded eponymous marches to be distributed among employees, however the Dodge Brothers record also delivered a rather morose inspirational message about the founders of the auto-making firm:

> *They were brothers - and it was not the mere physical fact of brotherhood that welded these two, John and Horace Dodge, together. It was a bond that had in it something of strange depth and purity and fineness; something that transcended the usual brother-bond of good fellowship and superficial understanding by a splendor hardly to beget by men who have known no such love, and became a thing richly spiritual and very beautiful. For the brothers loved each other as friends. They were friends. And it was not the mere comfortable badge of friendship that welded these two together. It was a bond which had in it something of a strange warmth and closeness, something that transcended the usual friendship. Throughout their childhood and their youth and manhood, the brothers worked and played together in an intimacy which on the part of each gave much and demanded much. The strange, spiritual beauty of their friendship grew with the years. There are those who knew them who say that each brother felt himself incomplete alone, that only in the companionship of his brother-friend did he feel himself an entity. But, to those who know the story of the Dodge Brothers, it is a matter of no surprise that the death of one followed so closely that of the other. The spiritual bond between them was so close, that, bereaved of his brother and his friend, Horace Dodge, though surrounded by the love of wife and family, felt himself still strangely alone. And, robbed of the companionship which had been so integral a part of his life, he lacked incentive to fight. It is a fact well known among their friends that always at midnight of the New Year, John and Horace Dodge left whatever friends and loved ones were merrymaking with them, and alone in the room of one of the brothers, each solemnly drank health and long life to the other. It may well be imagined the pain and loneliness with which Horace Dodge saw approaching the new year of 1921 - the first year in which there would be no pledge between brother-friend and friend-brother. One imagines the wistful bravery with which he planned to spend that midnight moment of pain with his family and friends. Smiling, and yet determined not to let them see the loneliness that ate at his heart. Loneliness worked its corroding evil on body and spirit more quickly than doctors and loved ones had thought, and the brothers are together.*

This couldn't be considered a promotional record, though it was obviously meant to "promote" an emotional message. However, the Dodge record is indicative of how mass communication was perceived at the time. It was seen as a tool of philosophical enrichment, more than salesmanship.

Having come this far along the inspirational tangent, it would be denying the readers a rare treat not to mention the "Psycho-Phone" records. The Psycho-Phone was a pop therapeutic device available in the late 1920s in either disc or cylinder format. The theory was that subconscious suggestion could ameliorate human behavior, much as hypnosis is used nowadays to treat smokers or over-eaters. The mechanism itself was simple – an electric motor turned the record, which reproduced acoustically through a small horn. The machine was placed within earshot at bedtime, and a timer triggered the record to play at a pre-set moment. The soothing voice of the narrator assured the sleeping "patient" that the Psycho-Phone was doing its work.

> *I am now having a wonderful rest. I will wake up in the morning feeling fine. I desire health, happiness and harmony in my life. I have complete confidence in the effectiveness of the Psycho-Phone for this purpose. The sound of the Psycho-Phone lulls me to sleep, but my unconscious mind hears and is deeply impressed by these affirmations. I am healthy in every way. Every organ in my body, every faculty of my mind is working perfectly. I eat only what is good for me, and I have thorough bowel movements every day. I am always happy and never worry about anything. I am in harmony with all the world, and see only the good in everything. I think only of what I want, and never of what I do not want. I am young, vigorous, happy, good-natured, healthy and prosperous.*

4-5. A 5 3/4" advertising disc for Colgate toothpaste. This double-faced marketing record is couched as a children's story about tooth care, beginning, "Once upon a time there were two young people – Mary and Walter..." The disc was "created by the Talking Book Corporation, New York. Copyright 1920." Talking Book Corporation produced a line of children's records laminated to die-cut lithographed cardboard figures of animals and objects. *Courtesy of the Charles Hummel collections.* (Value code: G)

4-6. Not a Victor record... exactly... This 5 1/2" diameter single-faced advertising disc was commissioned by Herschberg & Company, 339 Fifth Avenue, New York, to promote its line of "Victor" headwear. The record was "Manufactured by the Columbia Graphophone Manufacturing Company," circa 1920. It's helpful to remind the reader that the trade name "Victor," as in "victorious" over the competition, was employed by a number of firms selling vastly different products. *Courtesy of the Charles Hummel collections.* (Value code: G)

4-7. Calvin Coolidge had been President since August 1923, when, as Vice-President, he had succeeded the stricken Warren G. Harding. Coolidge was seeking election in 1924 when the American Record Company, New York City (no relation to the brand of the same name from 20 years earlier) manufactured this interesting record. The 4 3/4" diameter celluloid disc commanded attention by virtue of its unusual appearance, if nothing else. Sousa's famous march, "Stars and Stripes Forever" was recorded on the reverse side. *Courtesy of the Charles Hummel collections*. (Value code: F)

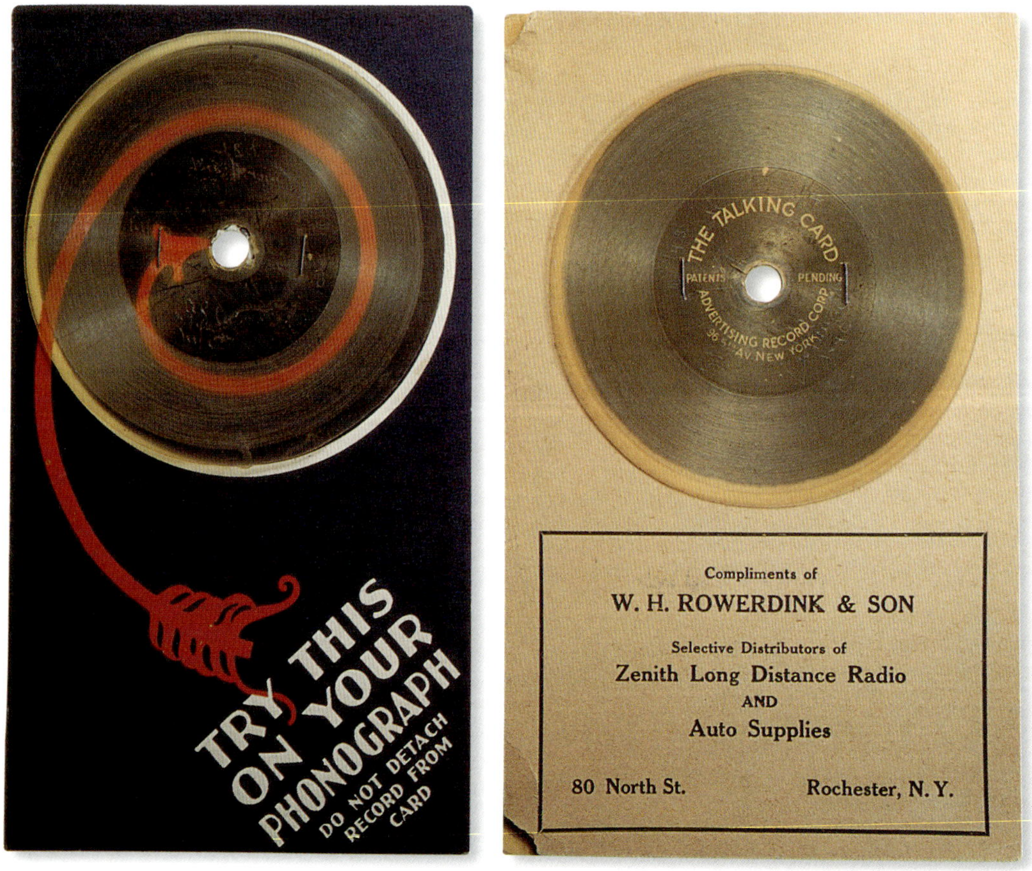

4-8. Advertising records from Rochester, New York, approximately 3 1/8" diameter. Left, advertising for F.P. Van Hoesen Company, paints and wallpaper. Right, W.H. Rowerdink & Son, auto supplies. The phonograph was not only the object of advertising, it was also the medium. *Courtesy of Alan H. Mueller.* (Value code: H)

4-9. Records continued to be a useful marketing tool. In 1932, Chevrolet mailed out this 4" diameter Durium record (a thin celluloid skin laminated to cardboard) in order to attract business. (Value code: H)

4-10. The reverse side of the Chevrolet marketing disc, with space at the top for an address label.

4-11. This small "Cayuga" (an extinct Indian tribe from central New York State) needle display (10" x 11") had its paper label applied over an existing "Wall-Kane" marking. *Courtesy of the Tom and Sandi McCarthy collection*. (Value code: F)

4-12. Another small needle display of the late teens was this 8" x 10" "Gilt Edge" dispenser. *Courtesy of the Tom and Sandi McCarthy collection*. (Value code: F)

4-13. The Jewel Phonoparts Company of Chicago was a manufacturer of disc talking machine accessories. As seen on the left, the "Jewel Tone" converter allowed 78s to be played on an Edison Diamond Disc Phonograph. The other brochures advertised various attachments including one that adapted Victors to play Edison or Pathé (vertical cut) discs. (Value code: H)

4-14. A Columbia Records counter display consisting of six revolving panels containing twelve 8" x 16 1/2" announcements. The major manufacturers stressed the importance of window treatments to their dealers, in order to get customers into the stores. Once inside, however, displays such as this one could alert patrons to new items of interest. *Courtesy of the Gfell family collection.* (Value code: VR)

4-15. The voice of Thomas A. Edison had never been offered for sale to the public, despite numerous requests over the years. The end of "the war to end all wars" prompted the great inventor to break his self-imposed "silence," in order to observe the momentous occasion. "Let Us Not Forget" expressed Edison's sentiments that, "…we must not forget…the part played by our gallant allies… I believe that the national airs of France, Great Britain, Italy and Belgium should for all time to come be as familiar to us as our own 'Star Spangled Banner.'" Released in June 1919, "Let Us Not Forget" remained in the Edison disc and cylinder record catalogues until October 31, 1929. This particular example is most unusual in that Edison himself autographed it, "To C.S. Reynolds, Orange [New Jersey], Dec. 20, 1924." The decorated advertising sleeve is rarely found with this record. *Courtesy of the Charles Hummel collections.* (Value code: autographed copy VR)

4-16. An Edison advertising calendar. The bulwark of Edison's 1919 disc line was the "C-19" "Chinese Chippendale." The family group shown here may seem arctically sedate, but the anthropomorphic ad copy soars, "Oh, wondrous Edison, do you know, why little children, always love you so…?" *Courtesy of Robin and Joan Rolfs.* (Value code: F)

4-17. Edison Diamond Disc Phonographs in the front window of the M. Doyle Marks Company, Elmira, New York, in 1919. At the left was the "D-25" "Jacobean," at $250.00 the least expensive instrument displayed. In the middle was the "French Gothic" Art Model (small cabinet), which recently had been reduced from $1,100.00 (with electric motor) to $800.00 (with spring motor). At the right was the "W-250" "William and Mary," introduced at $250.00 but up to $285.00 by this time. *Courtesy of the Gfell family collection.* (Value code: G)

4-18. A 1919 advertising calendar. Although a Victrola is pictured, the store also sold Columbia Grafonolas. The misspelling "Graphonola" was common, since the earlier Columbia machines had been known as "Graphophones." Furniture, undertaking, and talking machines – frequent bedfellows in small town America. *Courtesy of Robin and Joan Rolfs.* (Value code: F)

4-19. This Victor supplement from July 1919 illustrates how pervasive was the impact of the Great War, even eight months after the Armistice. *Courtesy of Alan H. Mueller*. (Value code: H)

4-20. A 34" long Victor felt pennant, available to dealers for 85 cents in 1919. *Courtesy of Robin and Joan Rolfs*. (Value code: F)

4-21. Christmas in an upper class neighborhood would not be complete without a Victrola "XVII." *Courtesy of Fred Guenther.* (Value code: F)

4-22. Opened, the Victor Christmas advertising flyer measures 8" x 12". In this instance, the Victor operatic artists perform their much-promoted "Red Seal" records in person, led by Enrico Caruso. *Courtesy of Fred Guenther.*

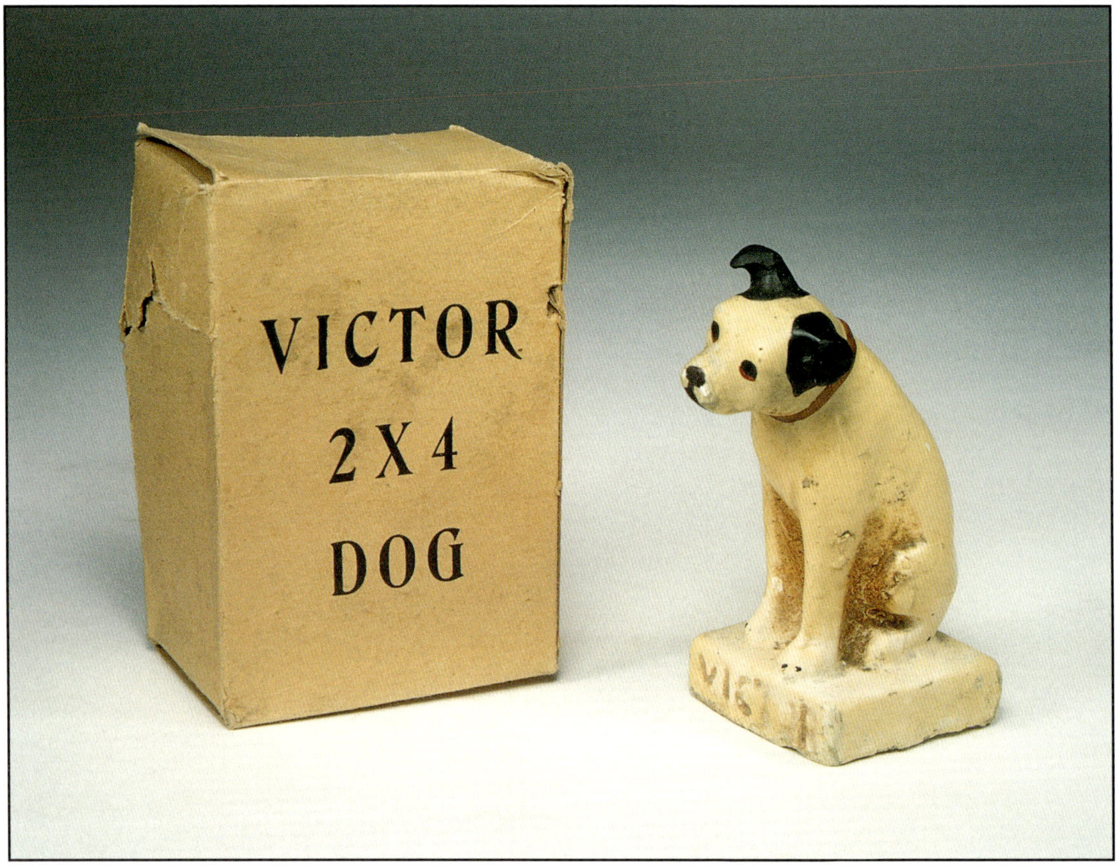

4-23. A 4" high plaster Nipper with its original box. These are sometimes found impressed with a dealer's name. *Courtesy of Robin and Joan Rolfs.* (Value code: with original box, F)

4-24. Foreign language catalogues in the vivid colors that became commonplace on phonograph advertising during the late teens. *Courtesy of the Scott and Denise Corbett collection.* (Value code: H)

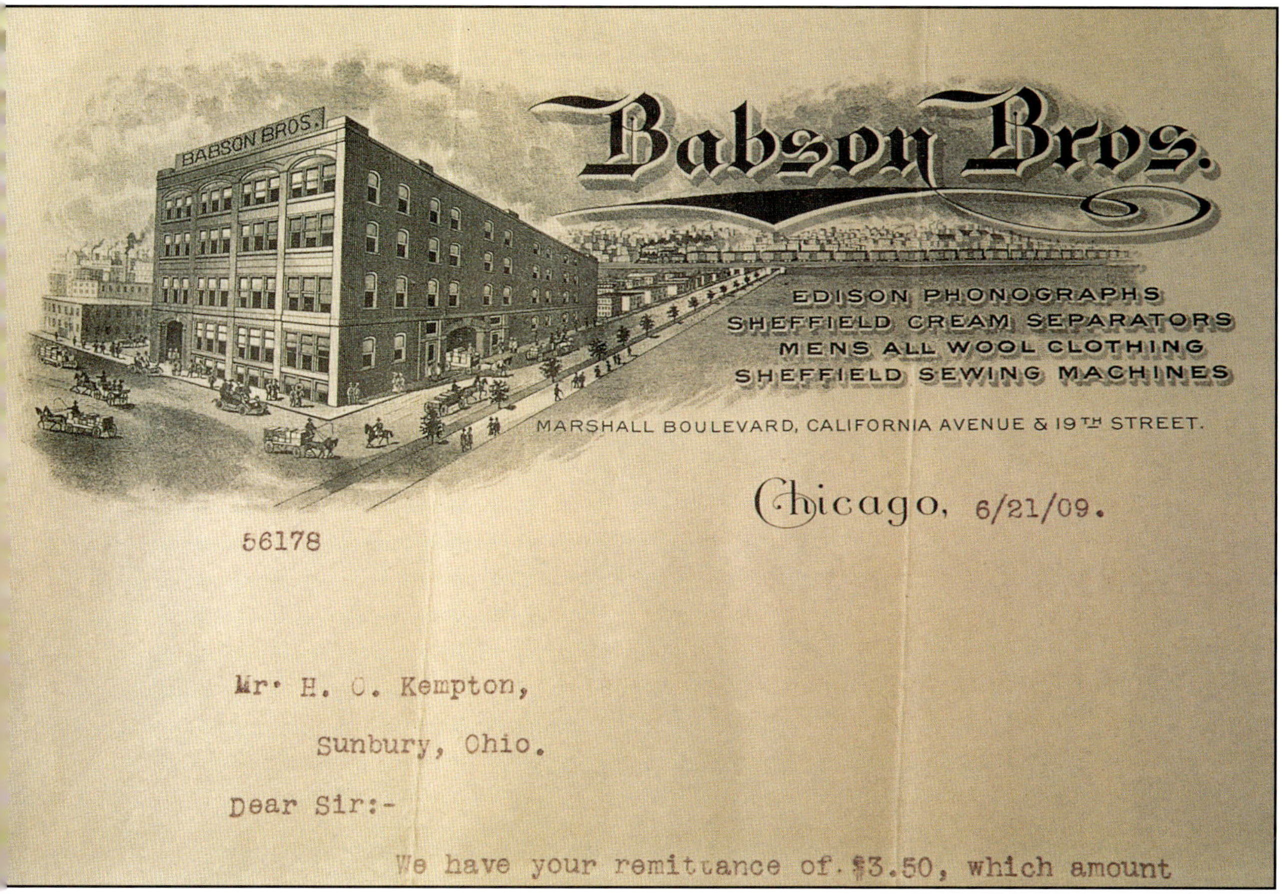

Babson Bros.

BABSON BROS.

EDISON PHONOGRAPHS
SHEFFIELD CREAM SEPARATORS
MENS ALL WOOL CLOTHING
SHEFFIELD SEWING MACHINES

MARSHALL BOULEVARD, CALIFORNIA AVENUE & 19TH STREET.

Chicago, 6/21/09.

56178

Mr. H. C. Kempton,

Sunbury, Ohio.

Dear Sir:-

We have your remittance of $3.50, which amount

4-25. Among Edison's staunchest supporters were the Babson's of Chicago. They distributed many thousands of Edison Phonographs during the first two decades of the twentieth century. However, by June 1923, they were selling "Embassy" disc talking machines, and the busy premises shown here no longer benefited the Edison company, which had grown out of dat. (Value code:H)

4-26. The Cheney Phonograph Company's claim to fame was the innovative design of its wooden internal horn ("Acoustic System" with "Air Chambers," as it was described). This Cheney brochure reflected the growing interest in "Art Models" (elaborate designs focused on existing furniture styles) during the late war years. *Courtesy of Charles McCarn*. (Value code: H)

4-27. It's a little much to imagine that the average trolley rider would know that Alethea was the ancient Greek goddess of truth. Small brands such as this, often manufactured by piano or furniture companies, were typical of the post-WWI boom. A trolley sign measuring 11" x 21". *Courtesy of David Werchen.* (Value code: G)

4-28. Identifying store decals and nameplates were common, but this particularly elaborate one, featuring the Nipper logo, graced the interior of a Circassian walnut Electrola "XVII."

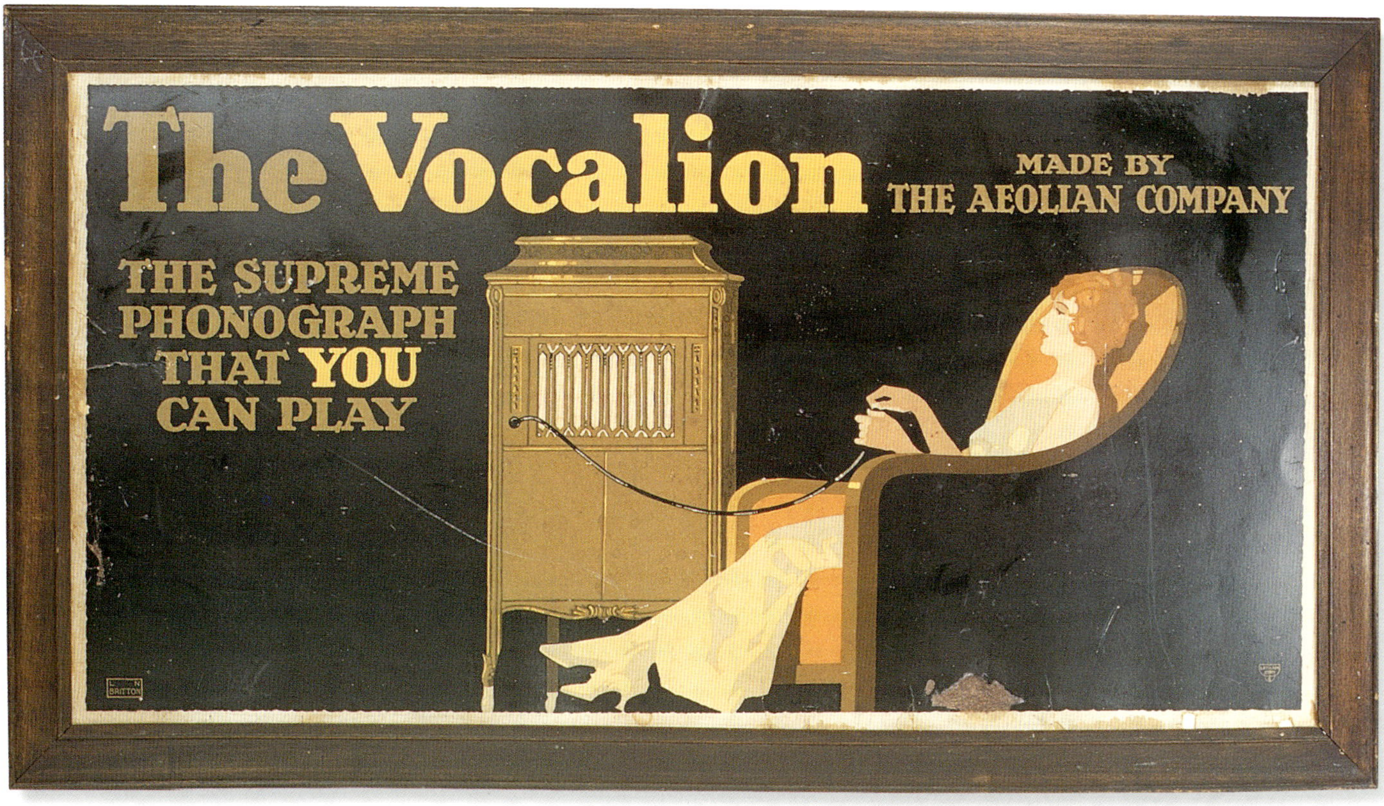

4-29. The Aeolian-Vocalion "Graduola," and "Volunome" attachments grew directly out of gizmos player piano companies created to involve the customer in the operation of the automatic mechanism. Various buttons, levers and slides allowed player piano owners to "participate" in the mechanical activity. Piano-maker Aeolian, which produced the Vocalion phonograph, dreamed-up the "Graduola," a cable-controlled device the primary function of which was to modify the volume of a recorded performance (whereas Aeolian's "Volunome" manipulated the *dynamics*). The listener could sit at some distance from the machine, and express his particular whims with impunity. A cardboard sign measuring 16 3/8" x 30". *Courtesy of Pat and Jamie Jones.* (Value code: C)

4-30. The Brunswick-Balke-Collender Company was already a prominent producer of commercial interiors and sports equipment when it embarked upon the manufacture of an eponymous line of disc talking machines in 1916. By the time this 9 1/2" x 20 1/4" metal sign was issued around 1919, Brunswick had introduced the "Ultona" soundbox, capable of reproducing lateral cut, Pathé-type vertical cut, and Edison discs. Note the references to "Plays All Records" and "All Phonographs in One," strong selling points. By 1921, Brunswick would become the third largest talking machine manufacturer in the industry. *Courtesy of the Tom and Sandi McCarthy collection.* (Value code: C)

4-31. This theatrical slide, created by the Flashagraph Company of Chicago, depicts a Columbia Grafonola "Favorite" atop a record storage cabinet. (Value code: F)

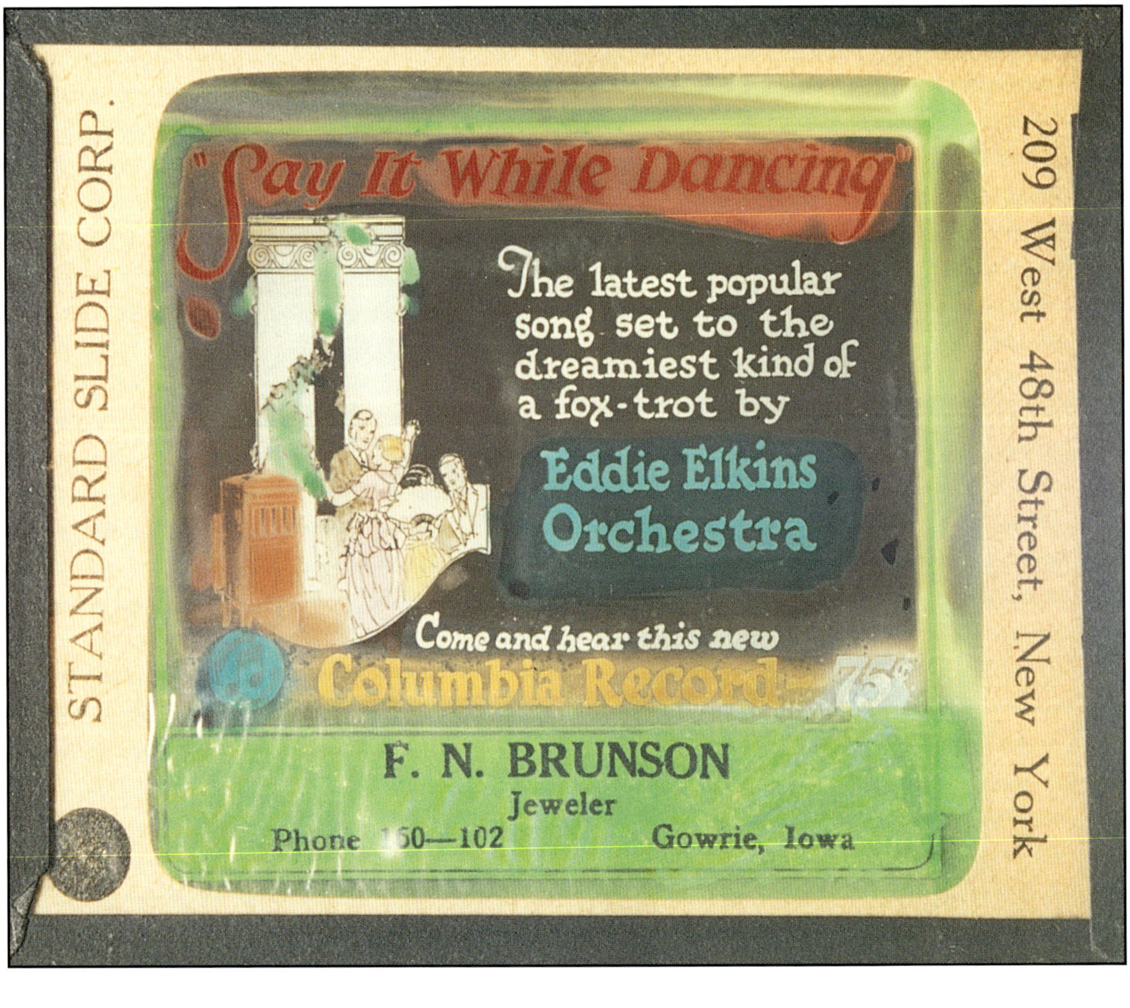

4-32. A theatrical slide from the Standard Slide Company of New York City, advertising Columbia records. (Value code: F)

4-33. A theatrical lantern slide that made a pitch for the installment plan. (Value code: F)

4-34. A Columbia advertising placard, featuring a rather bouffant Percy Grainger, 13 1/4" x 21 1/2". *Courtesy of the Domenic DiBernardo collection.* (Value code: F)

4-35. A postcard, circa 1920, showing the venerable Columbia factory (formerly the American Graphophone Company). The impact of brand recognition can be recognized in what is essentially a vacationer's souvenir postcard. (Value code: H)

4-36. Upper middle class domestic scenes were the frequent subjects of phonograph advertising calendars. This one was unusual, since it included additional ad copy for each individual month. *Courtesy of Robin and Joan Rolfs*. (Value code: F)

4-37. Although Victor has become associated with colorful, high-quality advertising lithography, Columbia also commissioned a varied array of attractive objects. This gift pack of Columbia discs reflected a Christmas theme. *Courtesy of the Domenic DiBernardo collection.* (Value code: F)

4-38. Another Columbia gift pack depicted stylized eighteenth century courtship. The flap at the top contained an appropriate greeting. *Courtesy of the Domenic DiBernardo collection.* (Value code: F)

4-39. A cardboard Columbia display. Items of so temporal a nature are seldom seen today. This piece was most likely intended to sit atop an opened Grafonola. *Courtesy of the Domenic DiBernardo collection.* (Value code: VR)

4-40. A large canvas banner by the Grinnell Sign and Poster Company – five feet wide! – to be hung outside a Columbia dealer's store. *Courtesy of the Tom and Sandi McCarthy collection.* (Value code: D)

4-41. A 17" x 23" lithographed metal chalkboard, for listing the latest Columbia hit. *Courtesy of Robin and Joan Rolfs.* (Value code: VR)

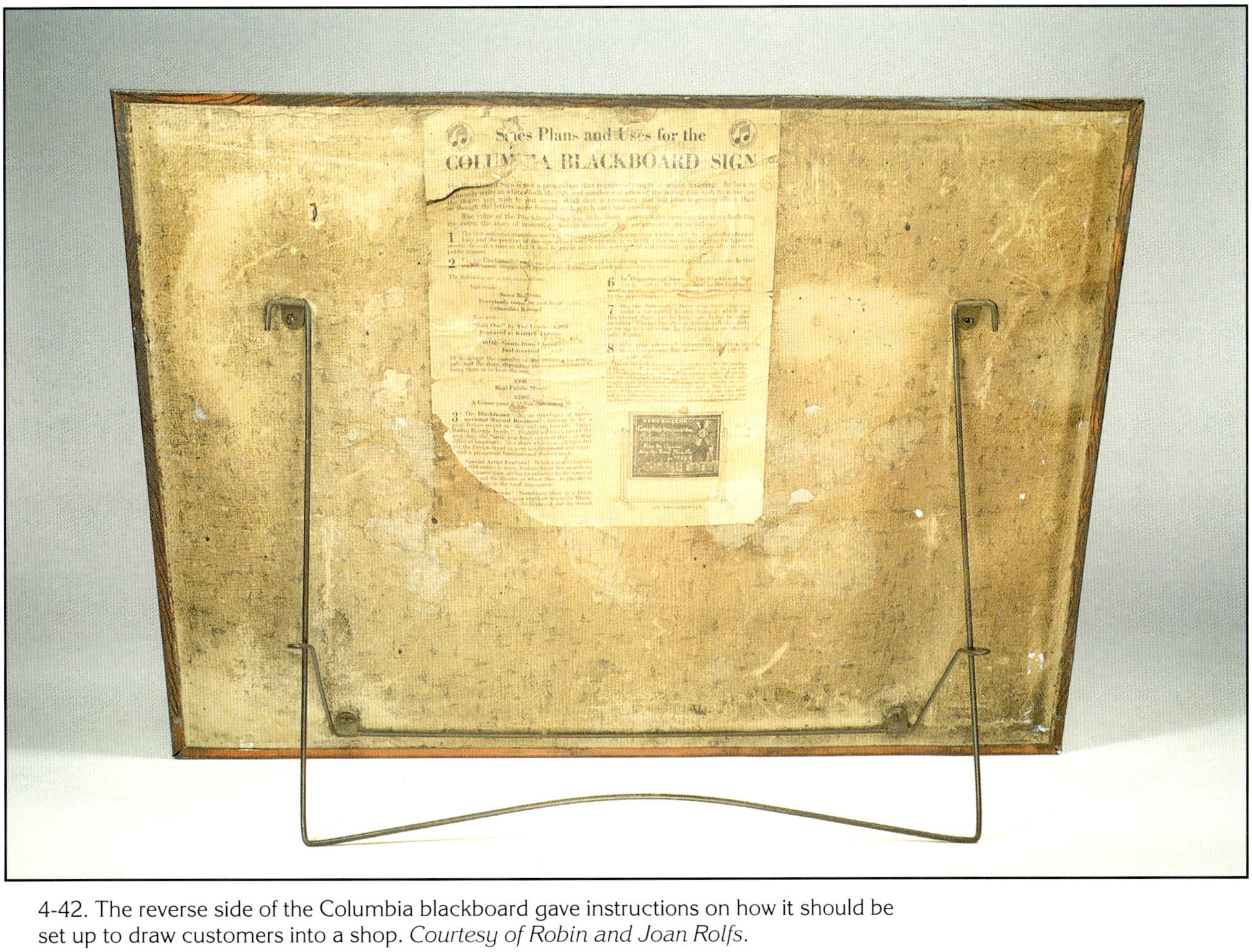

4-42. The reverse side of the Columbia blackboard gave instructions on how it should be set up to draw customers into a shop. *Courtesy of Robin and Joan Rolfs.*

4-43. Victor advertising fans in two typical shapes. The genuine practicality of these objects may not readily occur to us, in a widely air-conditioned world. *Courtesy of Robin and Joan Rolfs.* (Value code: G)

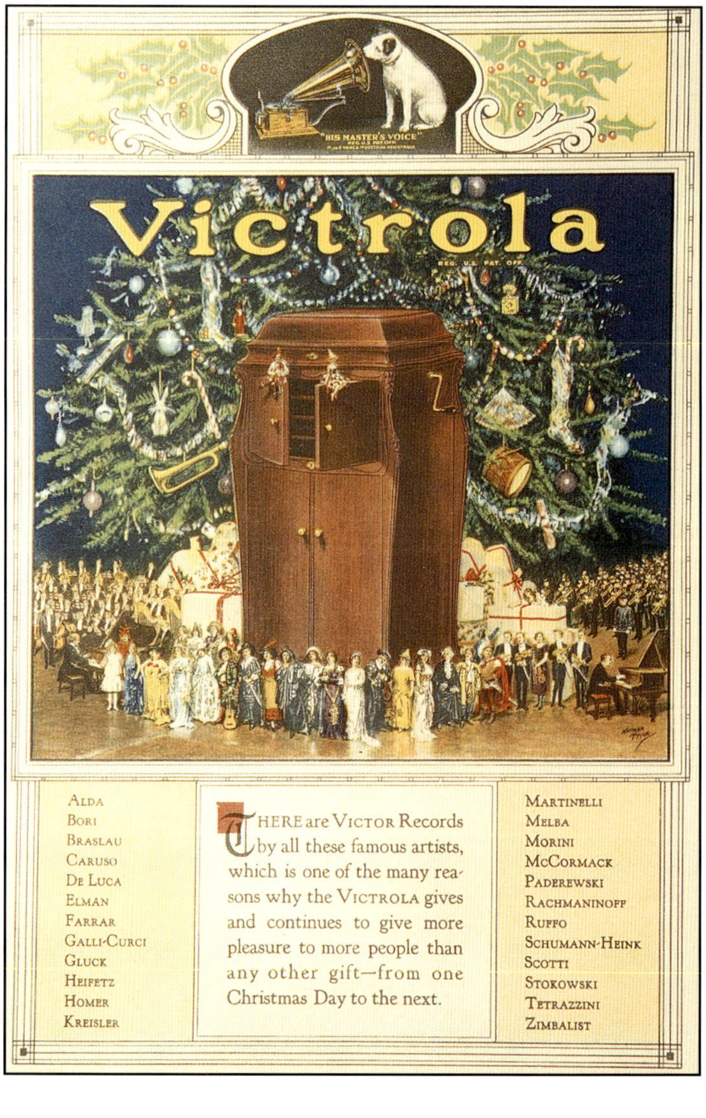

4-44. A flyer depicting a familiar Victor theme. A Victrola, in this instance next to an immense Christmas tree, is surrounded by a troupe of miniature singers and musicians, representing Victor recording artists. Columbia occasionally borrowed this premise in rival advertisements. Measures 6" x 9". *Courtesy of Fred Guenther.* (Value code: G)

4-45. Victor's stable of high-brow recording artists helped make it a Goliath of the industry. Topping the list of exclusive Victor stars was Italian tenor Enrico Caruso. His distinctive countenance appeared in Victor ads, and, in this instance, a framed portrait printed on canvas to resemble a painting. *Courtesy of Martin F. Bryan.* (Value code: E)

4-46. A dealer record display stand, cast in plaster, holding an autographed Tito Schipa disc. *Courtesy of the Tom and Sandi McCarthy collection.* (Value code: without disc, E)

4-47. Later, dealers used this cast metal stand to display a copy of the latest Victor hit record. *Courtesy of the Tom and Sandi McCarthy collection.* (Value code: E)

4-48. The "His Master's Voice" trademark achieved immeasurable impact worldwide. This enamel sign, 14 1/2" x 20", hailed from the former Czechoslovakia. *Courtesy of the Charles Hummel collections.* (Value code: A)

4-49. The interior of the Bergen Music Company, most likely on opening day. The flower arrangements wished "success," the lamp globes promised "We-Aim-To-Please" and, on the wall above compartments stocked with 78s, framed publicity photos of Victor artists were displayed. *Courtesy of the Tom and Sandi McCarthy collection.* (Value code: F)

4-50. A quiet day in July 1920 at the Bergen Music Company. *Courtesy of the Tom and Sandi McCarthy collection.* (Value code: F)

4-51. Despite Nipper's attraction to modern eyes, he is ignored by a group of school children admiring the front window of the Bergen Music Company, circa 1920. *Courtesy of the Tom and Sandi McCarthy collection.* (Value code: F)

4-52. Poshly attired families in high-toned settings was a theme again reflected in this Victor trolley sign, measuring 11" x 21". *Courtesy of Alan H. Mueller.* (Value code: E)

4-53. A soft-backed record cleaning brush bearing dealer advertising, a small celluloid pin in the likeness of Nipper, and a glass paperweight, 3 1/2" square. *Courtesy of the Scott and Denise Corbett collection.* (Value code: G)

4-54. Three circular advertising fans. The salutary effects of "good music" were widely referred to in phonograph advertising. *Courtesy of Bob and Karyn Sitter.* (Value code: G)

4-55.In a market awash in Victrola "look-alikes," the Sonora stood virtually alone. Although the company did produce some inexpensive and conventionally boxy models, the general image of Sonora was founded on the pneumatic appearance of its better instruments. A cardboard sign, measuring 10 1/2" x 20 1/2" (without mat). *Courtesy of the Tom and Sandi McCarthy collection.* (Value code: E)

4-56. A Sonora placard, 10 1/2" x 20 1/2", with space at the bottom left for the name of the dealer. Like Victor ads that often featured high-end Victrolas, Sonora exploited the "Highest Class Talking Machine" image. *Courtesy of the Tom and Sandi McCarthy collection.* (Value code: E)

4-57. This metal watch fob advertised Sonora's popular line of talking machines. *Courtesy of Steve and Ellie Saccante.* (Value code: F)

4-58. Sonora made a name for itself during the teens and early 1920s with its *zaftig* line of bombé cabinet models. *Courtesy of Steve and Ellie Saccente.*

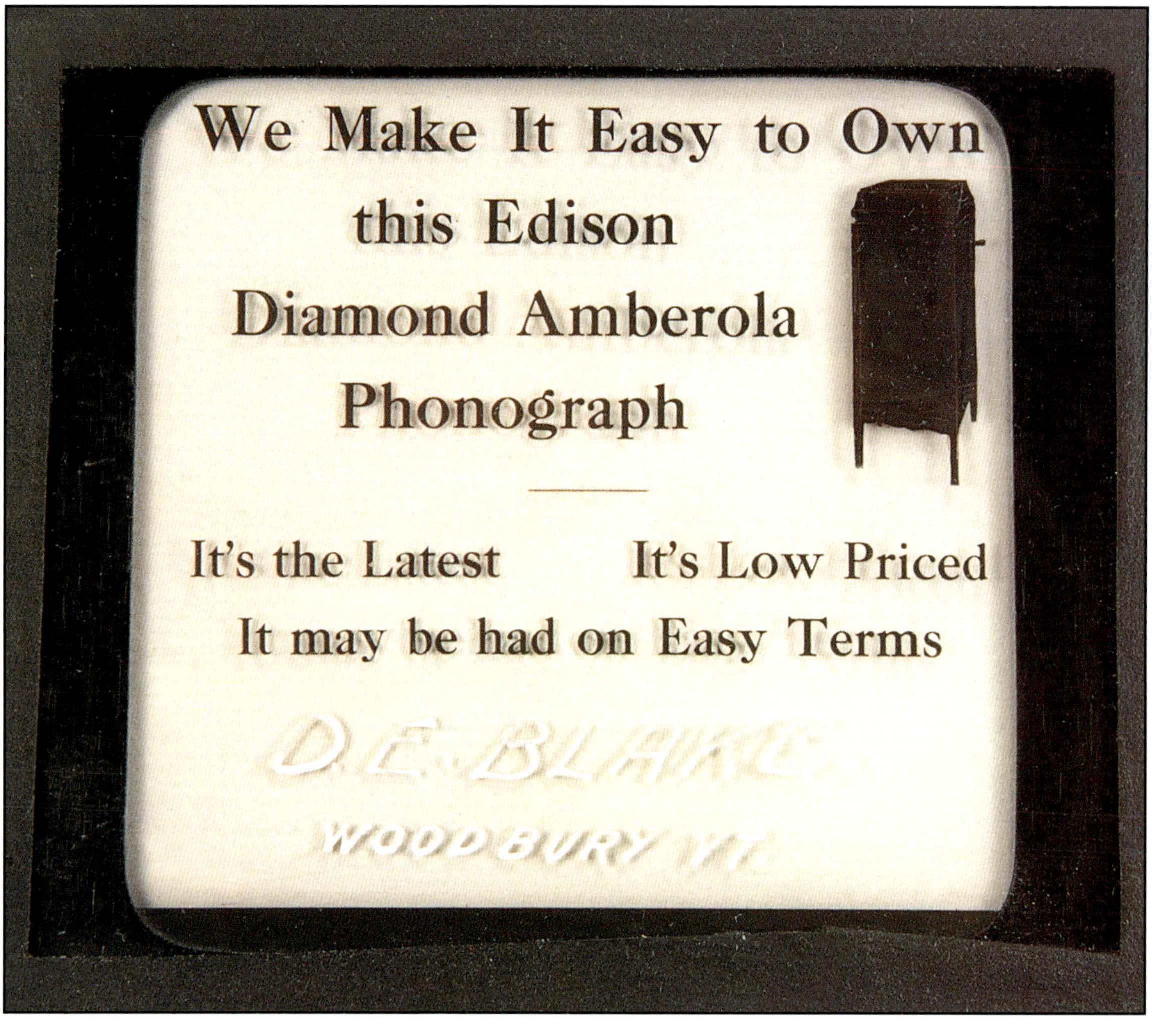

4-59. A theatrical slide promoted Edison Amberolas, circa 1920. Pictured is the "75," which had a sophisticated playing mechanism despite its egg-crate cabinetry. *Courtesy of Martin F. Bryan.* (Value code: F)

4-60. The image of a hand displaying an Edison cylinder was frequently exploited in Edison marketing. Less common, however, is this handy 2" diameter pocket mirror that one enterprising Michigan dealer distributed, circa 1920. "We give a floor lamp with every phonograph" must stand as one of the most unusual promotional slogans in the history of the industry. *Courtesy of the Babcock House Museum, John H. Perschbacher.* (Value code: F)

4-61. Two phonograph advertising rulers. The one at the top reminds us that talking machine repair was a trade that benefited as much from publicity as the purveying of the instruments. *Courtesy of Bob and Karyn Sitter.* (Value code: H)

4-62. This unusual sample packet of celluloid piano keys was given away by the Kranz-Smith Piano Company, which listed Victor products among the merchandise it carried. *Courtesy of Walter and Carol Myers.* (Value code: G)

4-63. An American city street scene, around 1920, with a Victor dealer at the left. *Courtesy of the Tom and Sandi McCarthy collection.* (Value code: G)

4-64. The covers of post-World War I Columbia record supplements were excellently rendered and printed in bright colors. The liberating effect of the war on America was evident in bobbed hair, short skirts and relaxed social attitudes. Compare this kinetically-charged scene to the static look of the advertisement in illustration 3-52. *Courtesy of the Tom and Sandi McCarthy collection.* (Value code: H)

4-65. The Invicta Spring Company of England chose a distinctive trade name for its products. A 9" x 12" advertising placard, circa 1920. *Courtesy of the Tom and Sandi McCarthy collection.* (Value code: H)

4-66. Practical household items, such as these small ink blotters, provided excellent locations for advertising. 3 1/2" x 6 1/4". (Value code: H)

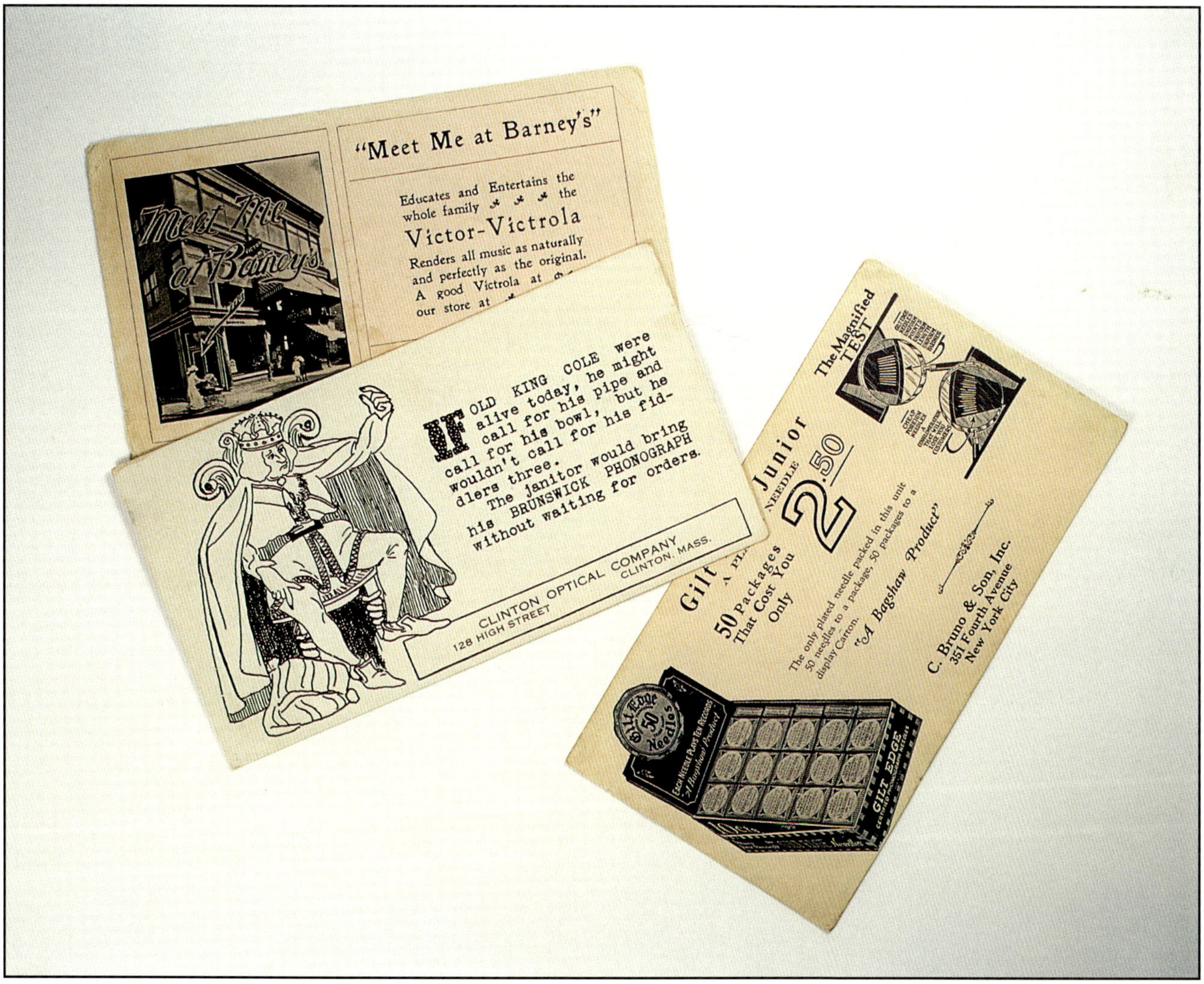

4-67. This 14" x 37" 1921 record list prominently featured an Emerson phonograph. Curiously, the company has emphasized the presence of the horn, (which was very reminiscent of an "old fashioned" external fixture) although the hinged front grille of the cabinet was meant to be kept closed, hiding the horn from sight. *Courtesy of Nina and Dave Heitz.* (Value code: F)

4-68. A fold-out brochure for the World phonograph, circa 1920. Note the pointed reference to "our own motors and tone arms." Many independent talking machine companies reduced costs by buying all mechanical parts from clearing houses specializing in generic equipment. World was attempting to distance itself from the cut-rate brands. The company's logo is also worthy of note. It might as well be called "Her Mother's Voice." (Value code: G)

4-69. A 3 1/2" x 5 1/8" catalogue of "Capitol" lamp phonographs from the Burns-Pollock Electric Manufacturing Company of Indian Harbor, Indiana. The fabric-covered shade served as a lid that, when closed, disguised the dual nature of the apparatus. The sound of the record emerged through the conical base and was reflected by the surface upon which the lamp was placed. (Value code: F)

4-70. Modern eyes have sometimes seen these tasseled artifacts of the teens and 1920s as "bawdy house lamps" – a serious error. The front cover of this catalogue depicted middle class family members enjoying the convenience and utility of a "Capitol."

"STUDIO"

MEASUREMENTS — Height, forty-five inches; width, seventeen inches; depth, twenty inches.

CASE—Brass Frame, Gold Plated; Choice selected Mahogany case, extra heavy Plate Glass Base, Turntable and Sides, Electric Light.

"SHERATON"

MEASUREMENTS—Height, forty-five inches; width, nineteen inches; depth, twenty-two inches.

CABINET—A most pleasing design, simple and rich. Made of choicest Mahogany, standard finish. All metal parts gold plated. Plate Glass Base and Turntable, Record Compartment, Electric Light

"CHIPPENDALE"

MEASUREMENTS—Height, forty-six inches; width, nineteen and one-quarter inches; depth, twenty-two and one-quarter inches.

CABINET—It is different—a great and noteworthy departure which places the "CHIPPENDALE" in a class distinctly apart from all others; it is a master creation of furniture architecture. Choice Selected Mahogany used; Hand Carved, Plate Glass Base, Turntable and Sides, Record Cabinet, Electric Light.

ENGLISH RENAISSANCE
DELUXE

CABINET—Antique Walnut or Polychrome. Cabinet width, 42 inches; height, 37 inches; depth, 20½ inches; antique gold trimmings.

TONE QUALITY—Is supreme, devoid of that rasping and scratching noise. Perfectly natural Tone-arm of special design, playing all makes of disk records.

MOTOR—Electric, AC or DC, 25 or 60 Cycle, it is Universal, and will not run hot, will run indefinitely.

TONE MODIFIER—Permits regulation without interfering with quality.

ANTOMATIC STOP—Is perfect.

"OLD ENGLISH"
DELUXE

CABINET—Antique Walnut or Polychrome. Cabinet width, 36 inches; height, 38 inches; depth, 20½ inches; antique gold trimmings.

TONE QUALITY—Is supreme, devoid of hat rasping and scratching noise. Perfectly natural Tone-arm of special design, playing all makes of disk records.

MOTOR—Electric, AC or DC, 25 or 60 Cyc'e, it is Universal, and will not run hot, will run indefinitely.

TONE MODIFIER—Permits regulation without interfering with quality.

AUTOMATIC STOP—Is perfect.

4-71. The Kurtzmann Phonograph Company of Buffalo, New York (loosely associated with Kurtzmann pianos) is best known for its "Studio" model – a machine largely constructed of plate glass, including a glass turntable. Included in this fold-out catalogue, however, are other never-seen models, which also featured unusual glass elements that, it was claimed, did not conduct extraneous sound. *Courtesy of Alan H. Mueller.* (Value code: F)

4-72. A Kurtzmann paperweight, appropriately of glass. Kurtzmann machines were electrically-driven, which at the time was considered the height of convenience. 3" x 5". (Value code: E)

4-73. Postcard advertising was an inexpensive and effective way to publicize a business. At the top, the Cadillac Phonograph Corporation offered a free trial of its instruments. In the center, the Wilson Seed Company included a "wonderful talking machine with four records" in its list of premiums. At the bottom, the Cooperative Record Club sold 16 records for $2.98. *Courtesy of Martin F. Bryan*. (Value code: H)

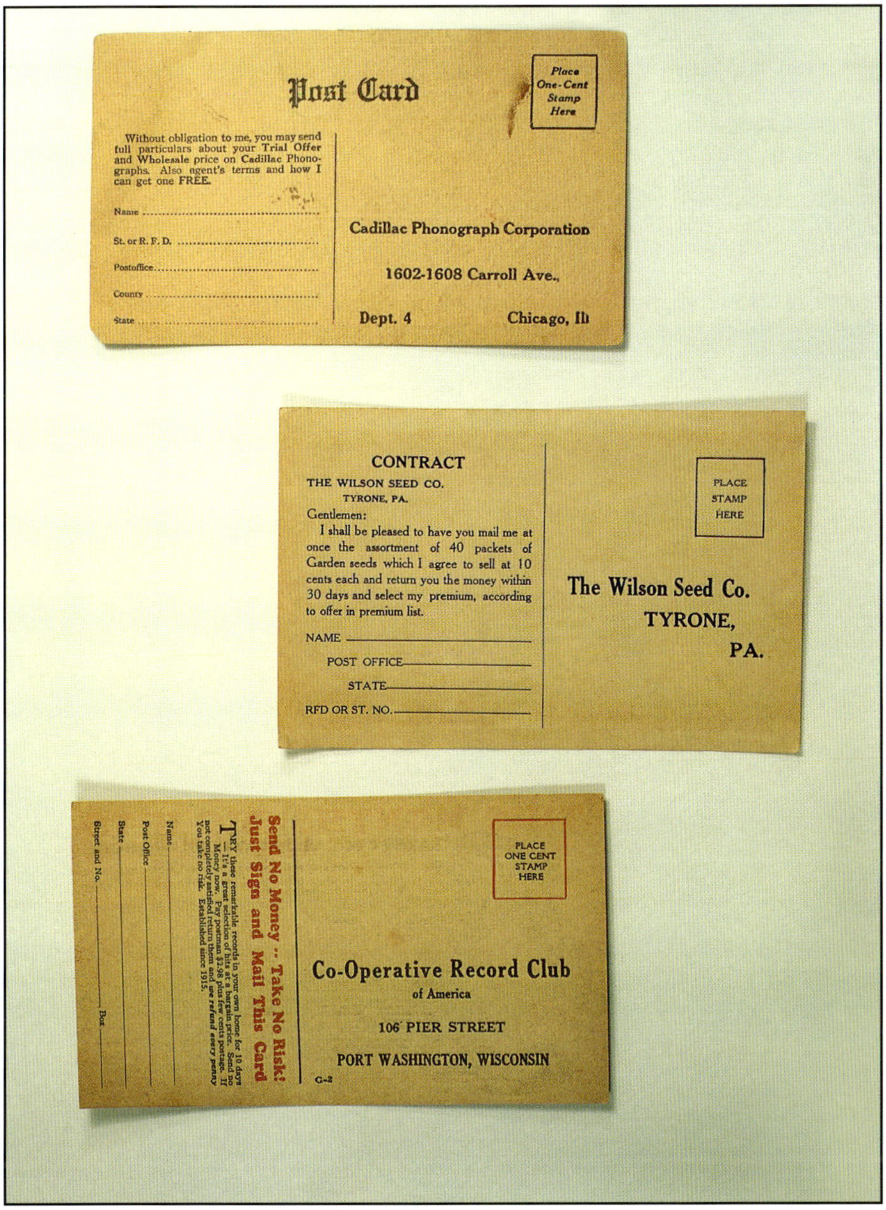

4-74. The reverse sides of the three previous postcard advertisements. *Courtesy of Martin F. Bryan.*

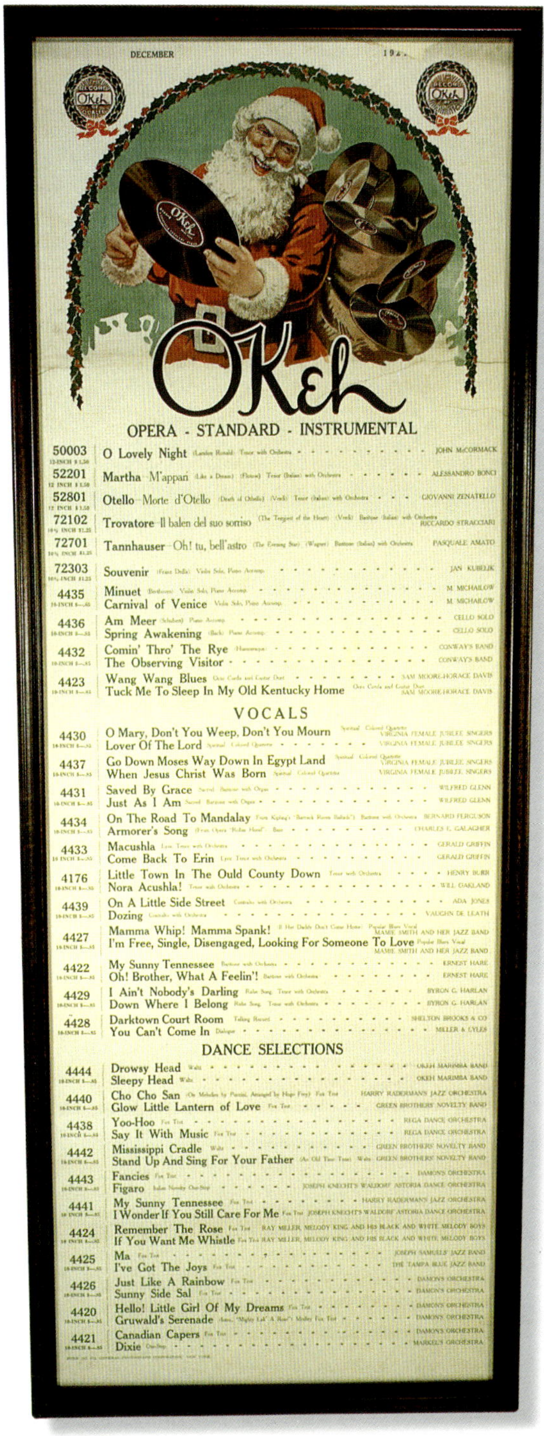

4-75. December 1921 Okeh records listed on a 14" x 34" sheet. *Courtesy of Nina and Dave Heitz.* (Value code: F)s

4-76. Okeh and Brunswick record supplements. (Value code: H)

4-77. Two examples of retail advertising needle tins, both with the dealers' names prominently featured. In these instances, it is not the product in the tin being advertised, but the merchant. The Landay Brothers tin is 2 1/2" in diameter. *Courtesy of the Charles Hummel collections*. (Value code: F)

4-78. Record cleaners offered larger surfaces for advertising than most needle tins. Here are three examples carrying dealer publicity, all 3 1/2" in diameter. *Courtesy of the Charles Hummel collections*. (Value code: F)

4-79. Dreams of the Old South invest this Columbia die-cut counter stand, 11" x 17". *Courtesy of David Werchen*. (Value code: F)

4-80. This theatrical slide for "The New Edison" featured a "WMC-33" ("William and Mary") of 1922, introduced at the tail-end of a "console" phonograph craze. "Console models from $135" was carefully phrased to disguise a basic weakness in the Edison Diamond Disc Phonograph line: there were no Edison disc instruments in the lower price range. Whereas Victor could boast of floor models starting at $100.00, and table models as low as $25.00, Edison's top-heavy line began at $95.00 (for the "B-19" table model) and rose upward in rapid increments. (Value code: F)

4-81. The Edison company's response to flagging sales of its Diamond Disc Phonographs was to introduce a cheesy line of machines that poorly represented traditional Edison quality. The "London" models of the mid-1920s were ill-conceived products at best. Shown in this copper newspaper die is the puny "LU-37" which retailed for $100.00. In the background is the imposing shape of the flagship "C-19" model ($295.00 at this time). *Courtesy of Charles McCarn.* (Value code: H)

4-82. Three practical advertising items: a screwdriver, a letter-opener and a highly unlikely tea strainer. *Courtesy of the Domenic DiBernardo collection.* (Value code: F)

4-83. This elegant matron may be relaxing before the Victrola, but she has decorously kept on her high-heeled shoes. *Courtesy of Robin and Joan Rolfs.* (Value code: F)

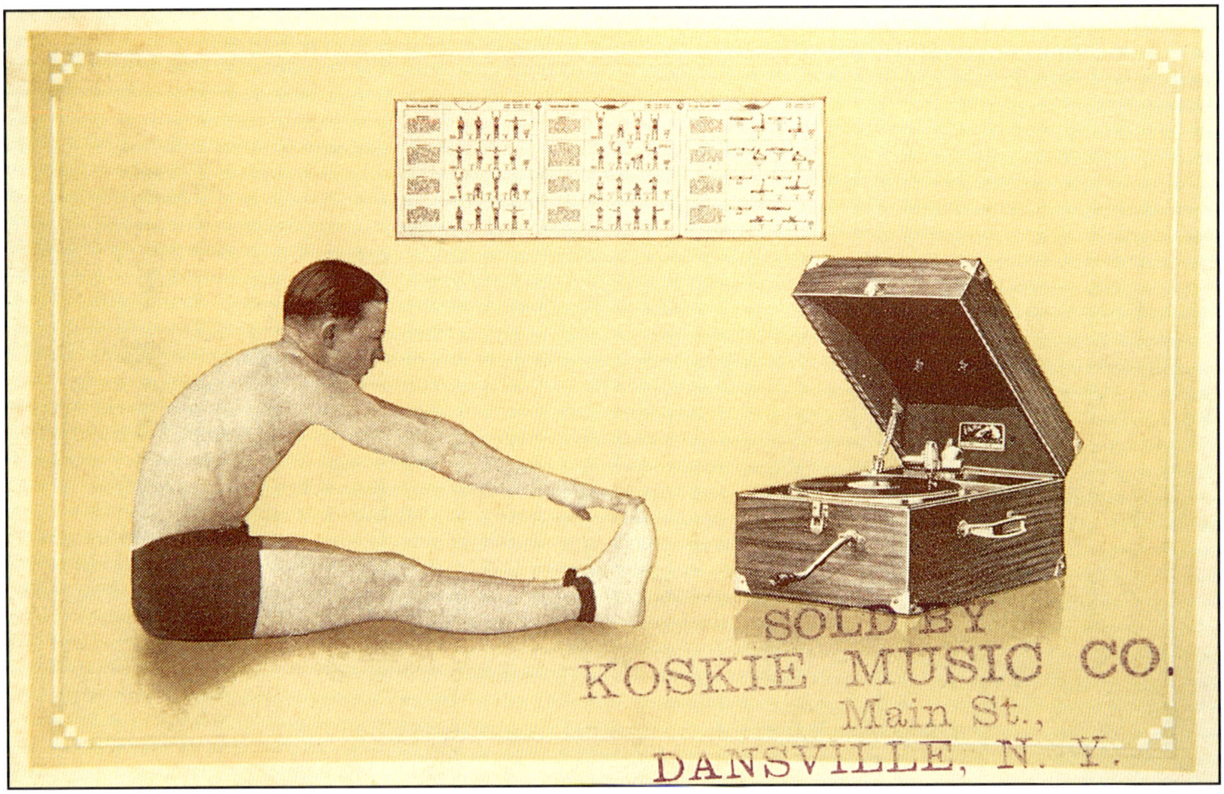

4-84. A small flyer promoting a series of Victor exercise discs. Illustrated was a "VV 50" portable, circa 1922. Measures 3" x 4 1/2". (Value code: H)

4-85. This Edison Diamond Disc Phonograph metal advertising sign may not be rare, but the accompanying dealer sales flyer certainly is! 100 of these signs, lithographed on tin-plated steel (colloquially known as "tin") could be ordered with store imprint for only $27.50. Sign measures 11 1/8" x 35 1/2". *Courtesy of Robin and Joan Rolfs.* (Value code: with flyer, VR)

4-86. The visual impact projected by this theatrical slide may be glimpsed from this specially illuminated view. (Value code: F)

4-87. Victor distributor, the Toledo Talking Machine Company, dispensed this handy 5" diameter thermometer to the dealers it serviced. (Value code: E)

4-88. A chilling image today, the swastika was once as harmless as the horseshoe and four-leaf clover depicted here with it. This "good luck" piece measures 1 1/4" diameter. *Courtesy of the Scott and Denise Corbett collection.* (Value code: F)

4-89. The good luck token, circa 1922, was included with each "Madame Hendren" baby doll. A year later, the "Madame Hendren" dolls began to be fitted with miniature cylinder phonographs capable of reciting nursery rhymes. *Courtesy of the Scott and Denise Corbett collection.*

4-90. A rare gift certificate with a Christmas theme, and a charming 6" long bookmark advertising Grafonolas. (Value code: H)

4-91. Two extensive catalogues of household products sold by the Larkin Company of Buffalo, New York. Below, Fall & Winter 1923-24, above, Spring & Summer 1920. The firm operated essentially as a buying co-operative, like the "wholesale clubs" popular today, although the stipulation that a certain minimum amount must be spent suggests further the record and book clubs of the 1950s and 60s that enforced monthly selections: "In the Premium Club, each Member buys at least a certain quantity of Larkin Products – usually $2 worth – each month or oftener." If Larkin had not gone out of business before the political witch-hunts of the 1950s, the next section of its credo might have been labeled "communism": "With each successive order of the Club, a different member receives the Premium of her [this was assumed] choice *given* with the total fixed monthly purchase of Products made by the Club. Members choose Premiums in turn until each has received a Premium, when the Club is reorganized and begins a new series." *Courtesy of Alan H. Mueller.* (Value code: H)

4-92. In 1925 Larkin distributed this 10 3/4" x 16 3/4" color flyer with "Symphonola" talking machines on one side and radios and player pianos on the other. In this instance, the firm was offering the instruments on easy terms: only a dollar down! (Value code: H)

Symphonola Records
SYMPHONOLA
PLAYABLE ON ANY PHONOGRAPH
Playable on any Phonograph
Enjoy the Latest
Dance Hits
Direct from Broadway
Symphon
50¢
POST PAID TO YOUR HOME
Dept. of BETTER HOMES

4-93. Graphically rich Larkin 10" record sleeves. Larkin emphasized the commonality of hearth and home. *Courtesy of Alan H. Mueller.* (Value code: H)

4-94. A 9" diameter "Symphonola" disc, pressed for Larkin by Emerson

4-95. *Along Broadway* was distributed to private individuals to promote Edison Diamond Disc Phonographs and records. Note the circulation that was claimed – nearly a quarter of a million copies. After having exhausted the novelty of the talking machine, marketers turned to varied quasi-medical mummery to support the importance of "elevating music" in the home. For a number of years, Edison pursued the theory that a person's mood could be ameliorated by properly administered doses of Edison records. The cover of this issue attests to that marketing campaign. *Courtesy of the Babcock House Museum, John H. Perschbacher.* (Value code: H)

4-96. Hail Columbia! The "Santa Maria" sails across the shallow waters of Ted Lewis' talent. A counter stand measuring 8" x 14 1/2". *Courtesy of David Werchen.* (Value code: F)

4-97. This 8 1/2" diameter embossed shop hanger advertised Winner Records, an English brand. The efficacy of riding a horse with a disc record in each hand has yet to be proven. *Courtesy of the Charles Hummel collections.* (Value code: F)

4-98. Die-cut Nipper figures attracted the eye and conveyed a message. On the right, two Nipper-shaped price tags for showroom use. Although Victor experimented with catchy advertising phrases ("look for the dog" and "the gift that keeps on giving" were two), nothing could top "His Master's Voice" for instantaneous impact. 3" to 5 1/4". *Courtesy of Robin and Joan Rolfs.* (Value code: G)

4-99. A Victor placard from a difficult period in the company's history. In 1924, the most recently introduced Victrolas had proved a failure, and the revolutionary "Orthophonic" machines and records would not be released until the following year. *Courtesy of Martin F. Bryan.* (Value code: G)

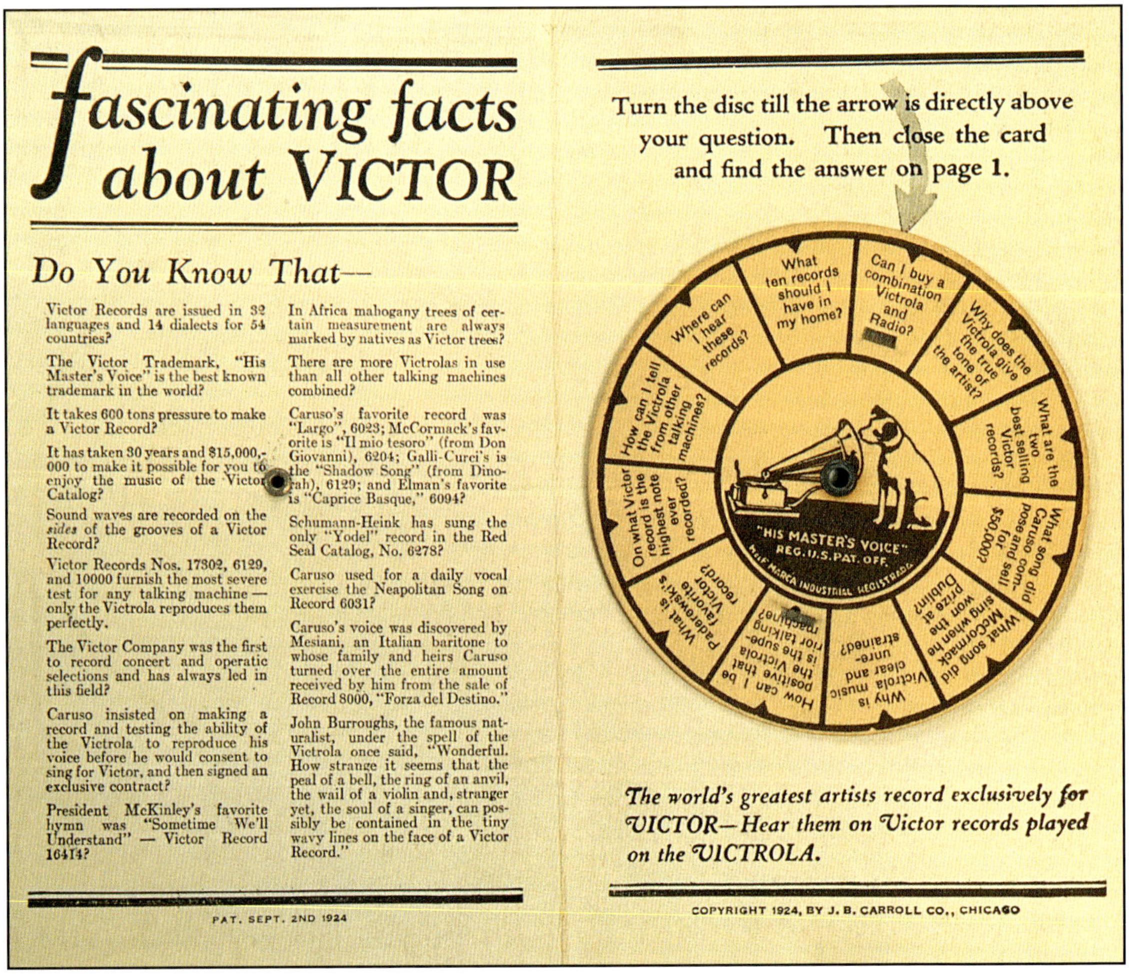

fascinating facts about VICTOR

Do You Know That—

Victor Records are issued in 32 languages and 14 dialects for 54 countries?

The Victor Trademark, "His Master's Voice" is the best known trademark in the world?

It takes 600 tons pressure to make a Victor Record?

It has taken 30 years and $15,000,000 to make it possible for you to enjoy the music of the Victor Catalog?

Sound waves are recorded on the *sides* of the grooves of a Victor Record?

Victor Records Nos. 17302, 6129, and 10000 furnish the most severe test for any talking machine — only the Victrola reproduces them perfectly.

The Victor Company was the first to record concert and operatic selections and has always led in this field?

Caruso insisted on making a record and testing the ability of the Victrola to reproduce his voice before he would consent to sing for Victor, and then signed an exclusive contract?

President McKinley's favorite hymn was "Sometime We'll Understand" — Victor Record 16414?

In Africa mahogany trees of certain measurement are always marked by natives as Victor trees?

There are more Victrolas in use than all other talking machines combined?

Caruso's favorite record was "Largo", 6023; McCormack's favorite is "Il mio tesoro" (from Don Giovanni), 6204; Galli-Curci's is the "Shadow Song" (from Dinorah), 6129; and Elman's favorite is "Caprice Basque," 6094?

Schumann-Heink has sung the only "Yodel" record in the Red Seal Catalog, No. 6278?

Caruso used for a daily vocal exercise the Neapolitan Song on Record 6031?

Caruso's voice was discovered by Mesiani, an Italian baritone to whose family and heirs Caruso turned over the entire amount received by him from the sale of Record 8000, "Forza del Destino."

John Burroughs, the famous naturalist, under the spell of the Victrola once said, "Wonderful. How strange it seems that the peal of a bell, the ring of an anvil, the wail of a violin and, stranger yet, the soul of a singer, can possibly be contained in the tiny wavy lines on the face of a Victor Record."

PAT. SEPT. 2ND 1924

Turn the disc till the arrow is directly above your question. Then close the card and find the answer on page 1.

The world's greatest artists record exclusively for VICTOR—Hear them on Victor records played on the VICTROLA.

COPYRIGHT 1924, BY J. B. CARROLL CO., CHICAGO

4-100. The Victor "Mystic Oracle" was remarkably clever. A magnet on the interior "question wheel" controlled a metal pointer on the face of the brochure. The interior wheel was coordinated so that the arrow always pointed to the correct "answer." 3 1/2" x 5 1/2" closed. *Courtesy of the Tom and Sandi McCarthy collection.* (Value code: VR)

4-101. Front cover of the Victor "Mystic Oracle." *Courtesy of the Tom and Sandi McCarthy collection.*

4-102. An 8" diameter Victor cardboard fan. The innate humor of this item is expressed by the partially visible but well-known at the time record title: "Her Bright Smile Haunts Me Still." With today's eyes, we are more likely to see only quaint flapper charm. *Courtesy of Fred Guenther.* (Value code: G)

4-103. An in-store clock, made by the Ingraham Company of Bristol, Connecticut. *Courtesy of the Tom and Sandi McCarthy collection.* (Value code: VR)

4-104. A mechanical pencil with the Victor logo. (Value code: E)

4-105. A parade float sponsored by Victor dealer, Balthaser Music House, Hamburg, Pennsylvania, circa 1924. Apparently the only external horn talking machine the dealer could locate was a rather out of place Columbia Disc Graphophone! Note the profusion of Nipper figures in various sizes. *Courtesy of the Tom and Sandi McCarthy collection.* (Value code: G)

4-106. An extremely unusual Victor item. This savings bank in the form of a leather covered volume opened to a Victrola catalogue, circa 1924. Many dealers distributed inexpensive practical appliances (such as banks cast in the shape of an upright phonograph) to inspire clients to put money aside toward the purchase of a talking machine. This bank is surely one of the best appointed. The 3 3/8" x 5 1/8" "book" was made by Bankers Thrift Book Company, Minneapolis, Minnesota, patented October 31, 1922. It was dispensed by dealer A.J. Lindgren of Duluth, Minnesota. *Courtesy of the Jerry Koch collection.* (Value code: VR)

4-107. This framed piece, 34" x 44" (including frame), commemorated the opening of a Utica, New York music store, August 3, 1925. Talking machines were featured merchandise. *Courtesy of Dom Coladonato.* (Value code: E)

4-108. These colorful cardboard figures (13 1/2" average height) contributed the formidable presence of Victor's "serious music" recording artists to dealer displays. Left to right: Emilio De Gogorza, Fritz Kreisler, Frances Alda, Sophie Braslau, Louise Homer, Antonio Scotti, Guiseppe DeLuca, Jose Mardones. *Courtesy of the Tom and Sandi McCarthy collection.* (Value code: each, H)

4-109. Grouped figures of Victor artists, many costumed in well-known operatic roles. Beginning at rear, left to right: Enrico Caruso, Willem Mengelberg, Amelita Galli-Curci, Feodor Chaliapin, Sergei Rachmaninoff, Rosa Ponselle, Geraldine Farrar, John McCormack, Maria Jeritza, Beniamino Gigli, Ignace Paderewski, Lucrezia Bori, Jascha Heifetz, Toti Dal Monte (in front). *Courtesy of the Tom and Sandi McCarthy collection.* (Value code: each, H)

4-110. The famous figure of Nipper the Victor dog made an excellent promotional item. There were small likenesses in many variations, some of which carried dealer identification. Miniature effigies were made of materials that included plaster, chalk and metal. The largest of this group of metal Nippers is 4" high. *Courtesy of the Tom and Sandi McCarthy collection.* (Value code: F)

4-111. There are Nippers… and then there are NIPPERS! A 19" papier mâché dog manufactured by the King Cole company dwarfed by a 42" papier mâché version with glass eyes. (Value code: A)

4-112. The antebellum look of this 14" x 28" Victor placard, and the "popular American" fare it advertised, might not have been commonly associated with opera star Galli-Curci, yet we can fairly feel the breeze that rustles the branches of this Old South reverie. *Courtesy of David Werchen.* (Value code: F)

4-113. So, *nu*? A rare cardboard sign fragment executed in Hebrew characters. (Value code: VR)

4-114. A nation of immigrants inspired Victor recordings in languages as obscure as Icelandic. (Value code: H)

4-115. A 20" diameter Victor enameled double-faced sign, to be suspended outside a shop, with a dealer identification plaque attached below. (Value code: C)

4-116. A metal sign, 2 3/4" x 6 3/4", advertising Songster (British) steel needles. *Courtesy of Leslie Rosenfeld.* (Value code: F)

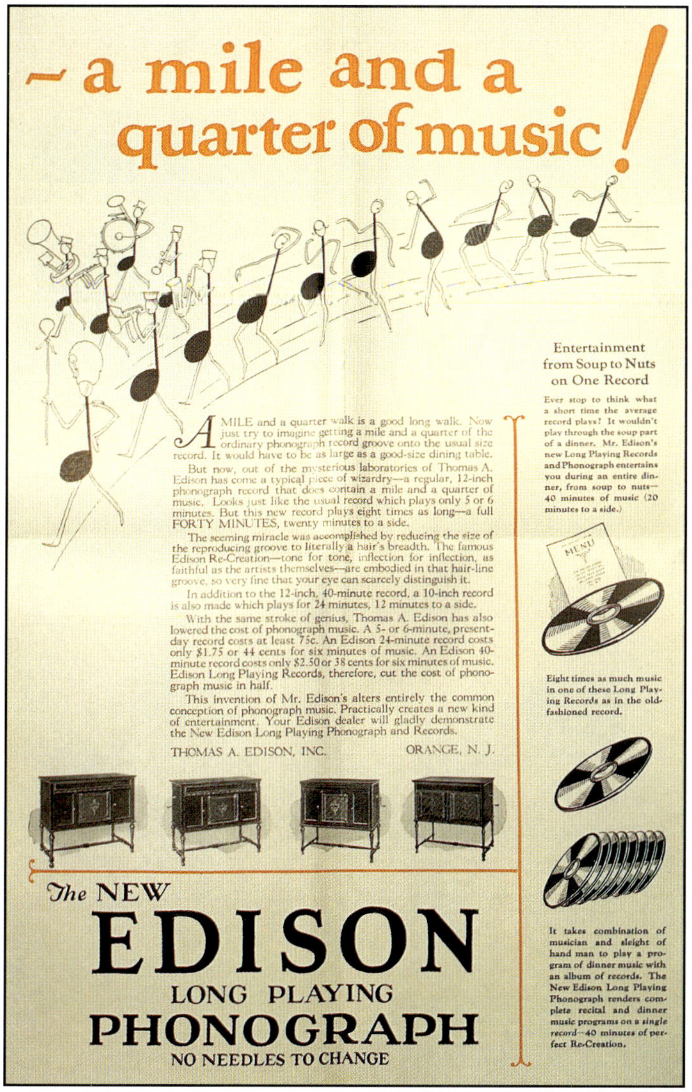

4-117. The technically-innovative Edison Long Playing disc records were offered in 1926 to an unenthusiastic public. The artistic content of each Long Playing disc was created by stringing together some of the most dated and deadly boring recordings from Edison's existing Diamond Disc catalogue. Catastrophically, none of the handful of Long Playing releases contained specifically-recorded material that might have showcased the new format. As can be seen here, four consoles, adaptable to Long Playing or regular Edison discs, were simultaneously introduced. The drab appearances of these confusingly similar machines certainly contributed to the rapid failure of the project. *Courtesy of Ray Phillips.* (Value code: G)

4-118. A Columbia counter stand from August 1926 advertising a snappy jazz-age hit. It's interesting to note that the name of the recording artists is itself an advertisement for radio sponsor Ipana toothpaste. *Courtesy of the Tom and Sandi McCarthy collection.* (Value code: E)

4-119. A 29 1/2" diameter store window sign in the image of a Victor "Orthophonic" recording (with disproportionately large interchangeable label). *Courtesy of the Tom and Sandi McCarthy collection.* (Value code: A)

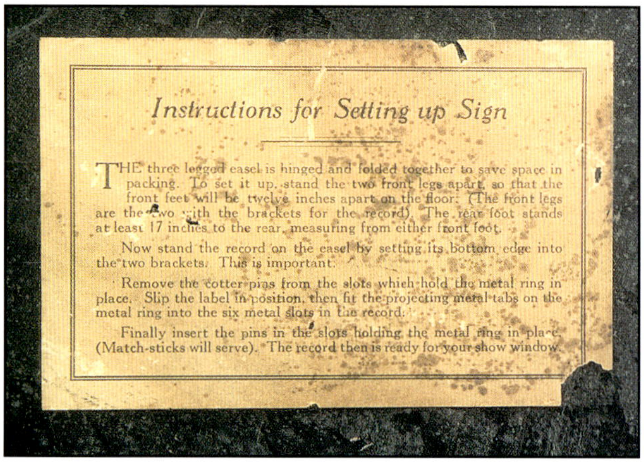

Instructions for Setting up Sign

THE three legged easel is hinged and folded together to save space in packing. To set it up, stand the two front legs apart, so that the front feet will be twelve inches apart on the floor. (The front legs are the two with the brackets for the record). The rear foot stands at least 17 inches to the rear, measuring from either front foot.

Now stand the record on the easel by setting its bottom edge into the two brackets. This is important.

Remove the cotter pins from the slots which hold the metal ring in place. Slip the label in position, then fit the projecting metal tabs on the metal ring into the six metal slots in the record.

Finally insert the pins in the slots holding the metal ring in place. (Match-sticks will serve). The record then is ready for your show window.

4-120. The "Orthophonic" record sign carried these instructions for setting it up. *Courtesy of the Tom and Sandi McCarthy collection.*

4-121. Brunswick record supplements from the late 1920s. At the outset of the electrical recording era, companies vied with one another for a catchy way to describe the new technology. Victor coined "Orthophonic" (literally "correct sounding"), while Brunswick capitalized on its own particular recording process (which involved photo-electric transference of sound impulses) as "musical photography." *Courtesy of Michael F. Khanchalian.* (Value code: H)

4-122. The Paramount record label was interestingly related to the United Phonographs Corporation discussed in illustration 3-77. Paramount discs, like Puritan phonographs, were produced by a subsidiary of the Wisconsin Chair Company of Port Washington. The Chair Company established the chic-sounding New York Recording Laboratories (the firm's first recording studio actually was located in New York City) and released records throughout the 1920s, including Puritan, Paramount, and Broadway. Eventually, a facility was set up in Grafton, Wisconsin to record and manufacture Paramount and Broadway discs. The term "sheik" became a popular male epithet following Rudolph Valentino's simmering performance in the 1921 film of that name. A 6 7/8" x 12" Paramount flyer with store imprint. *Courtesy of the collection of Michael S. Hatfield.* (Value code: VR)

4-123. Blues writers frequently employed sinister elements to give their compositions intrigue and depth: manifestations of bad luck, cemeteries, premonitions of death. In this 7" x 12" Paramount flyer, blues diva Ida Cox was depicted waking to a terrifying specter. Ms. Cox' usual fare was considerably more lighthearted. During 1929, her "Raisin' Cain" show troupe toured the South, where one of her chorus girls reported to a trade newspaper in January: "Little Ethel Jackson writes from the Ida Cox company and says that the show is still "Raisin' Cain." This is their third week at the Central of Dallas, Tex. Well one is certain they used their summer frocks [at] Xmas while we played in four feet of snow." *Courtesy of the collection of Michael S. Hatfield.* (Value code: VR)

4-124. Hip glossolalia from the 1920s. Papa Charlie Jackson was a medicine show singer and banjoist who also recorded a couple of duets with the renowned Ma Rainey on Paramount. Jackson joined the label in 1924 and achieved considerable success there until the end of the 1920s. A flyer with store imprint, 8 1/2" x 11", printed 7/29/27. *Courtesy of the collection of Michael S. Hatfield.* (Value code: VR)

4-125. The war between the sexes being waged in the kitchen. A 6 3/4" x 12" Paramount flyer. *Courtesy of the collection of Michael S. Hatfield.* (Value code: VR)

4-126. Country bluesman Blind Lemon Jefferson traveled north from Texas to record for Paramount in 1925. His unpretentious, plaintive vocals and fluid guitar work scored an immediate hit. Freud would have had a field day with the "black snake" symbolism (and blues vocalist Victoria Spivey's use of similar imagery in "Black Snake Blues"). 6 7/8" x 13 3/8". *Courtesy of the collection of Michael S. Hatfield.* (Value code: VR)

4-127. Blind Blake joined Paramount in 1926 and became nearly as popular as Blind Lemon Jefferson, then a well-established Paramount star. Printed 5/17/27, 8 7/8" x 13 3/4". *Courtesy of the collection of Michael S. Hatfield.* (Value code: VR)

4-128. Another Blind Blake publicity flyer, 6 3/4" x 14". The performer's success in "Race Records" continued through the later 1920s, and in 1929 Blake had ten new records released. *Courtesy of the collection of Michael S. Hatfield.* (Value code: VR)

4-129. "Negro Spirituals" were certainly the first expressions of African-American music widely recognized by white audiences (not counting minstrelsy or other examples tainted by racism). Those unfamiliar with ragtime, jazz, swing, folk music, or other idioms to which blacks contributed greatly, were likely acquainted with the soulful outpourings of black religious music. 7" x 11 3/4". *Courtesy of the collection of Michael S. Hatfield.* (Value code: VR)

4-130. Preaching, singing, and saving souls. 7" x 11". *Courtesy of the collection of Michael S. Hatfield.* (Value code: VR)

4-131. A 10" diameter Japanese Nipponphone record with decorative sleeve and accompanying printed sheet. It is difficult to imagine Lord Buddha, absorbed in contemplation, interrupted by a tune from the Nipponphone. What might this bizarre logo be called – "His Voice's Master?" (Value code: H)

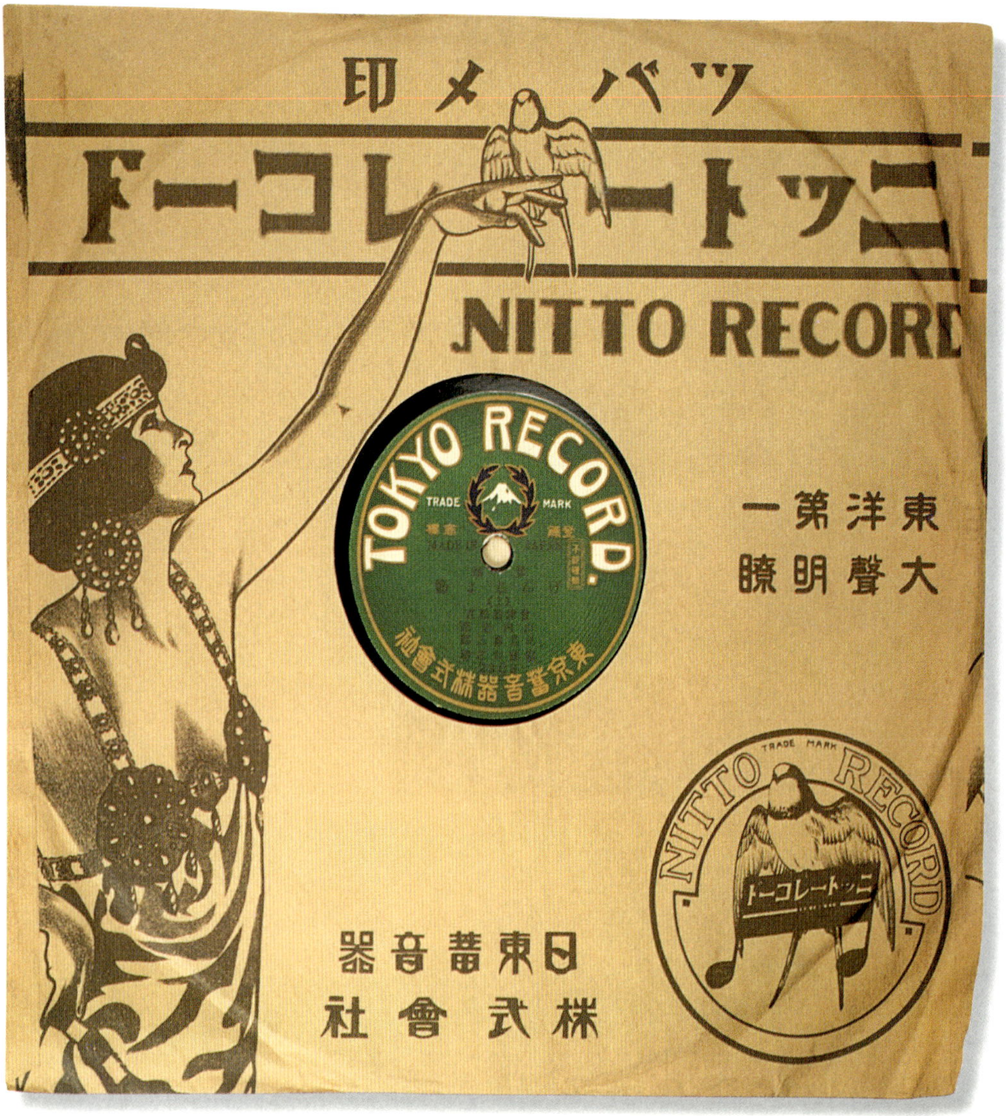

4-132. Another Japanese record with advertising sleeve. The vamp-ish oriental flapper is a surprise, since the Japanese are frequently viewed as sedate. (Value code: H)

4-133. Three unusual promotional items. Left, an eastern European matchbox holder with imagery right out of a "Grade Z" horror movie. Middle and right, pencils advertising steel needles. *Courtesy of Wilfried Sator.* (Value code: H)

4-134. The depiction of a phonograph with a "speaks for itself" slogan occurred to ad writers early on, and was widely exploited with slight variations. (Value code: H)

4-135. An 18" diameter Pathé enameled double-faced sign with mounting flange, announcing Pathé's up-dated audio products of the late 1920s. "Lateral cut (needle) discs, phonographs, wireless, electric pick-ups." (Value code: C)

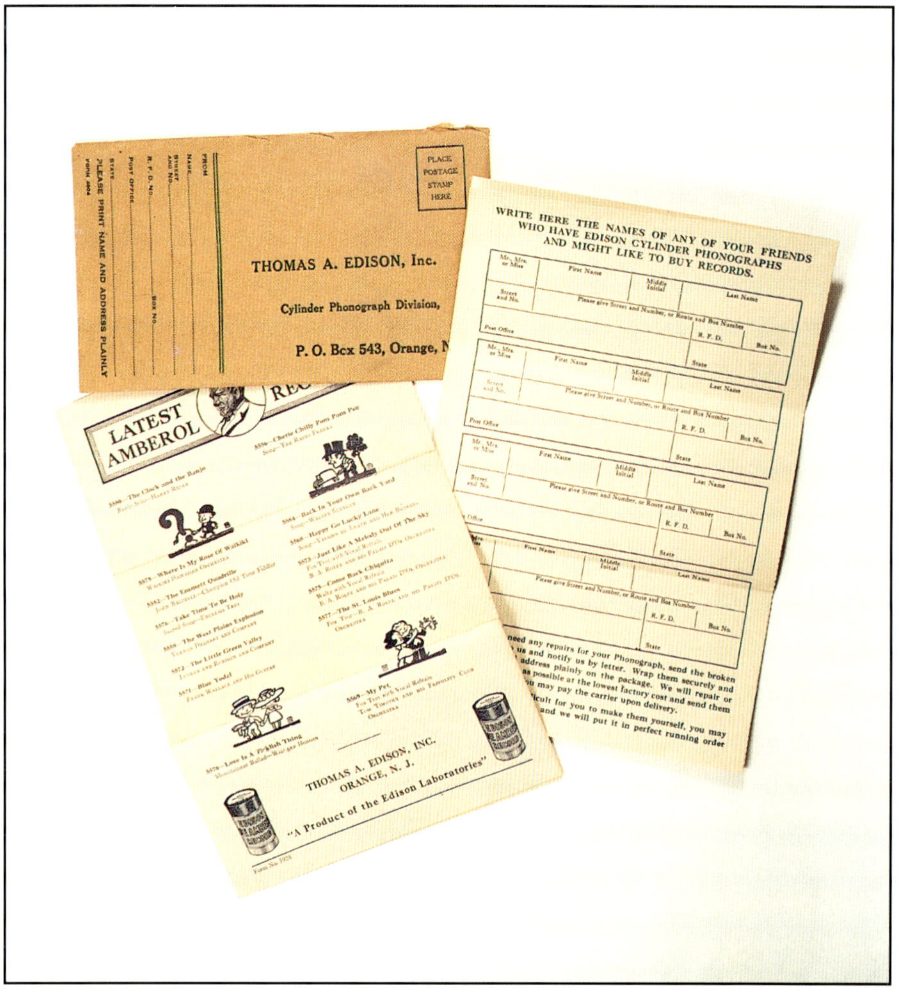

4-136. Edison dealers slowly bailed out during the late 1920s. The economy was going strong, but Thomas A. Edison, Incorporated had become mired in outmoded thinking and products that did not reflect the public's current taste. The sales of Edison machines and records nose-dived, especially Blue Amberol cylinders. At last, the firm that had prided itself on being the beneficent shepherd to legions of smiling and nodding dealers was forced to do the unthinkable – start selling cylinders by mail-order. Shown here, from September 1928, are mail-order materials as they would have been supplied directly to the customer. When these supplements were sent to those dealers who remained, the space between the two records was left blank for an identification stamp. (Value code: H)

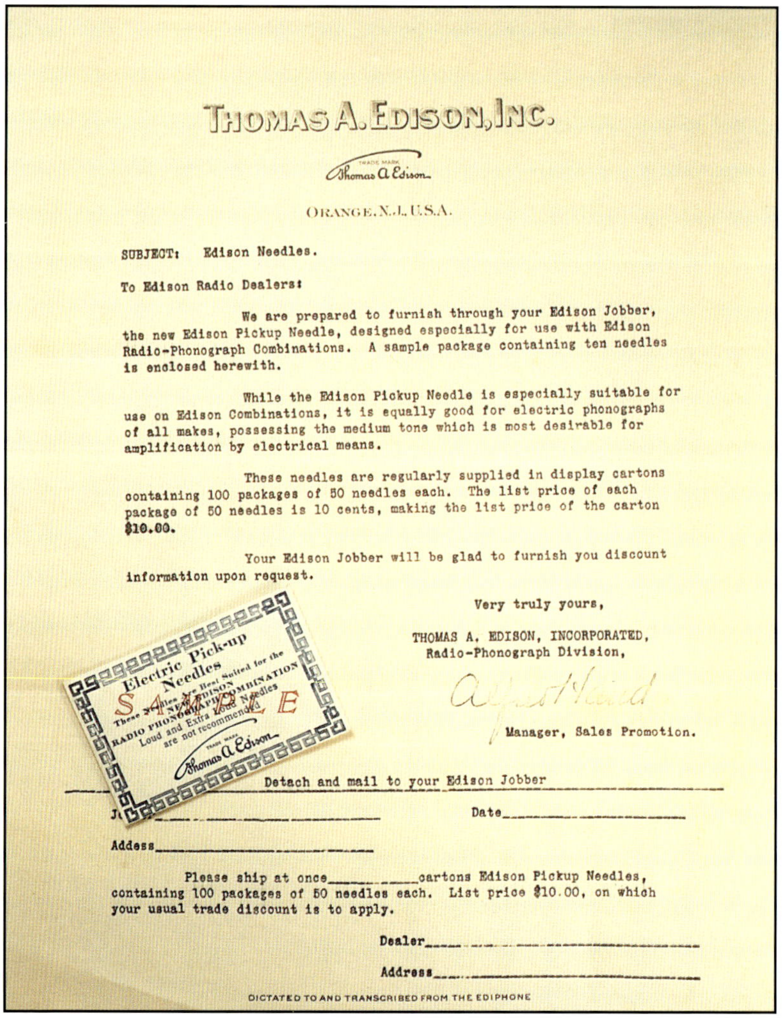
THOMAS A. EDISON, INC.

Thomas A. Edison

ORANGE, N.J., U.S.A.

SUBJECT: Edison Needles.

To Edison Radio Dealers:

We are prepared to furnish through your Edison Jobber, the new Edison Pickup Needle, designed especially for use with Edison Radio-Phonograph Combinations. A sample package containing ten needles is enclosed herewith.

While the Edison Pickup Needle is especially suitable for use on Edison Combinations, it is equally good for electric phonographs of all makes, possessing the medium tone which is most desirable for amplification by electrical means.

These needles are regularly supplied in display cartons containing 100 packages of 50 needles each. The list price of each package of 50 needles is 10 cents, making the list price of the carton $10.00.

Your Edison Jobber will be glad to furnish you discount information upon request.

Very truly yours,

THOMAS A. EDISON, INCORPORATED,
Radio-Phonograph Division,

Manager, Sales Promotion.

Electric Pick-up Needles
SAMPLE

Detach and mail to your Edison Jobber

J________ Date________

Address________

Please ship at once________cartons Edison Pickup Needles, containing 100 packages of 50 needles each. List price $10.00, on which your usual trade discount is to apply.

Dealer________

Address________

DICTATED TO AND TRANSCRIBED FROM THE EDIPHONE

4-137. In September 1928, Edison introduced radio-phonograph combinations, beginning with the "C-1" and "C-2." Venturing into lateral cut technology like a spinster on her first date, the firm put its name on conventional steel needles. *Courtesy of the Charles Hummel collections.* (Value code: H)

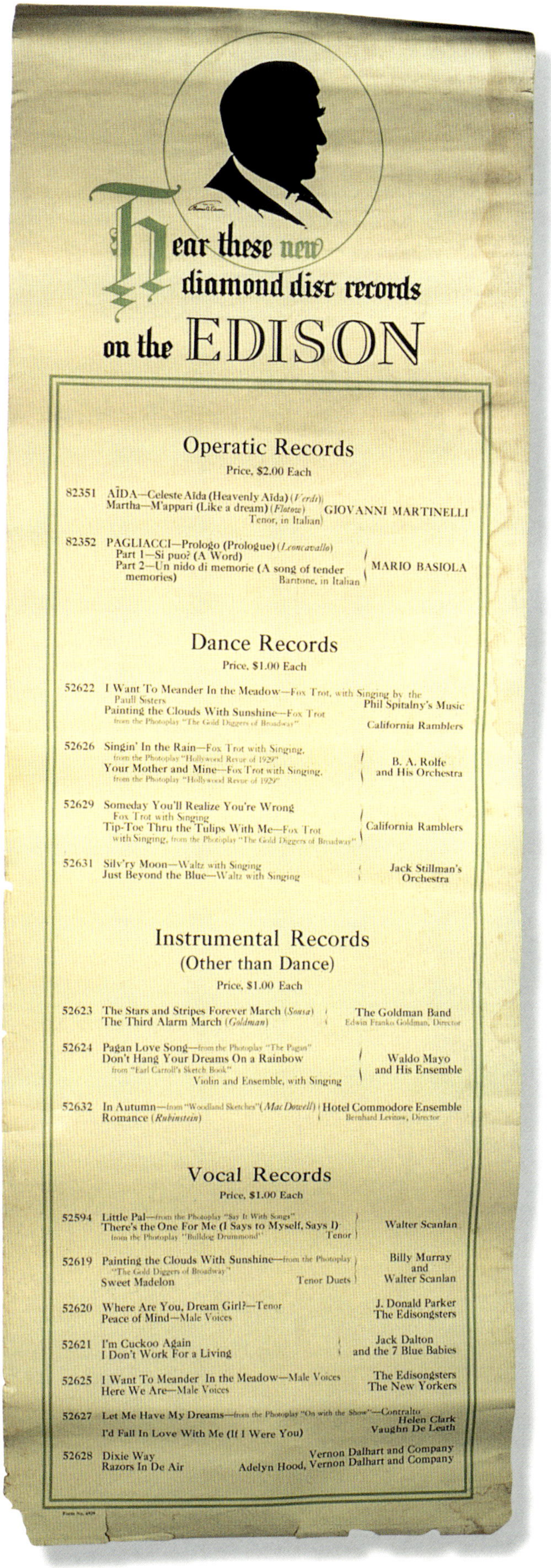
Hear these new diamond disc records on the EDISON

Operatic Records
Price, $2.00 Each

82351 AÏDA—Celeste Aïda (Heavenly Aïda) (*Verdi*)
Martha—M'appari (Like a dream) (*Flotow*)
Tenor, in Italian — GIOVANNI MARTINELLI

82352 PAGLIACCI—Prologo (Prologue) (*Leoncavallo*)
Part 1—Si puo? (A Word)
Part 2—Un nido di memorie (A song of tender memories)
Baritone, in Italian — MARIO BASIOLA

Dance Records
Price, $1.00 Each

52622 I Want To Meander In the Meadow—Fox Trot, with Singing by the Paull Sisters — Phil Spitalny's Music
Painting the Clouds With Sunshine—Fox Trot from the Photoplay "The Gold Diggers of Broadway" — California Ramblers

52626 Singin' In the Rain—Fox Trot with Singing, from the Photoplay "Hollywood Revue of 1929"
Your Mother and Mine—Fox Trot with Singing, from the Photoplay "Hollywood Revue of 1929" — B. A. Rolfe and His Orchestra

52629 Someday You'll Realize You're Wrong Fox Trot with Singing
Tip-Toe Thru the Tulips With Me—Fox Trot with Singing, from the Photoplay "The Gold Diggers of Broadway" — California Ramblers

52631 Silv'ry Moon—Waltz with Singing
Just Beyond the Blue—Waltz with Singing — Jack Stillman's Orchestra

Instrumental Records
(Other than Dance)
Price, $1.00 Each

52623 The Stars and Stripes Forever March (*Sousa*)
The Third Alarm March (*Goldman*) — The Goldman Band, Edwin Franko Goldman, Director

52624 Pagan Love Song—from the Photoplay "The Pagan"
Don't Hang Your Dreams On a Rainbow from "Earl Carroll's Sketch Book"
Violin and Ensemble, with Singing — Waldo Mayo and His Ensemble

52632 In Autumn—from "Woodland Sketches" (*MacDowell*)
Romance (*Rubinstein*) — Hotel Commodore Ensemble, Bernhard Levitow, Director

Vocal Records
Price, $1.00 Each

52594 Little Pal—from the Photoplay "Say It With Songs"
There's the One For Me (I Says to Myself, Says I) from the Photoplay "Bulldog Drummond"
Tenor — Walter Scanlan

52619 Painting the Clouds With Sunshine—from the Photoplay "The Gold Diggers of Broadway"
Sweet Madelon
Tenor Duets — Billy Murray and Walter Scanlan

52620 Where Are You, Dream Girl?—Tenor — J. Donald Parker
Peace of Mind—Male Voices — The Edisongsters

52621 I'm Cuckoo Again
I Don't Work For a Living — Jack Dalton and the 7 Blue Babies

52625 I Want To Meander In the Meadow—Male Voices — The Edisongsters
Here We Are—Male Voices — The New Yorkers

52627 Let Me Have My Dreams—from the Photoplay "On with the Show"—Contralto — Helen Clark
I'd Fall In Love With Me (If I Were You) — Vaughn De Leath

52628 Dixie Way — Vernon Dalhart and Company
Razors In De Air — Adelyn Hood, Vernon Dalhart and Company

Whether pragmatic, inspirational, or merely avaricious, phonograph promotion assumed a variety of mantles during its first fifty years. Boldly typeset posters advertising talking machine concerts evolved into refined inducements to buy a phonograph for the home. Simple catalogues stressing utility became treatises on "period design," describing the elevating influence that the phonograph would wield in the parlor. Exhibition handbills listing a handful of songs to be played became monthly lists of record releases. Ostentatious dealer advertising plaques and decals disappeared discreetly into the polished recesses of Victrola cabinets. Fanciful trade cards became advertising needle tins and record dusters. As the media changed, so did the message. Promises of jokes, brass bands, elocution, and realistic sound effects were swept away by the yearning to recapture the safety of the past. The novelty of entertaining young folks by the fireside was overtaken by the duty to "mould the American citizen of tomorrow." The need to have the "latest thing out" was supplanted by the perceived importance of observing classic designs.

It's an enduring question as to which, society or advertising, influences the other to a greater degree. Each *reflects* the other, and each in its turn *drives* the other in cyclical patterns. Frank Seaman's bold tactics in the 1890s undoubtedly influenced Americans' view of the talking machine, yet the passage of twenty years would see a world war relentlessly shape phonograph marketing. Advertising can be the chimera of public taste, as societal sensibilities can be sculpted by advertising.

Through it all, the talking machine was celebrated as an invention unlike any other; a device that kept loved ones close; an instrument that made homes happy. Those constants were presented in various ways over the years. However, the phonograph's promotion ultimately appealed to the ever-changing ideals most sacred in the hearts of the people. As both the object and the medium of marketing, the phonograph has transformed us with its singular magic.

4-138. Get them while you can – a rare object from the eleventh hour of the Edison Phonograph. A June 1929 dealer record supplement "hanger," 13" x 35 1/2", listing some of the last electrically-recorded Diamond Discs to be released (including No.52,632). *Courtesy of Charles McCarn.* (Value code: VR)

4-139. A 5" x 6 1/2" metal ashtray promoting Victrolas, and an RCA Victor matchbook that carried dealer identification on the reverse. *Courtesy of Rae Ann Rieping.* (Value code: H)

VALUE CODE KEY

One man's meat is another man's poison.

Preparing a value system for a large number of diverse items is a task fraught with concerns. We have dealt with the job as realistically as possible. Items which are extremely uncommon will be rated "very rare" (VR). The "VR" designation is not meant to indicate a price of any kind – it is only an expression of the infrequency with which the object changes hands.

Values will be expressed *in the individual captions* by the following letter codes:

- A $1500 and up
- B $1000 to $1499
- C $750 to $999
- D $500 to $749
- E $250 to $499
- F $125 to $249
- G $51 to $124
- H up to $50

This might seem to be a long list of prices. However, you will find that many of the values actually will fall within a small range of categories: E, F, G and H. Many illustrations contain a selection of objects. If these items are similar enough, a general value code will be shown. If there is sufficient disparity in the prices, they will be individually valued: always listed from left to right and clockwise, if applicable.

By employing price ranges instead of specific dollar amounts, we leave ourselves open to various "slings and arrows" of discontent. It is our feeling that ours is the only effective approach to the subject. However, this does add an element of discretion to the use of our book.

In using the value codes, we advise *conservatism*. If you are trying to establish the value of an object in your possession, the natural instinct is to seize upon the highest price in the given range, regardless of condition. This can be a mistake. The condition of the items in the book is nearly always excellent, but the condition of *your* item is the important issue. Condition can affect the value by up to 50% - and occasionally more. The bottom end of a price range has as much validity as the top, though it seems a less attractive prospect. Different examples of the same type of object may represent the entire range of a certain price category, due to condition. The ranges are also intended to be *comparative*. Certain objects in category "B," for instance, may *never* approach $1500, no matter how perfectly preserved they are.

Beyond condition, many, many factors affect the price of an "antique." Exact worth is something that cannot be fixed precisely in time. We can only hint at it. Our guide is intended to help you understand the value of the objects illustrated, but we vigorously discourage the use of the phrase, "It *books* for such-and-such a price." True worth is what the market will bear. Quoting books, auction results or what a shop is asking will probably not elevate the price higher than the general market will currently support.

Finally, in the area of phonograph advertising there are two distinct and sometimes considerably different markets: the phonograph collectors and the advertising collectors. Disputes between these two groups as to the value of certain objects never will be fully resolved – so we content ourselves by hoping to satisfy the needs of the most number of people.

BIBLIOGRAPHY

Association for Recorded Sound Collections, various editors *ARSC Journal*, various issues to present.

Barnum, Frederick O., III. *His Master's Voice in America*. Camden: General Electric Company, 1991.

Barr, Steven C. *The Almost Complete 78 RPM Record Dating Guide (II)*. Huntington Beach: Yesterday Once Again, 1992.

Baumbach, Robert W. *Columbia Phonograph Companion, Vol. II (Disc Graphophones and the Grafonola)*. Woodland Hills: Stationery X-Press, 1996.

_____. *Look for the Dog*. Woodland Hills: Stationery X-Press, 1996.

Bayly, E., editor. *The EMI Collection*. Bournemouth (GB): Talking Machine Review, 1977.

_____. *The Talking Machine Review International*, various issues beginning 1970. Bournemouth (GB).

Bayly, Ernie, and Michael Kinnear. *The Zon-o-phone Record*, Heidelberg (Victoria, Australia): Michael Kinnear, 2001.

Bill, Edward Lyman, editor. *The Talking Machine World*, New York, various issues 1905-1929.

Brooks, Tim, editor. *Little Wonder Records, a History and Discography*, St. Johnsbury (VT): New Amberola Phonograph Company, 2000.

Bryan, Martin, editor. *The New Amberola Graphic*, various issues 1973 to present. St. Johnsbury (VT).

Charosh, Paul, compiler. *Berliner Gramophone Records, American Issues 1892-1900*. Westport: Greenwood Press, 1995.

City of London Phonograph and Gramophone Society, various editors. *The Hillandale News*, various issues 1960s to present.

Conot, Robert: *A Streak of Luck*. New York: Seaview Books, 1979.

Dethlefson, Ronald, editor. *Edison Blue Amberol Recordings, 1912-1914*. Brooklyn: APM Press, 1980.

_____. *Edison Blue Amberol Recordings, 1912-1914* (paper cover). Woodland Hills (CA): Stationery X-Press, 1997.

_____. *Edison Blue Amberol Recordings, 1915-1929*. Brooklyn: APM Press, 1981.

_____. *Edison Blue Amberol Recordings, 1915-1929*, second edition. Los Angeles: Mulholland Press, 1999.

Dethlefson, Ronald, and George Copeland. *Pathé Records and Phonographs in America, 1914-1922*. Los Angeles: Mulholland Press, 2000.

Dixon, Robert, and John Godrich. *Recording the Blues*. New York: Stein and Day Publishers, 1970.

Edge, Ruth, and Leonard Petts. *The Collector's Guide to 'His Master's Voice' Nipper Souvenirs*. London: EMI Group, 1997.

Fabrizio, Timothy C., and George F. Paul. *Antique Phonograph Gadgets, Gizmos and Gimmicks*, Atglen (PA): Schiffer Publishing, Ltd., 1999.

_____. *Discovering Antique Phonographs*. Atglen (PA): Schiffer Publishing, Ltd., 2000.

_____. *Phonographs With Flair, a Century of Style In Sound Reproduction*. Atglen (PA): Schiffer Publishing, Ltd., 2001.

_____. *The Talking Machine, an Illustrated Compendium 1877-1929*. Atglen (PA): Schiffer Publishing, Ltd., 1997.

Fagan, Ted, compiler. *The Encyclopedic Discography of Victor Recordings, Pre-Matrix Series*. Westport: Greenwood Press, 1983.

Fagan, Ted, compiler. *The Encyclopedic Discography of Victor Recordings*. Westport: Greenwood Press, 1986.

Frow, George L. *Edison Cylinder Phonograph Companion*. Woodland Hills: Stationery X-Press, 1994.

_____. *The Edison Disc Phonographs and the Diamond Discs*. Sevenoaks, Kent (GB): George L. Frow, 1982.

_____. *The Edison Disc Phonographs and the Diamond Discs*. Los Angeles: Mulholland Press, paperback reprint 2001.

Gaisberg, Frederick W. *The Music Goes Round*. North Stratford (NH): Ayer Company Publishers, Inc., 1977 (1942 reprint).

Gelatt, Roland. *The Fabulous Phonograph, revised*. New York: Appleton-Century, 1965 (three eds. 1955, 1977).

Gracyk, Tim, with Frank Hoffmann. *Popular American Recording Pioneers, 1895-1925*. Binghamton (NY): Haworth Press, 2000.

Gracyk, Tim, editor. *Victrola and 78 Journal*. Roseville (CA): various issues 1994-1998.

Hatcher, Danny, editor. *Proceedings of the 1890 Convention of Local Phonograph Companies*. Nashville: Country Music Foundation Press, reprint, 1974.

Hazelcorn, Howard. *A Collector's Guide to the Columbia Spring-Wound Cylinder Graphophone, 1894-1910*. Brooklyn: APM Press, 1976.

_____. *Columbia Phonograph Companion, Volume I: Hazelcorn's Guide to the Columbia Cylinder Graphophone*. Los Angeles: Mulholland Press, 1999.

Hunting, Russell, editor. *The Phonoscope*. New York,:Phonoscope Publishing Company, various issues 1896-1900.

Johnson, E. R. Fenimore. *His Master's Voice Was Eldridge R. Johnson*. Milford (DE): State Media, Inc., 1975.

Koenigsberg, Allen, editor. *The Antique Phonograph Monthly*. Brooklyn: APM Press, various issues 1972-1993.

Koenigsberg, Allen. *Edison Cylinder Records, 1889-1912, 2nd ed*. Brooklyn: APM Press, 1988.

_____. *The Patent History of the Phonograph, 1877-1912*. Brooklyn: APM Press, 1991.

Laird, Ross. *Brunswick Records, a Discography of Recordings 1916-1931*, in four volumes. Westport: Greenwood Publishing Group, 2001.

Lorenz, Kenneth M. *Two-Minute... Cylinders of the Columbia Phonograph Company*. Wilmington (DE): Kastlemusick, Inc., 1981.

Maken, Neil. *Hand-Cranked Phonographs*. Huntington Beach: Promar Publishing, 1995.

Marco, Guy A., and Frank Andrews, editors. *Encyclopedia of Recorded Sound in the United States*. New York: Garland Publishing, Inc., 1993.

Martland, Peter: *Since Records Began: EMI: the First Hundred Years*. Distributed by Timber Press, Portland, OR: Amadeus Press, 1997.

Marty, Daniel. *Histoire Illustrée du Phonographe (Illustrated History of the Phonograph)*. Lausanne/Paris: Edita/Lazarus, 1979, (reprinted in various English language editions with slight modifications of the title).

Michigan Antique Phonograph Society, various editors. *In the Groove*, various issues to present.

Moore, Jerrold Northrop. *A Matter of Records*. New York: Taplinger Pub-

lishing Company, 1977.
Moore, Wendell, editor. *The Edison Phonograph Monthly*, various anthologies 1903-1916. New Albany (IN): Wendell Moore Publications.
Proudfoot, Christopher. *Collecting Phonographs and Gramophones*. New York: Mayflower Books, 1980.
Read, Oliver, and Walter L. Welch. *From Tinfoil to Stereo*, Indianapolis, Howard W. Sams and Company, Inc., 1959.
Reiss, Eric L. *The Compleat Talking Machine*. Chandler (AZ): Sonoran Publishing, (revised)1998.
Rust, Brian, and Tim Brooks. *Columbia Master Book Discography*, in four volumes. Westport: Greenwood Publishing Group, 1999.
Rust, Brian, compiler. *Discography of Historical Records on Cylinders and 78s*. Westport: Greenwood Press, 1979.
Seiter, Bessie and Floyd, and Robin and Joan Rolfs. *Phonograph Dolls That Talk and Sing*. Hortonville (WI): Audio Antique LLC, 2001.
Sherman, Michael W. (with William R. Moran and Kurt R. Nauck, III). *Collector's Guide to Victor Records*. Dallas: Monarch Record Enterprises, 1992.
Sherman, Michael W., and Kurt R. Nauck, III. *Note the Notes, An Illustrated History of the Columbia 78 rpm Record Label, 1901-1958*. New Orleans: Monarch Record Enterprises, 1998.
Stewart-Baxter, Derrick. *Ma Rainey and the Classic Blues Singers*. New York: Stein and Day Publishers, 1970.
Sutton, Allan. *Directory of American Disc Record Brands and Manufacturers, 1891-1943*. Westport: Greenwood Press, 1994.
Sutton, Allan, and Kurt Nauck. *American Record Labels and Companies, an Encyclopedia (1891-1943)* [with CD-ROM]. Denver: Mainspring Press, 2000.
Welch, Walter L., and Leah Brodbeck Stenzel Burt. *From Tinfoil to Stereo, 1877-1929*. Gainesville: University Press of Florida, 1994.
Wile, Raymond R.,and Ronald Dethlefson. *Edison Diamond Disc Recreations, Records and Artists 1910-1929*. Brooklyn: APM Press, 1985.

GLOSSARY

Amberol. The first four-minute cylinder developed by Edison, 1908-1912. These cylinders are black in color, made of especially hard metallic soap, and were usually sold in green and white containers.

Amberola. The name denoting Edison's line of internal-horn cylinder Phonographs, 1909-1929.

Back mount. A term used to describe a talking machine which uses a back bracket which supports the horn and thus removes its inertia from the **soundbox.**

Bedplate. The plate (usually metal) to which the upper mechanism of a cylinder talking machine is mounted.

Blank. A smooth, grooveless unrecorded cylinder.

Blue Amberol. The blue celluloid four-minute cylinder sold by Edison, 1912-1929. The containers for these cylinders were blue until 1917, orange and blue thereafter.

Carriage. The assembly which "carries" the **reproducer** of a cylinder talking machine across the recording.

Carrier arm. Edison nomenclature for the **carriage**. The **half-nut** and its flat supporting spring are attached directly to the carrier arm on nearly all Edison machines.

Combination attachment. Devices offered by Edison to convert pre-1908 Phonographs to play four-minute cylinders in addition to the two-/zminute variety.

Concert. Edison's trade name for the five-inch diameter cylinder and the Edison Phonograph designed to play it.

Crane. The support used to mount horns of 15-inch length or greater to cylinder talking machines.

Cylinder. A geometric form on which entertainment recordings were made, 1877-1929. The earliest sheets of tinfoil were followed by self-supporting cylinders of ozocerite-covered cardboard, stearic acid/paraffin, hard metallic soap, and celluloid. Advantages of the cylinder format included a constant surface speed and the ability to make home recordings.

Diamond disc. Edison's line of disc records and machines, 1912-1929. The Diamond Discs were vertically recorded, and the Diamond Disc Phonographs were one of the very few disc talking machines to use a **feedscrew.**

Diaphragm. The flexible, circular vibrating membrane of a **soundbox** or **reproducer** which converts mechanical energy to acoustic energy or sound waves. Mica, glass, compressed paper, copper and aluminum were commonly used as diaphragms in early talking machines.

Elbow. The connection between the horn and the **soundbo**x or **tone arm** of a disc talking machine. Earliest elbows are made of leather, gradually giving way to metal elbows after 1900.

Endgate. A swinging arm which supports one end of the **mandrel** on some cylinder talking machines. To mount or remove a cylinder it is therefore necessary to open and close the endgate.

Feedscrew. A threaded rod which usually drives a half-nut fixed to the carriage of a cylinder talking machine, thus guiding the reproducer across the record grooves. Certain disc machines used **feedscrews** to drive the **soundbox** across the record or to move the turntable beneath a fixed soundbox. Similarly, some cylinder machines used feedscrews to drive a mandrel longitudinally beneath a fixed reproducer.

Front mount. A term used to describe a disc machine where the horn attaches directly to the **soundbox**, and the support arm (or mount) runs directly below and parallel to the **horn**. In such an arrangement the support arm points in the same general direction as the bell of the horn.

Gramophone. Originally the name by which Emile Berliner's disc talking machine was known, it became a generic term to denote any disc playing talking machine, but fell out of use in the United States.

Grand. Columbia's trade name for the five-inch diameter cylinder and the various Columbia machines designed to play it.

Governor. The mechanical assembly in a talking machine motor which regulates the speed, usually by limiting the outward movement of spinning weights.

Half-nut. An internally threaded metal piece usually in the form of a nut which has been cut in half. The threads of the half-nut correspond to the threads of the **feedscrew**. As the feedscrew revolves, the half-nut will be propelled along it, thus driving the **carriage** of a talking machine.

Lateral recording. The type of disc talking machine recording where the information is encoded in sides of the groove. (see **Vertical recording**)

Mandrel. The tapered drum upon which the cylinder record is placed for playing.

Needle. The point (usually steel) of the **soundbox** which rides the grooves of the recording and transmits vibrations to the **diaphragm**.

Needle head. A colloquial term for the **soundbox** or **pick-up** which accepts vibrations directly from the record.

Needle tin. A container to store and dispense steel talking machine needles.

Needle sharpener (or **cutter**). A device for repointing disc talking machine needles of fiber, thorn or steel.

Phonograph. Originally, the name given by Edison to the sound recording/reproducing device he invented in 1877. In American usage, the term has been applied to sound reproducing equipment in general, regardless of age or type of record played.

Recorder. A device comprising a **diaphragm** and cutter stylus for recording cylinder or disc records.

Repeating attachment. A device for cylinder or disc talking machines which returns the **needle** or **stylus** to the beginning of the record after the selection has played.

Reproducer. The component comprising **stylus**, linkage and **diaphragm**, which reproduces the sound from the record grooves. This term is most frequently applied to cylinder machines. (See **soundbox**)

Shaver. On a cylinder talking machine, a device which holds a knife in position to pare the recorded surface from a wax cylinder.

Soundbox. The component comprising **needle**, linkage and **diaphragm**, which reproduces the sound from the record grooves. This term is most frequently applied to disc machines. (See **reproducer**)

Stylus. The point (usually sapphire or diamond) of the **reproducer** which rides the grooves of the recording and transmits vibrations to the **diaphragm** or **pick-up**.

Talking machine. A general term for sound reproducing devices playing either cylinder or disc records, made prior to the advent of electric reproduction. Specific brands such as Graphophone, Victrola or

Amberola all fall within the general category of talking machines. Modern American usage substitutes **phonograph** for the older term "talking machine." For the purposes of historical accuracy, both terms will appear frequently in this book.

Tone arm. A movable hollow tube which conducts sound to the **horn** from the **soundbox**.

Trunnion. Rightly, the sleeve visible on either side of the **carriage** which slides over the **feedscrew** shaft on a Graphophone, but commonly used to denote the entire carriage.

Turntable. The round platter which supports a disc record and revolves while the record is being played. After 1960, that separate component in a **sound system** which comprised the **turntable** and **record changer** was often referred to simply as the **turntable**.

Vertical recording. The type of cylinder or disc recording in which the sound vibrations are encoded in the bottom of the groove. (see **lateral recording**)

Wax. Although the material from which many cylinder records were made is generally referred to as "wax," it was more rightly various formulations of metallic soap. The resemblance of this material to conventional wax promotes the common descriptive term.

INDEX

EDISON RECORD
W. T. CRANE & CO.
PIANOS
PHONOGRAPHS AND RECORDS
SYRACUSE, N.Y.
WILL SAVE YOU MONEY
ON PIANOS
& ORGANS
No.
SCHWEGLER BROS
PHONOGRAPHS
BUFFALO, N.Y.
NEAR MICHIGAN ST.
RECORDS
219-221 GENESEE ST.
PHILIP SCHMITZ,
DEALER IN
Edison, Columbia, Victor & Zonophone Talking Machines
213 MARKET ST.,
Camden, N.J.
CATALOGUE NUMBER
Cash or Credit.
AMERICAN RECORD COMPANY
Music hath Charms
HAWTHORNE, SHEBLE & PRESCOTT
SPRINGFIELD, MASS. U.S.A.
SEMMENCE BROS.
EVERYTHING IN PHONOGRAPHS AND TALKING MACHINES
BICYCLES AND SPORTING GOODS